Artificial Intelligence Law

Artificial Intelligence Law

Edward J. Swan

Wolters Kluwer

Published by:
Kluwer Law International B.V.
PO Box 316
2400 AH Alphen aan den Rijn
The Netherlands
E-mail: lrs-sales@wolterskluwer.com
Website: www.wolterskluwer.com/en/solutions/kluwerlawinternational

Sold and distributed by:
Wolters Kluwer Legal & Regulatory U.S.
920 Links Avenue
Landisville, PA 17538
United States of America
E-mail: customer.service@wolterskluwer.com

ISBN 978-94-035-0987-7

e-Book: ISBN 978-94-035-0997-6
web-PDF: ISBN 978-94-035-1007-1

This book is dedicated to my daughters, Molly and Mary.

About the Author

Dr. Swan has been one of the world's leading lawyers advising major international financial businesses, international organizations, national governments, banks, exchanges, clearinghouses, markets, and tech companies.

He was Partner and Counsel in major international law firms, including Skadden Arps, Brown Rudnick, Cameron McKenna and Simmons and Simmons.

Professor Swan has been a Visiting Professor of Law at University College London, the Catholic University in Lille and Paris, France, and the IESEG School of Management in Lille and Paris. He has been a Member of the Board of the Institute of Advanced Legal Studies at the University of London.

Dr. Swan has published many law books and dozens of articles, including law books for Oxford University Press and Kluwer Law International.

Dr. Swan attended Rocky Mountain College and Harvard University and has a Juris Doctor degree from New York University and a PhD in law from the University of London.

Table of Contents

Acknowledgments

This book has been possible because of the kindness and help of friends, relatives, partners, acquaintances, colleagues, publishers, editors, officials, opponents and judges that I have encountered in my many years of immersion in law around the world. I thank them all for their contributions to my development with the utmost sincerity.

Also, I need to thank Vanna Fadda without whose loyalty and encouragement, my books would not get written.

Edward (Ned) Swan
Lille, France
November 2023

Introduction

Not Legal Advice

This book is not legal advice. It would be foolish, and probably impossible, to try to give a complete explanation of all the different ways that artificial intelligence (AI) and its uses are affected by the legal regulation that exists and is growing in the many jurisdictions in which AI assets are owned and used.

The purpose of this book is to provide a general understanding of the issues that participants in the AI asset world need to be aware of as they acquire, own, use and are affected by AI.

If any person or any entity finds it necessary to have legal advice about the regulatory effects of the policy and laws of any particular legal jurisdiction, it will be necessary for them to obtain advice from qualified legal advisors in that jurisdiction or jurisdictions.

The purpose of this book is to review those legal concepts, throughout the world, that currently govern the application of AI and to comment on modifications or extensions of the rule of law that are being proposed as necessary to serve and protect humanity in relation to the expanding applications of AI.

The chapters of this book will be divided into three types. The first type will discuss general legal concepts and how these are applicable to the uses of AI. The second will be an examination of a number of the world's largest commercial legal jurisdictions with a summary of how their legal systems may interact with the use of AI, and the third will be an examination of existing and proposed laws, regulations, treaties, conventions and agreements that are or will be applicable to AI in specific fields of law and how they may be affected by AI.

However, the reader must always keep in mind that this book does not provide legal advice on the application or effects of specific laws in any particular jurisdiction. Legal advice relating to the law of any jurisdiction must be obtained from qualified legal advisers permitted to give legal advice in the jurisdictions in question.

CHAPTER 1

Artificial Intelligence

§1.01 WHAT IS ARTIFICIAL INTELLIGENCE?

It is generally accepted that the modern understanding of the term "artificial intelligence" (AI) was first "coined" for the Dartmouth College[1] Summer Research Project held between June 18 and August 17, 1956:

> For six weeks in the summer of 1956, a group of scientists convened on the Dartmouth campus for the Dartmouth Summer Research Project on Artificial Intelligence. It was at this meeting of the term "artificial intelligence", was coined. ... The initial conference in 1956 paved the way for the future of artificial intelligence in academia, according to Cade Metz, author of the book "Genius Makers: The Mavericks Who Brought AI to Google, Facebook and the World." ... Conference participants John McCarthy and Marvin Minsky would establish AI labs at Stanford and MIT, respectively, while to other participants, Alan Newell and Herbert Simon, built an AI lab at Carnegie Melon. Taken together, the labs at MIT, Stanford and Carnegie Mellon drove AI research for decades. ... The goal was to build a machine that could do what the human brain could do, Metz said.[2]
>
> The conference mostly consisted of brainstorming ideas about how AI should work. However, "There was very little written work record" of the conference, according to computer science professor emeritus Thomas Kurtz[3], in an interview that is part of the Rauner Special Collections archives.[4]

1. Dartmouth University is one of the eight prestigious "Ivy League Schools" (Harvard, Yale, Princeton, Columbia, Cornell, Pennsylvania, Brown and Dartmouth) in the United States. Dartmouth is located in Hanover, New Hampshire.
2. Kent Friel, "A Look Back on the Dartmouth Summer Research Project on Artificial Intelligence," The Dartmouth, May 19, 2023, online at: thedartmouth.com.
3. Thomas E. Kurtz, a retired Professor of Mathematics and Computer Science, Dartmouth University.
4. Kent Friel, May 19, 2023, as cited above. The Rauner Special Collections Library holds rare books, manuscripts and archives of Dartmouth College. *See* citation online at: dartmouth.edu.

> Metz said that after the conference, two camps of AI research emerged. One camp believed in what is called neural networks, mathematical systems that learn skills by analyzing data. The idea of neural networks was based on the concept that machines can learn like the human brain, creating new connections and growing over time by responding to real world input data. [Other] conference participants would go on to argue that it wasn't possible for machines to learn on their own.[5]

> In about 2010, however, the neural network idea "was proven to be the way forward," Metz said. Neural networks allow artificial intelligence programs to learn tasks on their own, which has driven a current boom in AI research, he added.[6]

As can be seen, the modern understanding of "AI" is that AI systems are machines that can do some things the human brain can do, including modifying the performance of the AI system in response to data it encounters during the performance of its operations.

Of course, AI machines are not purely "mechanical" machines. They are machines that comprise or include "cyber" or "digital" elements.

§1.02 WHAT IS THE HUMAN IMPACT OF AI?

There is a huge amount of information about AI circulating in the media. It is difficult to know whether the consensus is that AI will benefit, harm or even bring an end to the human race.

Opinions of this kind make it difficult to know whether AI will be an extension of humanity or an opponent of humanity.

Examination of this quandary requires an injection of realism. From a legal point of view, there will be no division between humanity and AI. AI will not be able to create its own separate world in opposition to humanity.

§1.03 CORRECTING FUNDAMENTAL LEGAL MISCONCEPTIONS

In discussions of AI, there frequently arise misconceptions about the legal status of AI.

The first is that AI systems can exhibit such independence from their originators and produce such unexpected results in their operation that they constitute an independent being that is separate from humanity.

Indeed, it is sometimes argued that AI systems should be given a separate legal status that entitles them to acquire legal rights that are now only available to human beings.

The second is that one of the difficulties with AI systems is that they are currently "unregulated" and, therefore, not subject to legal restriction and control.

5. Kent Friel, May 19, 2023, as cited above.
6. *Ibid.*

Neither of these things is true. There will never be a separation between an AI system and human beings. Humans will be the designers, the creators, the operators, the distributors, the owners or the users of the AI systems in question.

From a legal point of view, the humans behind an AI system will always be legally responsible for the outcomes the system produces.

Far from being "unregulated," the creation, distribution and operation of AI systems are and will remain subject to a vast spectrum of existing laws and regulations all over the world.

§1.04 THE HUMAN CONNECTION

The real and, indeed, the legal status of AI flows from its connection to its creators, distributors and users.

This connection is shown in the phrase "AI."

The etymology of the current use of "artificial" traces from the Middle English "artificial" ("man-made") via Old French (the modern French word is "artificial"), that came from the Latin artificiālis from artificium ("skill"), from artifex, ars ("skill"), and -fex, and from facere ("to make"). The American *Merriam-Webster Dictionary* defines "artificial" as "man-made."

In the New Oxford Dictionary of English, "artificial" is defined as "made or produced by human beings, rather than occurring naturally."

In other words, the application of the word "artificial" indicates a direct connection between human creation and the thing created.

The term "AI" is defined as "systems able to perform tasks normally requiring human intelligence."[7]

A system that applies AI might be a computer or other contrivance that provides instructions, usually in digital form, directing the tasks in question. Such a device may be called an "AI machine." The word "machine" originates from the Greek word mekos, meaning "contrivance."[8]

Indeed, such devices are usually said to be operating in response to "machine code" or "machine language," which is defined as "a programming language consisting of binary or hexadecimal instructions."[9]

From a legal point of view, the question arises as to what circumstances will permit a break between the creator of an artificial object and the object itself.

The first question is one of legal responsibility. In legal systems, humans are usually assigned a level of responsibility for the results of their actions. The use of an artificial object complicates matters because it allows the creator of an artificial object

7. *The New Oxford Dictionary of English*, "artificial intelligence," (Oxford: 1998).
8. *The New Oxford Dictionary of English*, "machine," (Oxford: 1998).
9. *The New Oxford Dictionary of English*, "machine code," (Oxford: 1998).

an opportunity to project the results of a person's actions beyond their body through the use of the created artificial object.

§1.05 THE LAW OF MACHINES

Historically, as the artificial creations of humans grew more complex and the range of their effects extended further, legal systems were required to decide how far to extend legal responsibility for those effects.

To put it in a popular entertainment context, the "Terminator" was not legally responsible for its actions. Legal responsibility remained with the human creator(s) of the system that brought about the Terminator.

With the increasing use of things operating with "AI," there is much discussion about whether AI will ultimately be a useful tool or a destructive enemy of the human race. Some commentators even raise the possibility that AI could result in the extinction of humanity.

One continuing check on the operation of AI is the fact that the creators of artificially intelligent things will always be legally responsible for the outcomes of their artificially intelligent creations.

The traditional legal concepts of legal responsibility, including duty of care, negligence, and compensation for damages, will always be legally applicable to those humans who create and/or use artificially intelligent things or systems. Artificially intelligent creations will never obtain legal independence from those who launch them into the world.

However, because artificially intelligent creations will not automatically possess an understanding of geographic and jurisdictional boundaries, worldwide agreements on the legal responsibilities relating to the use of AI will need to be carefully defined and put into place.

That is not to say that there are no existing legal restrictions on the use of AI both within individual jurisdictions and internationally, but these will need to be reviewed to determine how they will apply to any new range of artificially intelligent creations.

§1.06 APPLICATION OF MACHINE LAW TO AI

The complexity and speed with which artificially intelligent things can operate have caused a level of unnecessary confusion with respect to their place in law. The confusion is that they can appear to be so "clever" that they seem to be operating in a sphere that has previously been assumed to belong only to human beings. That sphere is "creativity." The fact that their complexity can allow some AI products to build on and extend their instructions so that they achieve results that were not specifically ordered or even expected by their human creators causes some people to believe that they are in some ways, a type of superior being.

In some cases, these feelings have extended so far that some people argue that the sophistication of the operations of artificially intelligent things should cause human society to regard them as having legal rights that are now only available to human beings.

For example, in March 2023, a hearing was conducted before the United Kingdom Supreme Court in which an American scientist named Stephen Thaler argued that an artificially intelligent "creativity machine" that he had created should be granted patents for two things which the creativity machine produced without any intervention from him. In other words, he was seeking to require the British Patent Office to grant legal rights, in this case patent rights, to a machine.[10]

The fundamental flaw in his argument is that without his intervention (in originating the creativity machine), the two subsequent products produced by the creativity machine would not exist.

§1.07 THE HUMAN ELEMENT OF LAW

The purpose of law is to define relations between human beings. Law is intended to be a more desirable substitute for violence and other damaging behavior.

Many different definitions of law have been proposed, but essentially, laws are the rules created by the governors of a society that impose penalties for failure to obey those rules.[11]

Law is itself "artificial" because it is made by humans to govern the behavior of humans within a particular society. The duties and obligations it imposes on humans are not applicable to other objects or life forms. They are not transferable to machines. They stay with the humans that are responsible for the creation and operation of machines.

It is true that there are legal "persons" in the form of corporations (limited companies) or partnerships, but these are dependent for their creation and governance on the human shareholders and directors behind them. Like the machines discussed above, they are human creations and do not exist without human intervention and participation.

Machines should never have legal rights and responsibilities because no machine exists without a basic starting point of human intervention. The initial intervener has rights and responsibilities with respect to a machine and its operations. At different points in the life of a machine, other humans may intervene to purchase it or operate it in such a way that the original rights and responsibilities of the initial human creator are severed, transferred or modified with regard to others who may intervene in the operations of the machine. But at no point does the machine itself obtain legal rights and responsibilities. Those are always traceable to one or more human actors.

§1.08 A LOOK AT LEGAL RESPONSIBILITY FOR MACHINES

Essentially, AI machines are a new stage of evolution in the Industrial Revolution. They are a progression of the Age of Machines.

10. "Patent Law: Discovery Process," *The Economist*, March 11, 2023, p. 22.
11. P. Shears and G. Stephenson, *Introduction to English Law* (Butterworths, London, 1996), pp. 3-5.

To understand where legal systems currently stand in relation to AI machines and how the laws are likely to evolve, it is useful to see how legal systems dealt with the arrival of the Industrial Revolution and the interaction between humans and the machines that changed their lives then.

§1.09 THE INDUSTRIAL REVOLUTION

The history of the Industrial Revolution began with the invention of steam power. In England in 1778, James Watt and Matthew Bolton invented a steam engine that could power machines. It was quickly realized that using this source of power to operate machines that could process and weave textiles could greatly increase the volume of textile production and reduce costs, providing Britain with a competitive advantage in the commercialization of textile materials such as wool, flax and cotton.

For centuries, Britain had been an enormous producer of textile raw materials such as wool and flax, but these had been largely traded in raw form to markets in the Low Countries, where they were manufactured into textiles that Italian trading companies then marketed all over the known world. At that time, British manufacturers of cloth had been on a relatively small scale, largely done by hand and often at home using primitive spinning wheels and looms.

The introduction of large, powered textile processing and weaving machines meant that much larger quantities of textiles could be produced at much lower prices. These could be traded throughout the British Empire around the world at significant competitive advantages of speed of production, quantities and prices.

Whereas in 1778, there were no factories in Britain producing large quantities of textiles by powered machines, by 1830, there were over seven hundred such factories in operation.

§1.10 THE FACTORY ACTS

In the 1830s, the British Parliament began to impose laws in response to the changes wrought by the Industrial Revolution that are known as the Factory Acts. These were intended to protect human welfare from the detrimental effects of the expanding use of factories and machines.

There were five Factory Acts between 1833 and 1901.[12]

The first three applied to the textile industry and were aimed at protecting women and children.

The Factory Act of 1833 was aimed at limiting the employment of children in factories. The maximum workweek for children between the ages of 9 and 13 was limited to 48 hours. Their maximum daily workday was limited to 8 hours. For children between 13 and 18, the workday was limited to 12 hours. The employment of children under 9 years of age was prohibited, and children under 13 were required to

12. "The 1833 Factory Act," The National Archives, online, factory-artdoc.pdf.

receive two hours of schooling a day. Children under the age of 18 were not allowed to work at night. Government factory inspectors were appointed.

The Factory Act of 1844 reduced working hours for children between 8 and 13 years to 6 1/2 hours per day. This act also sought to extend protection to women by limiting their workdays to 12 hours and prohibiting women from working at night.

The Factory Act of 1847 limited the workdays of women and children under 18 years of age to 10 hours a day.

The Factory Act of 1867 extended those limitations to all working establishments in which more than five workers were employed.

The Factory Act of 1901 limited the minimum age for work to 12 years. Like the previous act, this rule applied to all working establishments that employed more than five workers.[13]

Although these rules were groundbreaking for their times, as the industrial age and the mechanical marvels it produced spread around the world, rules for the protection of workers, although they undoubtedly differed from country to country, were adopted to protect those employed to work in factories.

§1.11 THE AI REVOLUTION

The introduction of AI into commerce is imposing a similarly dramatic change on the relationship between humans and the means of production.

With the Industrial Revolution, things that were previously being done by humans, by hand, were now being done by machines. With the present AI Revolution, many intellectual tasks previously performed by humans are now being done by AI machines.

Prior to the Industrial Revolution, there had been no need for laws governing the operation of factories, and certainly no laws restricting the employment of humans in factories.

This is similar to the situation that currently exists with AI. The presence of AI in culture and industry is generally new enough so that significant legal thought as to how its use should be limited is just beginning. New statutes and regulations applying to AI are just beginning to be introduced. As with the early Factory Acts of the Industrial Revolution, a central goal is the protection of children.

§1.12 EXAMPLE: THE UTAH SOCIAL MEDIA LAW

For example. in the United States, the State of Utah has passed a comprehensive law to allow parents to control the exposure of their children to social media available on the Internet. This is the first law in the United States that gives parents the power to restrict their children's exposure to certain social media.[14]

---

13. Factory Acts, The National Archives, online, factory-artdoc.pdf.
14. Peter Stubley, "Utah Law Gives Parents Full Control of Children's Social Media," *The Times*, online, March 24, 2023.

The law gives parents complete access to their children's Internet accounts and permits parents to restrict Internet access from 10:30 p.m. to 6:30 a.m.. The governor of Utah wrote:

> We're no longer willing to let social media companies continue to harm the mental health of our youth.

A companion law was passed at the same time, making it easier for parents to bring legal action against social media companies for any financial, physical or emotional harm caused by their posts and imposes fines for any social media companies aiming advertising at persons under 18.

Although Utah is the first state to impose such laws, it is reported that Ohio, Texas and New Jersey are considering similar regulations and that California has imposed privacy restrictions to protect those under 18.

These things have followed President Biden's recent request for nationwide legislation preventing "big tech" companies from collecting the personal data of children and teenagers on the Internet and targeting children and teenagers with advertisements. In his State of the Union address, President Biden was reported to say, "We must finally hold social media companies accountable for the experiment they are running on our children for profit."[15]

However, such legislation has not been greeted with universal approval. Some civil liberties groups say that the new Utah law requires the collection of private information about children itself. An official of the political group NetChoice reportedly said that the Utah regulations are counterproductive and unconstitutional because they will require media companies to collect data about children, verifying their ages and parental relationships. This could put sensitive private data at risk from online hacking attacks.[16]

A significant tool that large Internet service providers (such as Google and Facebook, etc.) use to collect and process user data involves the use of sophisticated AI programs. Using AI gives them rapid insight into many aspects of the customer data they collect.

As the Marketing AI Institute points out on its website:

- "AI can help you predict outcomes and successful courses of action.
- AI powered systems can analyze data from hundreds of sources and offer predictions about what works and what doesn't.
- AI can also deep dive into data analytics about your customers and offer predictions about consumer preferences, product development and marketing channels.
- AI can be used to unify data across platforms. That includes using the speed and scale of AI to pull together all your customer data into a single, unified

15. David McCabe, "President Biden Will Call for More Limits on Social Media," *The New York Times*, online, March 21, 2022.
16. Peter Stubley, "Utah Law Gives Parents Full Control of Children's Social Media," *The Times*, online, March 24, 2023.

> view. Artificial intelligence is also capable of unifying data across different sources, even hard to track ones like call data."[17]

It is protection from this kind of comprehensive AI intrusion that the public, particularly children or other vulnerable people, may need or wish protection from.

17. Mike Kaput, "AI in Analytics: Top Use Cases and Tools," Marketing Artificial Intelligence Institute, online at: marketingaiinstitute.com, April 04, 2022.

CHAPTER 2

Concerns about AI

Laws and regulations restricting AI-assisted activities will continue to evolve, and considerable thought will need to be given to their formulation.

In an early fictional attempt in the 1950s, the science fiction writer Isaac Asimov published a story collection that contained the Three Laws of Robotics.[18]

First Law

A robot may not injure a human being or, through inaction, allow a human being to come to harm.

Second Law

A robot must obey the orders given by human beings except where such orders would conflict with the First Law.

Third Law

A robot must protect its own existence as long as such protection does not conflict with the First or Second Law.

The goal of these "laws," the protection of the human race from harm by robots was admirable, but their basic premise was false. They seem to imply that robots could be put in the position of legal responsibility for the welfare of humans.

That will never be the case.

The Laws of Robotics, as stated by Asimov, will need to be rewritten to work in human society. It should be remembered that he was a writer of science fiction, and his Laws of Robotics go beyond what is sociologically possible. It is undoubtedly true that, as time goes on, AI machines, including robots, will become more sophisticated in that they will be able to choose from a greater range of possible outcomes. However, from a legal point of view, they will never achieve legal separation from their creators. Legal responsibility will always ultimately rest with those creators, so the Laws of Robotics

18. Isaac Asimov, "Runaround," *I, Robot* (New York: Del Ray, 2008).

will need to be modified to reflect that. For example, the First Law should be that humans who create any artificial, intelligent tools, including robots, that may independently choose to harm a human being remain responsible for those actions. That is the most important issue.

We are already at the point where artificially intelligent machines, such as drones, are able to make decisions about whether to launch a strike on an identified target without additional human intervention.[19]

As time goes on, the choices that artificially intelligent machines will be allowed to make will be broader, perhaps in the context of international conflicts, more deadly, but it is always a human intervention that puts these things in operation, and, legally, always be those humans that bear ultimate legal responsibility.[20]

With the Industrial Revolution, things that were previously being done by humans, by hand, were being done by machines. With the present cyber revolution, intellectual tasks previously performed by humans are now, to some extent, being done by AI machines.

§2.01 DATA SWEEPING

There is no question that AI will impact on people's lives in many ways, some of which we cannot even foresee at this point. However, one impact that people are generally aware of, but do not usually realize all the details of, is how Internet Service Providers (ISPs) are gathering and using a colossal amount of data around the world from their customers' interaction with the Internet. People may be aware of some of this collection, but they may not be aware of all of it.

Although Utah is the first U.S. state to pass specific legislation against Internet exploitation by intrusive AI tools, concern about the harvesting of customer data is an issue that has been explored by the U.S. Federal Trade Commission (FTC) in a 2021 report entitled "Examining the Privacy Practices of Six Major Internet Service Providers" (ISPs). In their report, the key concerns that the FTC identified, in summary, are the following:

(i) Several of the ISPs in the study collect large amounts of sensitive customer data.

(ii) Several ISPs collect and use data in ways that customers do not expect and could harm the customers. For example, ISPs sometimes collect data not related to the services they are requested to provide, such as:
   - browsing data;
   - television viewing history;
   - contents of e-mail and search;
   - data from connected services;

19. Navy Productions, "What Happens when PIRATES attach MASSIVE US Navy Ships? Somali Pirates Documentary," U.S. Navy, online, YouTube, accessed September 14, 2023.

20. Or in the case of the military, the collective human organizations, governments, that operate them.

- location information;
- race and ethnicity data.

The FTC points out that such data could be used in ways that harm customers by: property managers, bail bondsmen, bounty hunters, or those who would use it for discriminatory purposes:

(i) Although ISPs may claim to offer customers choices, some are not clearly explained and may be intended to influence consumers toward more data sharing.

(ii) Many ISPs can be as intrusive as the largest advertising platforms (Google, Facebook and Amazon). The problem can be amplified across the Internet because many ISPs may have access to the following kinds of customer information:
   - consumers' unencrypted Internet traffic;
   - subscribers' identities;
   - consumers activities across websites and geographic locations;
   - some ISPs can combine browsing and viewing history with a broad range of information they may have from several integrated products, services and features that they may offer.[21]

The FTC Report on ISP internet collection activities has been startlingly revealing. The Report is something that should be carefully read by every lawmaker, around the world, who is charged with regulating the interaction between ISPs and their customers. ISPs are using a variety of AI tools to collect a huge swath of information about their customers.[22]

As the report points out, there is a significant amount of information that customers voluntarily provide during registration processes, such as their name, contacts and billing information which is often required to get requested services. In addition, there is also identification information that is often required, such as date of birth, identity verification and credit checks.[23]

These categories of information are things that customers usually knowingly and consciously provide. However, in addition to these, there is also a lot of information collected that is useful to the ISPs but which customers may not know is being collected, organized and used by the ISPs to allow them to make more money from their customers. This can include the technical specifications of the devices the customers are communicating with, including media access control addresses, device serial numbers, device type and operating system. In addition, records will often be made of the details of customers' communication sessions, including the volume of traffic sent and received.

21. "A Look At What ISPs Know About You: Examining the Privacy Practices of Six Major Internet Service Providers" An FTC Staff Report, Federal Trade Commission, online, October 21, 2021.
22. As cited above: "A Look at What ISPs Know about You: Examining the Privacy Practices of Six Major Internet Service Providers" An FTC Staff Report, Federal Trade Commission, online, October 21, 2021 (FTC Report).
23. *Ibid.*, at p. 15.

A number of ISPs were also found to collect and use internet protocol (IP) Addresses and the URLs consumers use when receiving and sending Internet traffic on their devices. Some ISPs also collect location data which they claim is necessary for telecommunication services or emergency support and to determine whether the network signal strength in the customers' geographic location is strong enough to serve customers in the area.[24]

The FTC also reports that ISPs may use the information they collect for purposes wholly unconnected to the services consumers thought they were receiving, including the ISP's compliance with legal obligations, law enforcement requests and court orders such as search warrants.

ISPs are sometimes required to provide law enforcement with personal information about consumers, such as location information. Many ISPs also use information such as names, telephone numbers, location information, device information, identifiers and mobile broadband usage information to prevent fraud or to protect the security of customer devices connected to a network. Sometimes, the ISPs are using the information to detect and prevent "botnets"[25] or other malicious actors from inserting themselves in customer networks.

Other times, the ISPs may be using the information collected to know how consumers are using equipment or certain features on their equipment. The ISPs may use that information for product development and testing.

The FTC report goes on to say that advertising services pose a serious risk to consumer data privacy. Many ISPs actively collect consumer data for advertising purposes. For example, some ISPs use the web browsing information of consumers to target adds to them. There is also a practice of buying consumer information from third party data brokers for advertising purposes. One example that the report gives is as follows:

> A sizable number of ISP's in our study also buy data from data brokers about their existing customers. For example, an ISP might send the data broker subscriber names and addresses, which the data broker would then append with demographic information (e.g., gender, age range, race and ethnicity information, marital status, parental status) and interest data (e.g., hiking, biking, gardening, bodybuilding, etc.) ... for those subscribers.[26]

§2.02 A MODEL ORDER

The report indicates in its conclusion that the FTC is seriously concerned that:

---

24. *Ibid.*
25. A "botnet" is a "robot network" of computers "infected by malware that are under the control of single attacking party. ... From one central point, the attacking party can command every computer on its botnet to simultaneously carry out a coordinated criminal action." Palo Alto networks, "What Is a Botnet," online at paloaltonetworks.com, accessed September 14, 2023.
26. FTC Report, pp. 18-19.

> Many of the ISP's in our study amass large pools of sensitive data, and that their uses of such data could lead to significant harms ... .[27]

Therefore, the FTC has ordered a number of ISPs to be more transparent as to what information they are collecting from consumers, how it is being collected, and how it is being used.

In aid of this Report, the FTC issued an Order permitting the FTC:

> To compile data concerning the privacy policies, procedures, and practices of Internet service providers and related entities, including the method and manner by which they collect, retain, use and disclose information about consumers and their Devices.[28]

In December 2020, the FTC announced that it was issuing orders to nine major ISPs, including Amazon.com Inc, ByteDance Ltd., TikTok, Discord Inc, Facebook Inc, Reddit Inc, Snap Inc, Twitter Inc., WhatsApp Inc, and YouTube LLC. These companies were given 45 days to respond from the date they received the Order.[29]

§2.03 ISP DATA AND AI

The way that this is affected by AI is that ISPs use AI to harvest and use customer data.[30] For example, Alibaba, the world's largest e-commerce platform, uses AI to predict what consumers may want to buy.

Amazon uses AI throughout its business:

> [An] innovative way Amazon uses artificial intelligence is to ship things to you before you even think about buying it. They collect a lot of data about each person's buying habits and have such confidence in how the data they collect helps them recommend items to its customers and now predict what they need even before they need it by using predictive analytics.[31]

§2.04 IS IA "OUT OF CONTROL"?

> Elon Musk and Steve Wozniak are among hundreds of high-profile technologists, entrepreneurs and researchers calling on AI labs to immediately stop work on powerful AI systems, urging developers to step back from an "out-of-control race"

27. *Ibid.*, p. 44.
28. *Ibid.*, *see*, Model Order at pp. A-1 through A-9.
29. "FTC Issues Orders to Nine Social Media and Video Streaming Services Seeking Data About How They Collect, Use, and Present Information," Press Release, FTC online at: ftc.gov, December 14, 2020.
30. Bernard Marr, "The 10 Best Examples of How Companies Use Artificial Intelligence in Practice," *Forbes*, online, December 09, 2019. Note that this article is more than 3 years old. It seems probable that the ISP use of AI in collecting, analyzing and using customer data has become even more extensive.
31. *Ibid.*

> to deploy ever more advanced products while we better assess the risks advanced artificial intelligence poses to humanity.[32]

This request for a pause was set out in an open letter published on the website of The Future of Life Institute and signed by over one thousand business and technology people. In part, the letter says:

> Contemporary AI systems are now becoming human-competitive at general tasks, and we must ask ourselves should we let the machines flood our information channels with propaganda and untruth? Should we automate away all the jobs, including the fulfilling ones? Should we develop non-human minds that might eventually outnumber, outsmart, obsolete and replace us? Should we risk loss of control of our civilization? Such decisions must not be delegated to unelected tech leaders. Powerful AI systems should be developed only once we are confident that their effects will be positive and their risks will be manageable. This confidence must be well justified and increased with the magnitude of a system's potential effects. Open AI's recent statement regarding artificial general intelligence, states that "at some point, it may be important to get independent review before starting to train future systems, and for the most advanced efforts to agree to limit the rate of growth of compute used for creating new models." We agree. That point is now. Therefore, we call on all AI labs to immediately pause for at least six months the training of AI systems more powerful than GPT-4. This pause should be public and verifiable and include all key factors. If this pause cannot be enacted quickly, governments should step in and institute a moratorium.[33]

This letter and knowledge of who the signatories are has been widely reported and may well influence government and business leaders to support a careful examination of the way that AI is developing and careful consideration of how it should be regulated both within legal jurisdictions and internationally. Such an examination may lead to international conventions and treaties to impose sensible AI regulation. What this will be remains to be seen.

§2.05 THE AI GOLD RUSH

Nevertheless, despite the concern about the progress of AI expressed by "technology experts," including Elon Musk, the growing interest in AI and the fact that it is increasingly being used for a number of tasks has stimulated many technologists to seek to build their own AI businesses. And, somewhat surprisingly, this group includes Elon Musk. It was recently reported that:

> Elon Musk is working on an artificial intelligence startup that will rival open IA, the ChatGPT maker, in silicon valley's race to build AI systems. ... Musk's move to

32. Robert Hart, "Elon Musk and Tech Leaders Call For AI 'Pause' Over Risks to Humanity," *Forbes*, online, March 29, 2023.
33. Future of Life Institute, "Pause Giant AI Experiments: An Open Letter," online at: futureoflife.org, March 28, 2023.

> enter the AI market will surprise analysts after he called for a pause on development of GPT style models over safety concerns.[34]

§2.06 HOW DANGEROUS IS AI?

The fact that "hundreds" of technologists are reported to fear the potential of AI has raised concerns around the world that AI systems could lead to the extinction of the human race.

There is no question that the unregulated development and abuse of AI systems do present dangers, just as the general unregulated production of any machine has the potential to cause injury and death to humans.

Machines cause many deaths to humans around the world every year. But that does not mean that we should not manufacture or use them. There are laws and regulations to prevent their legal or negligent production and use. Many of these laws and regulations will also already be applicable to the creation and use of AI systems. Human beings are required to conform to a legal "duty of care" in anything that they do that could impact on other people.

Are these hundreds of technologists arguing these existing laws and regulations don't already apply to AI? Of course not. Anything that people do, including the creation and operation of AI machines, is overseen by existing laws and regulations. Yes, there are always "outlaws," but if apprehended, they are subject to legal consequences. AI is not exempt from existing criminal and tort law.

With respect to all these "technologists" expressing fear over AI, one has to be a bit skeptical of their motives. Yes, it is true that most of us, technologists or not, do not want to see the human race exterminated by natural or man-made causes, whether they be asteroids or rogue AI machines. But we need to recognize that the dramatic development of AI systems has led to a "Gold Rush" mentality whereby nations and individuals want to not only realize the "quality of life benefits" that AI may provide us but may also want to make profits from the expansion of this new industry. There was a little doubt that one group that wants to share in the wealth that may be created by AI includes "technologists" who understand how to create and use AI. Is it possible that some of them are, in effect, saying to the world:

> Here I am an AI expert. I am telling you that if AI is not carefully handled, it may wipe out the human race. Would it not be a good idea to hire me, preferably at great expense, to protect humanity from the potential dangers of AI?

One of the best-known pioneers in the development of the Internet, Mark Andreessen who helped develop the first pre-Google Internet browsers, Mosaic and

34. Robert Miller, "Elon Musk joins 'dangerous' race to create chatbots," *The Times*, online, April 15, 2023.

Netscape, has spoken out against the hysterical "warnings that AI poses an existential threat."[35]

It is reported that in his essay, "Why AI will save the world," Andreessen wrote:

> "AI risk" has developed into a cult, which has suddenly emerged into the daylight of global press attention and the public conversation. This has pulled in not just cringe characters, but also some actual industry experts and a not small number of wealthy donors. It's not that they actually have secret knowledge that makes their extremism logical, it's that they've whipped themselves into a frenzy and really are ... extremely extreme. Their extreme beliefs should not determine the future of laws and society.[36]

Marc Andreessen is not the only technological pioneer who finds the warnings of the "Doomers" too extreme. A number of other well-known technology experts believe the potential risks of AI to be overstated by some other technologists.

Andrew Ng, a professor at Stanford University who is responsible for Google's Brain Division, is reported to have written, "I'd like to have a real conversation about whether AI is a risk for human extinction. Honestly, I don't get how AI poses this risk."[37]

In June 2023, the president of Microsoft, Brad Smith, is reported to have asked those commenting on AI to "dial down the rhetoric."[38]

Sandra Wachter, a professor at the Oxford Internet Institute, is reported as saying that the statement by a group of technologists and industry investors that AI systems could be a danger to humanity is a publicity stunt that could have the unfortunate effect of distracting policymakers from "real AI harms, such as bias and discrimination."[39]

Andreessen summarized his view of AI development as follows:

> My view is that the idea that AI will decide to literally kill humanity is a profound category error. ... AI is not a living being that has been primed by billions of years of evolution to participate in the battle for the survival of the fittest, as animals are, and as we are. It is math—code—computers, built by people owned by people used by people and controlled by people. The idea that it will at some point develop a mind of its own and decide that it has motivations that lead it to try to kill us is a superstitious and naïve. In short, AI doesn't want, it doesn't have goals, it doesn't want to kill you, because it's not alive. And AI is a machine—that is not going to come alive anymore than your toaster will.[40]

It is reported that much of the impetus behind the "tumor" view of AI is from a philosophical movement called "effective altruism" (EA) named by William MacAskill at Oxford University. Reportedly, EA focuses its efforts on dealing with what it regards as "long-term threats" to humanity, such as climate change, nuclear war and AI.[41]

---

35. Mark Sellman, "AI does not mean our end is nigh, internet pioneer insists," *The Times*, online, June 10, 2023.
36. *Ibid.* (emphasis added).
37. *Ibid.*
38. *Ibid.*
39. *Ibid.*
40. *Ibid.*
41. *Ibid.*

EA backer, Vitalik Butterin, also apparently funded something called The Future of Life Institute which sponsored the highly publicized open letter about the necessity for pausing AI development to protect against the possibility of human extinction by AI.

It is worth noting that AI has suffered from being associated with the criminally charged CEO of the collapsed crypto exchange, FTX, Sam Bankman-Fried.[42]

42. *Ibid.*

CHAPTER 3

AI Legal Issues

The development of AI systems and the publicity and discussions surrounding it are happening so rapidly that it is useful to look at what new AI applications are being offered and what are being projected to be developed in the future.

It seems as though every day, there is news about the marvels and dangers that AI is presenting to the human race. Some of these may be exaggerated or inaccurately reported, but a review of what is on offer is useful to decide how these new systems and their creators and operators will need to be regulated.

Among the new AI inventions that have been reported, one finds the following.

§3.01 ChatGPT

The AI system that has probably been the subject of the most publicity and discussion is ChatGPT, an AI-powered analysis and response system that was created by a company called OpenAI.

This was introduced in November of 2022 and rapidly gained over a hundred million users. It takes the form of a "chatbot" which is a computer app that a user can pose questions to and get relevant responses. Among the tasks that ChatGPT is reported to be capable of doing:

> It can answer complex and nuanced questions, refine its answers, summarize dense information or write essays, poems, stories and workable computer code.[43]

It is projected that this sophisticated tool will be able to do many complex and time-consuming tasks in a fraction of the time that human workers can complete them and consequently may eliminate or modify jobs where humans are currently paid to do those tasks.

43. Juliet Samuel, "It's common sense to use artificial intelligence," *The Times*, online, April 05, 2023.

Like any significant invention, ChatGPT offers both significant benefits and significant problems. Many tasks may be completed in much less time than they had been before the application of this AI, but many jobs may be eliminated.

Also, the power and speed of this chatbot may enable users to cheat on examinations more easily or to pass off work completed by the chatbot as their own. School homework is a frequently cited example.

There was also the problem that the speed and sophistication of AI of this kind would aid users in breaking the law. For example, by aiding the rapid circumvention of confidentiality protections, the production of realistic seeming false documents, false video and audio presentations, creating credible falsehoods, gathering large amounts of personal private data, and aiding in the planning and execution of complex cybercrimes.

The potential of AI to produce both good and bad results has caused governments to consider how AI can best be used to aid their governing processes and economic development while, at the same time, considering ways to control it to prevent damaging misuse.

Balancing these things is a complex problem, but nevertheless, it must be done. It is not particularly useful to conclude that the nature of AI is so complicated that it is not possible to regulate it effectively or to prevent it from being misused.

However, it will forever be the case that legal regulation cannot totally prevent antisocial behavior. The creation of even the most enlightened penal laws cannot prevent crime, but it does provide a society with a considered and consistent method of responding to it.

Laws may not entirely prevent anti-social behavior, but they may deter it. Those considering misusing AI may be persuaded to behave in legally compliant ways after considering the penalties they may incur from breaking the law.

It does no good to argue that attempts to create laws to regulate AI will come too slowly or be inadequate to prevent all misuse of this new and powerful tool. As with any situation that a society considers necessary to control, the anti-social use of otherwise useful tools can never be entirely prevented, but it is sensible to provide laws that are perceived to encourage the benefits of inventions while limiting the damage they can do.

It is always necessary for any civilization to create a regulatory system that allows the benefits of the activities of their citizens to outweigh the harm that people may do. Laws are never perfect, but they are essential for human interaction.

It makes sense to limit the uses of something like ChatGPT, but it is equally sensible to encourage its beneficial uses.

§3.02 CHABOT PROBLEMS

Some countries, including China, Russia and Italy, have banned the use of ChatGPT entirely. Would it not be better to ban some uses of it rather than make it impossible for their citizens to benefit from using it in ways not deemed harmful to society?

However, there are problems with AI systems like ChatGPT relating to invasions of privacy and inaccuracies that can make such systems untrustworthy and even dangerous.

Unfortunate examples of this potential have been reported. In April 2023, ChatGPT was said to have falsely accused a law professor of sexually harassing a student.[44] The accusation was apparently made by ChatGPT as the result of research by another academic:

> The AI claimed he made sexually suggestive comments and attempted to touch a student during a class trip to Alaska. It cited an article from The Washington Post as evidence.

The accused professor said:

> It was a surprise to me since I have never gone to Alaska with students, The Post never published such an article, and I have never been accused of sexual harassment or assault by anyone.

About the same time, it was also reported that an Australian mayor threatened to sue the developer of ChatGPT for defamation "after the chatbot falsely claimed that he had been imprisoned for bribery."[45]

Unfortunately, these reports are also consistent with a report by *The Guardian* newspaper that there were instances when ChatGPT was quoting articles purportedly from that newspaper that *The Guardian* had never published.[46]

Those are the kinds of things that require carefully considered regulation, of which there will be more detailed discussion in the following chapters.

Obviously, the law needs to apportion responsibility to those who cause or negligently permit AI systems to publish false and damaging information about individuals and organizations. Legal responsibility needs to be assigned to technologists creating AI systems who fail to make certain that their systems contain controls that prevent AI systems from simply making things up and representing them as supported facts. Such false reports are not only damaging to those falsely accused but also severely damaging to the sources that chatbots may falsely refer to as support for their false accusations and to those relying on research produced by chatbots.

§3.03 MICHAEL SCHUMACHER

Another very disturbing story was published in April 2023. A German magazine, *Die Aktuelle*, was reported to have published what it claimed was an interview with

44. Mark Sellman, "ChatGPT falsely accuses law professor of sex assault," *The Times*, online, April 06, 2023.
45. Mark Sellman.
46. Alex Farber, "BBC News chief fears 'frightening' impact of AI on audience trust," *The Times*, online, April 11, 2021.

Michael Schumacher, the famous Formula One driver who was badly injured in a skiing accident some years previously:[47]

> The article itself, under the headline "my life has completely changed" and framed in a question-and-answer format, discussed "Schumacher's" feelings about the 2013 accident, his children and his future.[48]

This so-called interview was reportedly completely false and was believed to have been created using an AI chatbot from a website named Character.ai. Reportedly, this chatbot:

> simulates answers from a range of famous, figures including Albert Einstein, Paul McCartney and JRR Tolkien, extrapolating from their writings and statements in the public domain.[49]

If this report is accurate, it is clearly another shocking example of using AI to make money by deceiving people with false information artificially created.

The legality and morality of such behavior are clearly unacceptable in a society seeking to promote peaceful and civilized relationships between its human members. Successfully maintaining such a society requires honesty, transparency and curtailment of fraudulent deception. It is surprising that some governments and their regulatory bodies seem puzzled about how to respond to such activities. Perhaps this is because they have not clearly decided how they should respond to the remarkable new machines that comprise AI. This is surprising. It is not clear why AI should provoke any response different from the legal response to other human-made machines. The benefits should be encouraged, and the unacceptable risks should be legally barred. There seems little doubt that a known and demonstrated potential for fraud should be eliminated by the constructors of AI systems under penalties of law. If they find themselves unable to write the code to do this, they should recognize that their AI system may be entirely banned.

A radical solution to such problems that has been adopted by some countries is to ban the use of certain chatbots entirely, but that also eliminates the opportunity to use them for productive and beneficial projects. As with other machines, a balance needs to be achieved between the risks posed by chatbots and the benefits they can bestow. Perhaps that balance is better achieved by legal regulation that sensibly assigns responsibility for limiting the potential of chatbots to respond to inquiries with false information. The potential for legal liability would undoubtedly cause technologists developing such AI systems to carefully consider whether the instructions they give such systems will produce accurate and safe results for all potential users and those affected by AI system outcomes.

47. Oliver Moody, "Michael Schumacher 'interview' in German magazine was made up with AI chatbot," *The Times*, online, April 18, 2023.
48. Oliver Moody, April 18, 2023, cited above.
49. Oliver Moody, April 18, 2023, cited above.

§3.04 HARM TO YOUNG PEOPLE

One of the principal objections to the world of cyber technology is that many of its products, such as apps, games and social media, are designed to be addictive to young people, such as children and teenagers, and that they cause them to spend a lot of time looking at screens which interferes with their education, social development and family life.

To date, much of this criticism has been aimed at games and social media apps, but the advent of sophisticated AI products is causing additional worry about the impact these things will have on young people:[50]

> Generative AI is about to reshape the processing power, capability needs and creative output of the entire telecommunications, social media and gaming industries.
>
> What does it even mean to "be smart" in a world powered by generative AI? What should we be teaching children to prepare them for an uncertain future? What is the role of the teacher if a super-intelligent chatbot can offer an entirely personalized learning experience?[51]
>
> It is reported that educators and legislature have taken serious action to limit the exposure of young people to social media and there is a view that they will react in the same way or even more strongly to the exposure of young people to AI products.
>
> For example, it is reported that in March 2023, the superintendent and school board of San Mateo County, California, a location closely associated with the Silicon Valley tech industries, filed suit in the U.S. Federal court alleging that companies such as Alphabet (which owns YouTube), Snapchat and ByteDance (which owns TikTok) are using sophisticated AI to design products that are "addictive and deliver harmful content to youth."

§3.05 HARMS OF OPPOSING AI DEVELOPMENT

One of the issues with the development of AI is that those who are critical of it seem to take the view that all AI is the same—all presenting an equal danger to the human race. That is like saying that all machines are equally dangerous. It is important that we think of AI systems as sophisticated machines. Some will be more helpful than others. Some may be unacceptably dangerous, and others may be critically necessary. Most AI systems will fall somewhere in between.

This is why it is essential that a well-thought-out legal system for regulating them needs to be instituted across the world. Like other machines, those that developed them will have the responsibility for restricting, and in some cases eliminating, those characteristics that can cause harm.

50. Kathryn Parsons, "Think social media is bad for young people? Just wait for AI," *The Sunday Times*, online, April 09, 2023.
51. Kathryn Parsons, cited above.

As with any human-created product, some contain acceptable risks, and others may offer unacceptable risks. As with any product or activity, the level of risk must be matched, by appropriate laws and regulations, to those who are allowed to use it.

For example, only licensed drivers are allowed to operate the powerful and dangerous machines that we call automobiles. Only trained and licensed radiologists are allowed to operate X-ray machines. Under the control of the wrong persons, either of these can cause serious or fatal injuries. That does not mean that it makes sense for us to entirely ban their use. We have concluded that the benefits of having them built to acceptable specifications and operated by qualified persons outweigh the risks that their existence poses.

Appropriately regulated AI systems can make dramatic improvements to our lives that could not be achieved by other means. For example:

> We've already seen how AI can drive progress that humans couldn't achieve alone. The London-based team at Deep Mind recently used AI to crack what is called the protein-folding problem, which had flummoxed researchers for decades and which may be a springboard for developing important new drugs.[52]

The same article points out that there are other critical medical research projects that would benefit greatly from the use of AI in analyzing collected data. The author says that it is now possible to collect thousands of genomes from sequencing DNA and link them to the medical records of UK National Health System (NHS) patients. It is argued that employing AI to analyze these records would lead to possible breakthroughs in developing cancer drugs for providing personal medical treatment. AI could also lessen the pressure on doctors by providing basic diagnosis and then booking appointments with doctors specializing in relevant areas.[53]

However, there is reportedly serious resistance to using AI in medical treatment, with the resistance apparently being due to concerns about privacy and safety:

> Instead, British legislators, no doubt under pressure from the medical establishment, are slapping down heavy-handed rules that make it hard for AI to be used in our [the British] health system.
>
> As the tech entrepreneur Balaji Srinivasan, wrote in response to red tape here: "The regulatory choking of AI begins. You'll be able to use it for engineering and design, but not bring down the cost of medicine. Not in the West, at least."[54]

This is unfortunate. Public health systems around the world are already struggling under the pressures of increasing population, longer life expectancy, and shortages of trained medical staff. AI is already showing that it can reduce the burdens of medical care by making the use of medical resources more efficient. For example, there has been a recent report about how the Israeli health tech firm Genetika + is using AI to match the most useful medications to particular patients:

52. Rohan Silva, "We'd be mad to slow the progress of AI now: With schools and hospitals under more pressure than ever before, this game-changing technology has to be embraced," *The Times*, online, April 10, 2023.
53. *Ibid.*
54. *Ibid.*

> [T]he company says its technology can best match antidepressants to patients, to avoid unwanted side effects, and make sure the prescribed drug works as well as possible. "We can characterize the right medication for each patient the first time," adds Dr. Cohen Solal.[55]

Historically, excessively fearful legislative response to game-changing inventions has not been unusual.

§3.06 THE RED FLAG LAWS

In the late 19th century, "red flag laws" were enacted in both the UK and some parts of the U.S. to restrict the operation of newly introduced automobiles (or so-called self-propelled vehicles or locomotives). These laws did not apply to rail traffic but to self-propelled vehicles (referred to then as "locomotives") operating on roads. The first "Red Flag Act" was the British Locomotives Act of 1865, which said:

> [A person], while any locomotive is in motion, shall proceed such locomotive on foot by not less than 60 yards, and shall carry a red flag constantly displayed, and shall warn the riders and drivers of horses of the approach of such locomotives, and shall signal the driver thereof when it shall be necessary to stop, and shall assist horses, and carriages drawn by horses, passing the same.[56]

A similar red flag law was introduced in the U.S. state of Vermont in 1894.[57]

It is possible that one of the important reasons for the introduction of such laws was safety, although there may also have been concerns about the competitive dangers that automobiles presented to the important horse and carriage-related businesses of the time.

Nevertheless, there is no question that automobiles are one of the most important inventions the world has ever seen and that they have hugely changed lives and the environment in ways that were probably impossible to foresee in the 19th century.

Despite the fact that automobiles are powerful and dangerous to the point of being involved in approximately 1.5 million traffic deaths annually around the world,[58] there is currently too great an acceptance of the importance of cars to forbid or over-restrict their use. And this does not even count the damage that their use does to the environment, or the damage they do to human health and fitness by replacing walking and/or cycling.

Yet, most people do not fear the existence and use of cars. They have become an important and, in some cases, a critical part of human life. Yes, there are significant risks of injury and death, but society has decided those are acceptable risks to enjoy the benefits that automobiles provide.

---

55. Natalie Lisbona, "How artificial intelligence is matching drugs to patients," BBC New, online, April 17, 2023.
56. Olyslager, P. and Sir J. Brabham, *Illustrated Motor Cars of the World*, (New York: Grosset & Dunlap).
57. *Ibid.*
58. Centers for Disease Control and Prevention, online at: cdc.gov.

It is unfortunately the case that media organizations and commentators seek sensational stories or points of view to publish. They may do this in order to sell publications or attract "clicks" on their websites to make money. Unfortunately, this ambition has led to reports about the potential for AI to control or even wipe out the human race. There is not much evidence that such things are likely. Indeed, as of this writing, the only reported death due to AI is a story about an unfortunate man who committed suicide, possibly in response to the urging of a chatbot that he had formed an unhealthy relationship with.

However, if it were reported that it was likely that AI systems would, like automobiles, contribute to approximately 1.5 million deaths of people a year, people would be terrified. Nevertheless, despite the annual fatality totals of automobiles, people seem to feel that this is an acceptable risk that has to be endured in order to benefit from the advantages of using automobiles.

With respect to AI, legislators should learn from their past mistakes and avoid senseless "knee-jerk" reactions to sensational media stories about how AI is endangering the existence of the human race.

Like any powerful invention, AI needs to be sensibly regulated to promote its benefits and reduce its dangers. However, the human race has managed to control new inventions and novel ways of interacting many times in the past through carefully thought-out regulation. This is how we must proceed with AI. Reacting to extraordinary media reports that may be intended to attract "clicks" or sell publications does not promote effective, successful legal systems.[59]

It makes no sense to talk about forbidding the use of AI now. It is already being used in many fields to make tasks more efficient and more effective.

An article in *The New York Times* in April 2023 listed 35 ways that AI is being used already.[60] The things being done with AI are reported to include:

- Planning gardens
- Planning workouts
- Planning meals
- Making gifts
- Designing spaceships
- Organizing messy workspaces
- Composing wedding speeches
- Composing emails
- Editing written material
- Constructing opposing arguments
- Designing a clock that creates a new poem every minute
- Organizing thesis research
- Summarizing scholarly articles
- Helping overcome ADHD

59. Rhys Blakely, "Rogue AI 'could kill everyone'," *The Times*, online, January 26, 2023.
60. Francesca Paris and Larry Buchanan, "35 Ways Real People Are Using A.I. Right Now," *The New York Times*, online, April 14, 2023.

- Helping overcome the dyslexia
- Sorting picture archives
- Transcribing doctors' notes
- Appealing an insurance denial
- Writing Excel formulas
- Writing literary criticism
- Helping with homework
- Learning Chinese
- Learning English
- Coding apps
- Debugging computer code
- Playing computer games
- Providing existing computer games
- Creating new computer games
- Teaching sports training
- Designing new proteins
- Identifying plant diseases
- Copying art styles
- Creating Dungeons and Dragons worlds
- Making musical playlists
- Improving use of language.

What this demonstrates is that AI is very useful in responding to the human imagination's ability to design tasks. In this sense, it is obviously a supplement to human imagination and not a replacement for it.

Legal regulation needs to encourage and guide this relationship, not prevent it.

§3.07 LOSS OF POWER

Concern has been expressed that AI systems may take from humans the power to control their own lives. Given the rapid expansion of AI systems to assist decision-making in a variety of situations, is it the case that "we may soon find that much of the real power in our society is wielded by algorithms?"[61]

The truth of the matter is that in the field of human relations, people become powerless to the extent that they agree to give up their power over their life choices. True, political power can sometimes be given up in the face of threats of violence, but that is not what we are currently facing from AI systems. AI systems are created by people. In all societies, people are subject to governmental laws and regulations. Those things determine the limits within which people are permitted to act.

The sensible response to the creation of AI systems is to impose legal restrictions and the potential of legal liability on those creating AI systems. The introduction of AI

61. Josh Glancy, "The real AI threat: how powerless it makes us," *The Sunday Times*, online, April 16, 2023.

systems could perhaps be restricted to those who are licensed to do so after having passed rigorous examinations on their intentions and skills. The licensees will need to guarantee that their AI systems will be constructed to reduce or eliminate threats of deceptive, damaging or dangerous outcomes.

The most effective legal regulation of any activity, including technological creativity, is not to focus legal restrictions solely on the AI machines themselves but on the people creating them. Appropriate legal penalties should be applied to those who fail to create AI machines where the benefits of employing them substantially outweigh the risks. This is not significantly different from the laws that apply to automobiles, airplanes, ships and other mechanical machines that offer both benefits and risks. Law has always been able to make the responsibilities of inventors clear, to take advantage of useful inventions, but to protect the public against unacceptable risks. The same legal responses should be put in place now before AI systems are allowed to injure the public.

§3.08 TRANSPARENCY

One important issue that attaches to the creation of AI systems is the issue of transparency.

Scientists and technicians involved in the development of AI are striving to create AI systems that mimic human behavior as closely as possible.

Digital game creators have reached the point where they are able to create AI communities where individual AI "citizens" react to their roles in ways reminiscent of human behavior. The creators of these systems say that their purpose is to make computer games more realistic and immersive.[62]

This highlights one of the important legal steps that must be taken in response to AI. That is, AI systems must always be accompanied by a clearly stated explanation that their products, whether written, video or audio, are created by AI systems and, therefore, may not be representations of reality or truth.

For example, in April 2023, *The Guardian* newspaper contained a report that ChatGPT has been producing articles and citing reports from that newspaper that do not exist:[63]

> The AI had simply made them up. Its fluency, and the vast training data it is built on, meant that the existence of the invented piece even seemed believable to the person who absolutely hadn't written it.[64]

In response to the potential of the public being "bombarded with disinformation," the head of BBC News proposes:

62. Rhys Blakely, "AI 'humans' in virtual world plot and gossip like us' *The Times*, online, April 14, 2023.
63. Alex Farber BBC News chief fears 'frightening' impact of AI on audience trust," *The Times*, online, April 11, 2021.
64. *Ibid.*, citing Chris Moran, *The Guardian's* head of editorial innovation.

> [T]he creation of a "forensic journalism hub" that will house teams dedicated to fact-checking, including verifying still and video images from social media and satellite tracking.[65]

This is certainly a worthy effort on the part of the BBC, but it seems to be acceptance of responsibility by victims of misinformation rather than by those responsible for creating misinformation. True, news organizations should make efforts to avoid spreading disinformation created by others, but the principal legal responsibility for the effects of disinformation should be on those who create systems that are shown to have the potential to lie or misinform.

The creators need to construct their AI systems to prevent their creations from publishing potentially harmful disinformation. They should be legally required to do so and penalized for their failures to do so under applicable tort law.

For example, on Friday, April 21, 2023, *The Times* published an "in depth" article entitled "How worried should we be about the rise of the AI 'monster'."[66] It was accompanied by garishly colored illustrations that seemed to herald a heartless dystopian future. This was apparently an attempt to grab people's attention. The first paragraph quotes an MIT professor as saying:

> The evil thing about this monster is even though everybody sees it and understands it, they still can't get out of the race.

The second paragraph begins by posing the question:

> Are we really in an unavoidable battle with an AI monster to stay alive?

It goes on:

> Sam Altman, the head of open AI, which developed ChatGPT, is a "little bit scared" of the technology, which in the worst-case scenario could mean "lights out for all of us."

This approach seems excessively sensationalist in light of the fact that, as of this writing, AI has not even begun to approach causing the toll of death or damage inflicted on humans by the many long-existing human-made machines on our roads, in our skies, in our factories, on our seas, on our farms, in our energy systems, on our building sites, and in our homes.

Accidents attributable to machines in common use contribute to millions of deaths every year around the world. Yet we continue to use them every day because we have concluded that their benefits outweigh the risks they present.

Our solution to controlling these "monsters" is a highly developed legal system which requires the construction and operation of dangerous machines by competent practitioners who are required to exercise legally mandated duties of care and who face legal penalties if they fail in their duties.

---

65. *Ibid.*
66. Mark Sellman, "How worried should we be about the rise of the AI 'monster'" *The Times*, online, April 21, 2023.

If we conclude that the benefits of using AI machines outweigh the risks of using them, then the same approach should be applied to the creation and use of AI systems. Banning them entirely before we determine that there is a reasonable balance between the benefits and risks of AI seems absurd.

This is particularly true because the world of AI systems is already subject to many existing laws and regulations, including laws that require reasonable care, regulations on education and licensing of competent operators, laws against fraud and misrepresentation, laws protecting intellectual property, laws protecting privacy, laws requiring informed consent, tort law, and laws imposing penalties and compensation requirements for injuries caused by breach of duties.

The control and regularization of AI do not necessarily require the creation of a whole new regulatory system to prevent it from being inappropriately used. It seems that some regulators are baffled by the newness of AI and fail to understand that many of the legal tools necessary to control AI and punish its misuse already exist to a significant extent. The startling newness and cleverness of AI machines should not prevent existing legal requirements from being applied.

It is clear that some of the reported abuses of the use of AI systems, such as privacy violations, "fakes" and other misrepresentations and frauds, should already attract civil and criminal penalties. It is somewhat surprising that these are not already being widely used against those who use AI to damage individuals and organizations.

CHAPTER 4
Current AI Regulation

There seems to be a view expressed by some that AI is largely unregulated. However, nothing could be further from the truth.

In fact, AI is heavily regulated by a very large number of existing laws throughout the world. As discussed in the previous chapter, human activity within any society is regulated by many laws governing the many different areas of human life, particularly those areas where people interact with other humans. These include:

- Constitutional and administrative law
- Laws that require reasonable care
- Regulations requiring the education and licensing of competent operators
- Criminal law
- Contract law
- Laws against fraud and misrepresentation
- Laws protecting intellectual property
- Laws governing personality, status, and legal capacity
- Laws protecting privacy and personal data
- Laws protecting minors and other vulnerable groups
- Laws requiring informed consent
- Health and safety laws
- Welfare law
- Property law
- Family law
- Investment law
- Banking law
- Tort law
- Laws imposing penalties and compensation for injuries caused by breach of legal duties.

Many aspects of these areas of law affect the freedom of technologists to create and use AI. They also affected the ability of third persons to distribute or use their products. However, it is certainly the case that the creation of AI machines is a relatively new and rapidly growing area of endeavor. Consequently, new regulations may need to be created to regulate the specific activities of creating and using AI to interact with other persons within one's own society and around the world.

A significant complication that affects the world of AI, which affects many other digital businesses, is the fact that digital communication via the Internet has become almost unavoidably international. This means that no set of national laws can govern and protect all the persons who are impacted by AI machines.

It is critically important that the countries and legal jurisdictions that exist throughout the world undertake to cooperate in imposing consistent and reasonable regulations on the creation and use of AI machines within their own societies and that they recognize the importance of having laws that sensibly respond to the international impact of AI machines created within their own nation and those created abroad that impact on their society.

One goal of this book is to identify those international organizations that have an interest in employing international cooperation to create and enforce reasonable and effective laws and regulations governing the creation and use of AI machines.

§4.01 DUTY OF CARE

Anything human beings do is to a greater or lesser extent under the scrutiny of the law of some jurisdiction. This is more completely true with respect to anything done that impacts on others.

A basic legal concept that covers everything we do that impacts on others is the principle of "duty of care." This is a legal concept that originated in common law but is now reflected internationally in the legal systems of other jurisdictions and international organizations.

The UN System Chief Executives Board for Coordination provides the following definition on its website.

> "Duty of care" (DoC) is a legal concept that comes from common law and can be defined as a legal obligation requiring adherence to a standard of reasonable care while performing any acts that could foreseeably harm others. Another definition for DoC would be a legal obligation to act towards others with prudence and vigilance in order to prevent any risk of foreseeable damage. ...The legal consequence of a breach of such a duty is a legal liability imposed upon the author (of the breach) to compensate the victim for any losses they occur. ...This means that the author must take all appropriate measures to behave in an appropriate way in order to avoid causing harm to third parties. That being said, the fact that harm is done does not necessarily mean that the duty of care was breached (or, in other words that the author was negligent), as certain events are beyond the control of

> the author (because they were unforeseeable or unavoidable despite proper care being taken).[67]

The requirement of duty of care will be applicable to all activities relating to the creation, distribution and use of AI systems in almost any jurisdiction. It is a fundamental concept of law.

Historically, legal systems have taken account of that and have extended the concept of "duty of care" from the creator of an artificial thing to the effects caused by a person's artificial creations.

The application of the concept may, of course, vary under the laws of non-common law jurisdictions.

> The actual measure, scope or content of the "care" that is required in each situation depends primarily on two factors: (i) the relationship between the parties and (ii) the applicable law.[68]

Under systems of international private law, duty of care will always be applicable with modifications as referred to above. The UN recommends that in international situations, a good standard of reference for determining the application of duty of care is the Swiss Code of Obligations, Article 328. The UN points out:

> Article 328 CO has a very wide scope, going beyond the duty of care as it is understood in other legal systems. The extent of the protection effectively provided by article 328 CO must be examined on a case-by-case basis.[69]
>
> Article 328 CO covers the following issues:
>
> - The protection of overall health, both physical and mental, including a duty of prevention in relation to the work environment;
> - The safeguarding of personal and professional honor;
> - An employer's duty of aid and assistance, for example in the event of interpersonal disputes within the enterprise;
> - A ban on psychological and sexual harassment;
> - The protection of privacy;
> - Equal treatment.

§4.02 INTERNATIONAL IMPACT

AI systems can impact numerous legal jurisdictions. Decisions will have to be made as to how AI systems will need to comply with the duty of care across many jurisdictions which may, for domestic purposes, have laws and regulations defining the concept of duty of care differently.

---

67. United Nations System Chief Executives Board for Coordination, "ICRC Duty of Care: elements of definition" online at: unsceb.org., accessed June 26, 2023.
68. *Ibid.*
69. *Ibid.*

However, for purposes of the regulation and control of digital products such as AI systems that are easily distributed internationally, it seems sensible to create an agreed international standard defining the scope of the legal requirements of duty of care to be applied in transnational situations. The Swiss Code appears to provide a good starting point for the development of a universal standard.

CHAPTER 5
International Law

§5.01 EARLY PROPOSALS

Although the release of Open AI's ChatGPT in late 2022 has brought about a great deal of discussion about the capabilities of AI and what its impact is likely to be on human society, discussion of how AI should be regulated internationally has already been going on for some time.

§5.02 ASSOCIATION FOR THE ADVANCEMENT OF ARTIFICIAL INTELLIGENCE

The Association for the Advancement of Artificial Intelligence (AAAI) describes itself as:

> The premier scientific society dedicated to advancing the scientific understanding of the mechanisms underlying thought and intelligent behavior and their embodiment in machines.[70]

The AAAI was founded in 1979 and is still active in running conferences and providing information about AI.

Their website does not indicate that they are directly involved in promoting any particular form of legal regulation for AI, but their information and guidance would undoubtedly be helpful for those interested in controlling AI.

AAAI lists its goals as:

- Promoting research in, and responsible use of, AI
- Increasing public understanding of AI
- Improving the teaching and training of AI practitioners

70. "About the Association for the Advancement of Artificial Intelligence (AAAI)," at their website online at: aaai.org.

- Providing guidance for research planners and funders concerning the importance and potential of current AI developments and future directions.

The AAAI's activities are listed as including:

- Organizing and sponsoring conferences, symposia, and workshops
- Publishing a quarterly magazine for all members
- Publishing a series of proceedings, including annual proceedings for the AAAI conference on AI
- Advocating for members throughout the world through educational programs and governmental outreach
- Awarding grants and scholarships.

Based on the information provided on their website, it seems that the AAAI is one of the most active international organizations seeking to increase the knowledge about and the responsible use of AI.

§5.03 ERDELYI AND GOLDSMITH

In February 2018, two academics, Olivia Erdelyi of the University of Canterbury, New Zealand and Judy Goldsmith of the University of Kentucky, co-authored a paper proposing a "global solution" for the regulation of AI.[71] In their publication, they sought to address the "legal and ethical issues" faced by society as a result of the widening use of AI systems. They proposed the creation of an international AI Regulatory agency that:

> Could create a unified framework for the regulation of AI technologies and inform the development of AI policies around the world.

The authors point out that AI has many useful applications already being applied in fields such as data collection, law enforcement and medicine. However, they identify a number of uses that are troubling and need to be controlled, such as, among others:

- AI systems that produce discriminatory biases.
- Overly intrusive data collection applications that threaten privacy.
- "Childlike sex bots."
- AI weapons systems that are programmed to make "kill" decisions.

They argue that:

> The AI community has long been calling for policy action with respect to AI, and criticism is getting louder on the growing legal vacuum in virtually every domain affected by technological advancement.[72]

71. Olivia J. Erdelyi and Judy Goldsmith, "Regulating Artificial Intelligence: Proposal for a Global Solution," AIES'18, February 2-3, 2018, New Orleans, LA, U.S.A., online for download as PDF at: https://dll.acm.org/dol/pdf/10.1145/3278731, accessed April 26, 2023, DOI: 10.1145/3278721.3278731.
72. *Ibid.*, p. 95.

They also argue that courts that have handled some of the early AI cases have not had sufficient technical expertise.

There is a significant amount of truth in these arguments in that there is getting to be an increasingly loud demand that governments exercise effective control over the uses of AI systems that may constitute abuses and/or threats to the rights and well-being of individuals.

However, it does need to be recognized that there is by no means a "legal vacuum" with respect to AI systems. AI systems are human-created products and, as with respect to any human-created products, there is a vast spectrum of laws and regulations that require their creators and operators to exercise a range of legal duties with respect to them and to penalize those who fail in those duties. These include criminal law, tort law, privacy law, laws against fraud and misrepresentation, intellectual property law, and investment law, among many others.

AI systems must not be seen, because of the efficiency with which they operate and the range of choices that they are permitted to make, to be detached from other human-created products. As explained above, they are "machines." True, they are not mechanical machines. They are digital machines. But that does not excuse them from the application of existing law.

However, the authors are right that there needs to be an extension and adjustment of policy to make certain it is recognized by governments, regulators and judicial bodies that these AI machines are subject to existing law. There may also be a need to introduce specific policies and regulations that make this relationship clear.

The area in which AI systems make a significant difference to the application of existing laws and regulations is that, like other computer-created elements, they have nearly unlimited international reach over the internet. This means that a significant degree of international cooperation will be needed in order to effectively regulate them and curtail the misuse of these remarkable tools.

To deal with these international issues, Erdelyi and Goldsmith propose the establishment of an:

> Intergovernmental organization which could be named [the] International Artificial Intelligence Organization (IAIO)—to serve as an international forum for discussion and engage in standard-setting activities. The IAIO should unite a diverse group of stakeholders from public sector, industry, and academic organizations whose interdisciplinary expertise can support policymakers ... .[73]

The formation of such an international organization was certainly a good idea, but it does not appear to have been taken up. However, the AAAI mentioned above was already in existence.

§5.04 OEDC

In 2019, the Organization of Economically Developed Countries (OEDC) indicated its concern with the developing use of AI by publication of a book entitled *Artificial*

73. *Ibid.*, pp. 95-96.

Intelligence in Society. Among the issues that the book says need addressing are a number of legal and ethical issues. The book points out that AI offers many possible benefits, however:

> At the same time, AI is also fueling anxieties and ethical concerns. There are questions about the trustworthiness of AI systems, including the dangers of codifying and reinforcing existing biases, such as those related to gender and race, or of infringing human rights and values, such as privacy. Concerns are growing about AI systems exacerbating inequality, climate change, market concentration and the digital divide. No single country or actor has all the answers to these challenges. We therefore need international cooperation and multi-stakeholder responses to guide the development and use of AI for the wider good.
>
> Looking ahead, we must progress together on AI-related technical, ethical and legal issues in order to foster the alignment of standards and codes of conduct while ensuring the interoperability of laws and regulations. This is urgent, given the speed of developments and the breadth of applications. It is thus no surprise that AI is a top priority on national and international agendas including in the G7 and the G20.[74]

§5.05 G20

At the G20 meeting in September 2023, Indian Prime Minister Narendra Modi said:

> I suggest we establish a framework for responsible human centric AI governance. India will also give suggestions. It will be our effort that all countries get the benefits of AI in areas like socioeconomic development, global workforce and research and development.

The New Delhi Declaration published at that meeting said that the G20 countries would seek AI regulation that would provide certainty of "responsible AI development, deployment and use. ... [while promoting risk/benefit aware regulation that followed] a [pro-innovation regulatory/governance approach."[75]

§5.06 G7

At a meeting on April 29, 2023, the digital and technology ministers of the G7 agreed that member nations should adopt "risk-based regulation" of AI. But, they cautioned that such regulation should not prevent the responsible development of AI.

In their meeting in Japan, they recognized that members would have some differences in the way AI was regulated, but there would have to be overall recognition that AI apps such as ChatGPT were gaining popularity at an unprecedented rate.

74. OECD (2019), *Artificial Intelligence in Society*, OECD Publishing, Paris, https://doi.org/10.1787/eedfee77-en.
75. "G20 leaders bat for 'responsible Artificial Intelligence' eye ethics-based regulation," *The Times of India*, online, September 11, 2023.

Privacy policy regulators should examine the extent to which privacy is being threatened by AI developments.

Italy, which had previously banned ChatGPT, removed its ban on Friday, April 28, 2023.[76]

§5.07 THE UNITED NATIONS

In order to foster cooperation among members on the expansion of the digital world, the UN has published "The Secretary-General's Road Map for Digital Cooperation" (RMDC).[77]

In its introduction, the UN Secretary-General, Antonio Gutierrez, says:

> Digital technology is shaping history. But there is also the sense that it is running away with us. Where will it take us? Will our dignity and rights be enhanced or diminished? Will our societies become more equal or less equal? Will we become more, or less, secure and safe? The answers to these questions depend on our ability to work together across disciplines and act across nations and political divides. We have a collective responsibility to give direction to these technologies so that we maximize benefits and curtail unintended consequences and malicious use.

The RMDC covers eight important areas for action. One of those is "supporting global cooperation on artificial intelligence."

On AI, the UN's summary view is that:

> AI brings enormous benefits to the digital era, but it can also significantly compromise the safety and agency of users worldwide. Enhanced multi-stakeholder efforts on global AI cooperation are needed to help build capacity for the development and use of AI in a manner that is trustworthy, human rights based, safe and sustainable, and promotes peace.

However, the UN recognizes that there are a significant number of problems in achieving the digital cooperation necessary to achieve the stated goals:

> There are significant gaps in global digital cooperation, and digital technology issues are too often low on political agendas. Even where there has been cooperation, it is frequently fragmented and lacks tangible outcomes or sound follow-up processes. As a starting point, the Internet Governance Forum must be strengthened in order to make it more responsive and relevant to current digital issues.[78]

The RMDC is a follow-up to the Report of the Secretary-General, Roadmap for Digital Cooperation, published in June 2020.[79]

76. Kantaro Komiya, "G7 should adopt 'risk-based' AI regulation, ministers say," Reuters, online, May 1, 2023. Oh buck.
77. United Nations, "Secretary-General's Road Map for Digital Cooperation," online at: un.org.
78. "Secretary-General's Road Map for Digital Cooperation," online at: un.org, cited above.
79. UN, "Report of the Secretary-General Roadmap for Digital Cooperation," online at: un.org, June 2020.

The Report addressed a number of issues relating to the growth of digital communication and the importance of international cooperation in directing and controlling its growth so that its development provides maximum benefits and minimal harm.

In its section on AI, the Report predicted:

> Its use is forecast to generate nearly $4 trillion in added value for global markets by 2022 … .[80]

However, problems were pointed out:

> Artificial intelligence can also significantly compromise the safety and agency of users worldwide. For example, lethal autonomous weapon systems may be able to make life and death decisions without human intervention, while artificial intelligence tools such as synthetic media—also known as deep fakes—have been used to influence public opinion.[81]

The Report noted:

> While interest in artificial intelligence is overwhelmingly high … . There is a gap in international coordination, cultural collaboration and governance.[82]

The recommendations of the Report included:[83]

- a call for a global ban on lethal autonomous weapons systems;
- recognition of the work of the United Nations Educational Scientific and Cultural Organization on the ethics of AI;
- the achievement of sustainable development goals such as those proposed by the Artificial Intelligence for Good Global Summit convened annually by the International Telecommunications Union in partnership with UN organizations; and
- prevention of facial recognition software and digital identification from eroding human rights, deepening inequality and exacerbating existing discrimination.

A key conclusion was that "life and death decisions should not be delegated to machines."[84]

The Secretary-General says that with respect to Artificial Intelligence:

> To address the issues raised around inclusion, coordination and capacity-building for member states on artificial intelligence, I intend to establish a multistakeholder advisory body on global artificial intelligence cooperation to provide guidance to myself and the international community on artificial intelligence that is trustworthy, human rights based, safe and sustainable and promotes peace. The

80. *Ibid.*
81. *Ibid.*, p. 17.
82. *Ibid.*, p. 17.
83. *Ibid.*, pp. 17-18.
84. *Ibid.*, p. 17.

advisory body will compromise member states, relevant United Nations entities, interested companies, academic institutions and civil society groups.[85]

The discussions and recommendations that provide the basis for the report were provided by:

> [A] high level panel on digital cooperation of 20 independent experts ... convened by the UN Secretary-General to provide recommendations on how the international community could work together to optimize the use of digital technologies and mitigate the risks. In June 2019, the Panel published their report "The Age of Digital Independence" and with it a series of recommendations to improve digital cooperation. In a follow-up to the report, eight virtual Roundtable groups were convened to discuss if and how the recommendations can be advanced.[86]

§5.08 UNESCO AGREEMENT

Since the Secretary-General's report, the UN has promoted a number of initiatives relating to the development and control of AI. One of the most significant was the UNESCO Agreement, which is described as defining "common values and principles needed to ensure the healthy development of AI."

This was adopted by the 193 members of the UN Educational, Scientific and Cultural Organization (UNESCO) in November 2021. The central focus of the Agreement was "the ethics of artificial intelligence" (UNESCO AI Agreement).[87]

Although the UNESCO AI Agreement does not have the force of law, it was intended "to guide the construction of the necessary legal infrastructure to ensure the ethical development of this technology." It was hoped that this legal infrastructure would overcome some of the problems that UNESCO saw as arising in the development of AI, including the following:

> We see increased gender and ethnic bias, significant threats to privacy, dignity and agency, dangers of mass surveillance, and increased use of unreliable artificial intelligence technologies in law enforcement, to name a few. Until now, there were no universal standards to provide an answer to these issues.

UNESCO intended its AI Agreement to provide such a standard, although it was up to the members to apply this standard to legal reforms at each member's national level.[88]

Key provisions of the UNESCO AI Agreement call for:[89]

- guaranteeing individuals protection, transparency agency and control over their personal data;

85. *Ibid.*, p. 25.
86. *Ibid.*, p. 27. For more information, *see also*, https//www.un.org/en/digital-cooperation-panel/.
87. UN News, "193 countries adopt first ever global agreement on the Ethics of Artificial Intelligence," online at: news.un.org, November 25, 2021.
88. *Ibid.*
89. *Ibid.*

- banning the use of AI systems for social scoring and mass surveillance;
- ensuring that AI becomes a key tool in the fight against climate change and environmental deterioration;
- protecting against increasing inequalities and intensifying environmental damage.

The UN has urged that legal regulation of AI should be directed at focusing AI on solving problems where AI can make significant contributions. These have included urging:

- Countries and investors to step up the development and use of AI to improve road safety to a level where road deaths can be halved by 2030.[90]
- The use of AI to improve the health of populations around the world.[91]

§5.09 WHO

In June 2021, the World Health Organization (WHO) released its first report on AI.[92]

The principal concern of the WHO report is AI's effect on health. The Report says:

> Artificial intelligence (AI) holds great promise for improving the delivery of healthcare and medicine worldwide, but only if ethics and human rights are put at the heart of its design, deployment and use, … .

It points out that AI was already being used in a number of countries to improve disease diagnosis and screening, improve clinical care, assist health research and drug creation and support a variety of health interventions, including surveillance of diseases, response to outbreaks and management of health systems.[93]

WHO points out that one of the possible future benefits of AI is that it will give individuals greater control over their own healthcare.

But, some significant ethical problems are also raised by AI, including improper collection of health data and unethical uses of that data such as encoding biases in algorithms. These things can lead to dangers to patient safety, cybersecurity and world health, and the environment generally.

There is also an inherent problem in the way that health data is collected and used. Because AI is developing and being used principally in wealthier countries to date, the health data of their populations collected to train AI systems may not be as applicable in countries that are less developed.

The report recommends that:

---

90. UN Affairs, "Artificial intelligence can help have road deaths by 2030," online at: news.un.org, October 7, 2021.
91. UN News, Health, "WHO guidance on Artificial Intelligence to improve healthcare, mitigate risks worldwide," online at: news.un.org, June 28, 2021.
92. World Health Organization, News, "WHO issues first global report on Artificial Intelligence (AI) in health and six guiding principles for its design and use," WHO online at: who.int, June 28, 2021, accessed May 04, 2023.
93. *Ibid.*

AI systems should therefore be carefully designed to reflect the diversity of socioeconomic and healthcare settings.

In aid of achieving that goal, WHO proposes:

Six principles to ensure AI works for the public interest in all countries. ... WHO provides the following principles as the basis for AI regulation and governance.[94]

In summary, these are:

(1) *Protecting human autonomy.* Humans need to remain in control of both healthcare systems and medical decisions. Also, privacy and confidentiality need to continue to be protected. Patients need to be able to provide informed consent to both their medical treatment and the use of their medical data.
(2) *Protecting human well-being and safety and the public interest.* Regulatory requirements for safety, accuracy and usefulness should be internationally established for AI technologies. There should also be standards of quality control and quality improvement applicable at all times.
(3) *Ensuring transparency, explainability and intelligibility.* This should be a key condition for the acceptance of AI technology. Adequate information about them and their names to be published and documented before AI systems are created and used. Relevant information should be easily accessible for public consultation and discussion on how a particular AI technology is designed and whether it should be used.
(4) *Fostering responsibility and accountability.* Those responsible for the creation and application of AI technology should make sure that AI technologies are used only under appropriate circumstances and only by adequately trained operators. Opportunities need to be provided to question whether these standards are being met, and there need to be provisions for allowing persons and organizations that are adversely affected by the application of AI systems and algorithms to challenge them.
(5) *Ensuring inclusiveness and equity.* Measures should be undertaken to assure that AI systems providing beneficial health benefits should be available as widely as possible. They should be available to all regardless of age, sex, gender, income, race, ethnicity, sexual orientation, abilities or other protected characteristics of those who seek to use them. Human rights must be respected.
(6) *Promoting AI that is responsive and sustainable.* The creators, operators and users of AI systems should continually and transparently review whether their AI applications meet appropriate requirements and expectations. In their design, AI systems shouldn't minimize environmental impact and be as efficient as possible in their use of energy. Both those that regulate and use AI systems should be sensitive to impacts on the working environment where AI systems are employed. Workers who find their jobs modified or affected by AI systems, including healthcare workers, need to receive proper information and training to be able to employ appropriate AI systems effectively. If there are job losses due to the introduction of AI systems, both governments and employers need to put in place appropriate responses to protect the health and well-being of those affected.

94. *Ibid.*

All of these principles incorporate worthy goals. It is hoped that officials at WHO are able to interact effectively with governments, regulators and legislators to assure that new regulation applicable to AI recognizes such goals and incorporates mechanisms to achieve them.

§5.10 FIVE EYES COOPERATION

There is an intelligence-sharing agreement between Australia, Canada, New Zealand, Britain and the U.S. called the "Five Eyes" intelligence-sharing alliance.

It has been suggested that this alliance:

> Presents a unique opportunity to pool resources and expertise to create a secure, government-led language learning model AI systems. Last year The US National Security Commission on AI called for $40 billion to "expand and democratize federal AI research and development." In the UK, a more modest commitment was made in March with up to £1 billion. A combined effort from Five-Eyes countries would show serious intent.[95]

§5.11 NATO

It is frequently said that one of the most dangerous and worrying uses of AI will be to attack or wage cyber war on those considered to be enemies. More details of these dangers are given in the chapter on cyber war to follow.

Consequently, in this context, one of the most important international organizations that will need to consider how to deal with AI is the North Atlantic Treaty Organization (NATO).

One of the principal goals of NATO is to contain possible aggression by Russia. Unfortunately, Russia is reported to be one of the principal locations of Internet hacking and ransomware attackers. It is alleged that some, if not all, of such organizations operate with the knowing approval of the Russian government.

Consequently, NATO considers it a priority to defend against such activities by adopting an effective cyber strategy. The purpose of this is both to protect NATO members against aggression from non-member nations and to allow NATO members, where appropriate, to use AI to counterattack those who seek to use AI to damage NATO members.

In a meeting in October 2021, the defense ministers of NATO adopted a NATO AI strategy.[96] They expressed the view that:

> (C)ooperation is inherently needed to equally mitigate international security risks as well as to capitalize on the technology potential to transform enterprise functions, mission support, and operations.

95. Adam Hadley, "We need a Five Eyes for AI to give us the safest and best tech," *The Times*, online, Monday 24, 2023.
96. Zoe Stanley-Lockman and Edward Hunter Christie, "An Artificial Intelligence Strategy for NATO," NATO Review, online at: nato.int, October 25, 2021.

One of the key planks of the NATO strategy is their statement of "Principles of Responsible Use," in which NATO and its allies are required to commit to making certain that the AI applications that they develop and use will comply with the following six principles:[97]

(i) *Lawfulness*: "AI applications will be developed and used in accordance with national and international law, including international humanitarian law and human rights law, as applicable."
(ii) *Responsibility and Accountability*: "AI applications will be developed and used with appropriate levels of judgment and care. Clear human responsibility shall apply in order to ensure accountability."
(iii) *Explainability and Traceability*: "AI applications will be appropriately understandable and transparent, including through the use of review methodologies, sources, and procedures. This includes verification, assessment, and validation mechanisms at either a NATO and/or national level."
(iv) *Reliability*: "AI applications will have explicit, well defined use cases. The safety, security, and robustness of such capabilities will be subject to testing and assurance within those use cases across their entire life cycle, including through established NATO and/or national certification procedures."
(v) *Governability*: "AI applications will be developed and used according to their intended functions and will allow for appropriate human machine interaction; the ability to detect and avoid unintended consequences; and the ability to take steps such as disengagement or deactivation of systems, when such systems demonstrate unintended behavior."
(vi) *Bias mitigation*: "Proactive steps will be taken to minimize any unintended bias in the development and use of AI applications and in data sets."

These six principles constitute a comprehensive system of regulation and assignment of responsibility with respect to all developments and applications of AI.

§5.12 APPLICABILITY OUTSIDE NATO?

These principles are intended for NATO members and allies, but they represent the basis of a rational system of control of AI that should be the minimum adopted by any system of legal governance.

It would be sensible to compare any other international or national system of AI regulation that is proposed or adopted with these six principles. Any system which does not, at a minimum, include such principles may not be adequate to realize the benefits and minimize the risks posed by the use of AI.

97. *Ibid.*

§5.13 EUROPEAN UNION

The European Union, with its 27 Member States, is a natural place to evolve an international regulatory system for something as international as AI. Indeed, it has been said that the EU has ambitions to be the worldwide model for AI regulation.[98] The EU has drafted a proposed Artificial Intelligence Act (AIA).[99]

The details and a discussion of that Act are set out in the following chapter devoted to a discussion of EU law on the subject.

98. "The EU wants to become the world's super regulator in AI," *The Economist* online at economist.com, April 24, 2021.
99. "The Artificial Intelligence Act," Future Life Institute, online at: artificialintelligenceact.eu. This is a website maintained by the Future of Life institute (FLI). The FLI claims that it has two key priorities: first, to promote the beneficial development of artificial intelligence and, second, to regulate lethal autonomous weapons.

CHAPTER 6
EU Law

There is no doubt that the EU is keenly interested in the progress of the development of AI. As early as April of 2021, The Economist reported that the EU was interested in becoming "the world's super regulator in AI." As a regulatory body, the EU is strongly influential, with many of the tech regulations they have adopted being copied around the world.[100] This is the so-called Brussels effect, where EU policies have become a global standard.

On April 21, 2021, the European Commission published its proposed regulations on AI. The EU was the first major regulator to propose an overall legal regulation for AI.[101]

§6.01 EU DRAFT AIA

The EU draft of a proposed AIA is the first major jurisdiction legislation proposed for comprehensive regulation of AI.

The AIA divides AI systems into three categories.

The first includes applications and systems which present an "unacceptable risk." These include government social scoring systems similar to those used in China. These are banned under the AIA.

The second includes "high risk" applications, such as one that scans CVs and ranks job applicants according to specific legal requirements.

The third applies to those applications and systems that are neither banned nor listed as high risk. This category will be largely unregulated.[102]

---

100. "The EU wants to become the world's super regulator in AI," *The Economist* online at economist.com, April 24, 2021.
101. *Ibid.*
102. "The Artificial Intelligence Act," Future Life Institute, online at: artificialintelligenceact.eu. This is a website maintained by the Future of Life institute (FLI). The FLI claims that it has two key priorities: first, to promote the beneficial development of artificial intelligence and, second, to regulate lethal autonomous weapons.

The EU's Future Life Institute (FLI) describes AI applications as follows:

> AI applications influence what information you see online by predicting what content is engaging to you, captures and analyzes data from faces to enforce laws or personalized advertisements, and are used to diagnose or treat cancer. In other words, AI affects many parts of your life.

On its website, the FLI expresses the view that its AIA could become a "global standard" for AI regulation. They point to a law proposed in Brazil in late September 2021 that is influenced by the EU AIA.[103]

At a meeting of the G7 in Japan in late April 2023, the EU's technology regulation head, European Commission Executive Vice President Margrethe Vestager, reportedly said that the G7 meeting showed that Europe was not alone in wanting sensible AI regulation.[104]

§6.02 SECOND DRAFT

On April 27, 2023, it was announced that the EU had a preliminary agreement on the second draft of the AIA. Executive Vice-President Vestager announced that the EU will be able to reach an agreement on AI law within 2023.

Additions in the new draft included specific copyright protection for "generative AI" (AI that creates things such as documents or songs) and such things as transparency obligations for AI-generated music and pictures as well as copyright issues, and it noted that perceived educational risks would reportedly be covered by the legislation.[105]

The final EU AI Act is projected to deal with such things as fake news and other disturbing products that generative AI is seen to be able to create.

At the G7 meeting in Japan in April 2023, the French Minister for Digital Transition, John Noel Barrow, was reported to have said that France intends to provide relevant exceptions for small AI developers in the final EU AI Act.[106]

§6.03 JUNE 2023 AMENDMENTS

In June 2023, EU legislators agreed to add stricter amendments to the AI Act.[107]

These included:

- A ban on using AI for biometric surveillance.
- The requirement that any copyrighted data used to train AI systems, such as generative systems like ChatGPT needed to be disclosed.

103. FLI, online at: artificialintelligenceact.eu.
104. Kantaro Komiya, "G7 should adopt 'risk-based' AI regulation, ministers say," Reuters, online, May 01, 2023.
105. *Ibid.*
106. *Ibid.*
107. Foo Yun Chee and Supantha Mukherjee, "EU lawmakers vote for tougher AI rules as draft moves to final stage," Reuters online at: reuters.com, June 14, 2023.

Thierry Breton, the EU head of Industry, also agreed to travel to the U.S. in June 2023 to meet with OpenAI's CEO Sam Altman and with the Meta CEO Mark Zuckerberg.[108]

Following that meeting which took place at the end of June 2023, both Altman and Zuckerberg expressed support for the EU's proposed regulation of AI.[109] Breton said:

> [T]hat he and Zuckerberg... were "aligned" on the EU's regulation of AI, ... They agreed on the bloc's risk-based approach and to measures like watermarking.

It is reported that Altman was also in agreement with the EU's approach. He praised the EU for having the foresight to take AI developments seriously and said he looked forward to working with the EU.

Breton was reported to be satisfied with his discussions, saying that Meta was willing to submit to "stress tests" on the responses of Meta platforms to AI.

Breton also reported a meeting with Jensen Huang, the CEO of Nvidia, the chipmaker producing powerful platforms that are important to power AI systems. Huang was also reported satisfied with the meeting and indicated that Nvidia may well invest in Europe.[110]

§6.04 PROGRESS ON THE AI ACT

As of the beginning of September 2023, it was the goal of the EU to reach a final agreement on the AI Act before the end of 2023. This goal is subject to the EU MPs' position (adopted in June of 2023) that they will negotiate with the Member States over the final form of the law.

As of June 14, 2023, the European Parliament's statement of the state of the rules under the AI Act was as follows:[111]

> AI Act: different rules for different risk levels
>
> The new rules establish obligations for providers and users depending on the level of risk from artificial intelligence. While many AI systems pose minimal risk, they need to be assessed.

The description of the proposed rules under the AI Act below is largely copied from the website of the European Parliament (updated as of June 14, 2023). On that website, they also offer an online PDF copy of the AIA which is available for download.[112]

108. Chee and Mukherjee, June 14, 2023, as cited above.
109. Jillian Deutsch, "Zuckerberg, Altman Offer Support for EU Regulation of AI," Bloomberg online at: bloomberg.com, June 24, 2023.
110. Thierry Breton, "Excellent exchange in Santa Clara with Nvidia CEO Jensen Huang," Posted online at @ThieryBreton, June 24, 2023.
111. European Parliament, "AI Act: first regulation on artificial intelligence," online at: europarl.europa.eu, created June 08, 2023, updated June 14, 2023.
112. European Parliament, News, "EU AI Act: first regulation on artificial intelligence," online at: europarl.europa.eu, created June 08, 2023, updated June 14, 2023.

§6.05 AI ACT: DIFFERENT RULES FOR DIFFERENT RISK LEVELS

The new rules establish obligations for providers and users depending on the level of risk from AI. While many AI systems pose minimal risk, they need to be assessed.

§6.06 UNACCEPTABLE RISK

Unacceptable risk AI systems are systems considered a threat to people and will be banned. They include:

Cognitive behavioral manipulation of people or specific vulnerable groups: for example, voice-activated toys that encourage dangerous behavior in children.

Social scoring: classifying people based on behavior, socioeconomic status or personal characteristics.

Real-time and remote biometric identification systems, such as facial recognition.

Some exceptions may be allowed: For instance, some remote biometric identification systems where identification occurs after a significant delay will be allowed to be used to prosecute serious crimes but only after court approval.

§6.07 HIGH RISK

AI systems that negatively affect safety or fundamental rights will be considered high risk and will be divided into two categories:

(1) AI systems that are used in products falling under the EU's product safety legislation. This includes toys, aviation, cars, medical devices and lifts.

(2) AI systems falling into eight specific areas that will have to be registered in an EU database:
   - biometric identification and categorization of natural persons;
   - management and operation of critical infrastructure;
   - education and vocational training;
   - employment, worker management and access to self-employment;
   - access to and enjoyment of essential private services and public services and benefits;
   - law enforcement;
   - migration, asylum and border control management;
   - assistance in legal interpretation and application of the law.

All high-risk AI systems will be assessed before being put on the market and also throughout their lifecycle.

§6.08 GENERATIVE AI

Generative AI, like ChatGPT, would have to comply with transparency requirements:

Disclosing that the content was generated by AI.
Designing the model to prevent it from generating illegal content.
Publishing summaries of copyrighted data used for training.

§6.09 LIMITED RISK

Limited risk AI systems should comply with minimal transparency requirements that would allow users to make informed decisions. After interacting with the applications, the user can then decide whether they want to continue using it. Users should be made aware when they are interacting with AI. This includes AI systems that generate or manipulate image, audio or video content, for example, "deepfakes."

§6.10 NEXT STEPS

On June 14, 2023, MEPs adopted the Parliament's negotiating position on the AI Act. The talks will now begin with EU countries in the Council on the final form of the law.

The aim is to reach an agreement by the end of [2023].[113]

The EU's Expanding Digital Role:

It is certainly clear that the EU is holding itself out as a model for AI regulation. However, this is not an isolated interest.

The EU has passed a significant amount of legislation relating to the development and control of the cyber markets. More information about these can be found through the following links:

- Cyber currency dangers in the benefits of EU legislation.[114]
- Fighting cybercrime, new EU cyber security laws explained.[115]
- Boosting data sharing in the EU, what are the benefits?[116]
- EU Digital Markets Act and the Digital Services Act.[117]
- Five ways the European Parliament wants to protect online gamers.[118]

113. European Parliament, News, updated to June 14, 2023, accessed September 05, 2023, as cited above.
114. European Parliament, News, "Cybercurrency dangers and the benefits of EU legislation," online at: europarl.europa.eu, created April 01, 2023; updated May 30, 2023.
115. European Parliament, News, "Fighting cybercrime: new EU cybercurrency laws explained," online at: europarl.europa.eu, created November 10, 2022; updated May 30, 2023.
116. European Parliament, News, "Boosting data sharing in the EU: what are the benefits?," online at: europarl.europa.eu, created April 06, 2022; updated March 16, 2023.
117. European Parliament, News, "EU Digital Markets Act and Digital Services Act explained," online at: europarl.europa.eu, created December 14, 2021; updated August 24, 2023.
118. European Parliament, News, "Five ways the European Parliament wants to protect online gamers," online at: europarl.europa.eu, created January 17, 2023; updated January 18, 2023.

It will remain to be seen how many other jurisdictions follow the models and advice set out in EU legislation, regulation and analysis.

One advantage of the EU legislation is that it does benefit from the input of a process of negotiations between 27 developed European countries. The process of agreeing to EU legislation does demonstrate how technically advanced countries can achieve consensus on the regulation of the economically important and rapidly developing cyber markets.

On December 09, 2023, the EU announced that Members of the European Parliament had agreed an acceptable deal with the EU Council on AI safeguards. This included six key points:

(1) Biometric categorization systems that rely on "sensitive characteristics" such as race, religion, etc., would be banned.
(2) Bans on social scoring and manipulation user vulnerabilities.
(3) Consumer rights to complain and get proper explanations.
(4) Fines for violations from EUR 35 million up to 1.5% of turnover.

For details see EU press releases such as "Artificial Intelligence Act: deal on comprehensive rules for trustworthy AI" (December 9, 2023).

The EU will undoubtedly continue to refine its AI regulations as time goes on.

CHAPTER 7

U.S. AI Law

Because much of the pioneering work on AI originated in the United States, it would be surprising if the U.S. government did not consider what type of regulation makes sense for AI.

The U.S. government has taken a number of steps to impose policies and formal regulations to allow U.S. entities to benefit from the positive elements of AI development while seeking to reduce the risks that AI might pose.

§7.01 NATIONAL AI INITIATIVE ACT OF 2020

On January 1, 2021, the National AI Initiative Act of 2020 became law (AI Act 2020). Its purpose was to establish a coordinated AI program throughout the U.S. The AI Act of 2020 established the national AI initiative as a central coordination point for AI research and application in the U.S.:[119]

> The mission of the national AI initiative is to ensure continued US leadership in AI research and development, lead the world in the development and use of trustworthy AI in the public and private sectors and prepare the present and future US workforce for the integration of AI systems across all sections of the economy and society.[120]

Essentially, the National AI Initiative website acts as a central repository of AI information, including publications, AI development, and sections on:

- Innovation
- Advancing Trustworthy AI
- Education and Training
- Infrastructure

119. National Artificial Intelligence Initiative, online at: ai.gov, accessed May 15, 2023.
120. *Ibid.*

- Applications
- International Cooperation.

It provides information about the more than 20 U.S. government agencies that are dealing with AI.

It also provides news about noteworthy developments in AI, such as a February 13, 2023, report that a U.S. Department of Defense (DoD) team has piloted a fighter jet using AI.[121]

§7.02 BLUEPRINT FOR AN AI BILL OF RIGHTS

In the fall of 2022, the U.S. issued a Blueprint for an AI Bill of Rights (Blueprint) that addressed the issues presented by the development of AI systems. The Blueprint set out how the United States expected to encourage and regulate these new Digital products.

The Blueprint was issued by the Office of Science and Technology Policy of the United States (OSTP). The OSTP was established by the National Science and Technology Policy, Organization, and Priorities Act of 1976. The purpose of that Act was to provide the President's office and other government officials with appropriate advice on the scientific, engineering, and technological aspects of U.S. government concerns touching on economy, national security, health, and resources, among other things.[122]

The Blueprint is used to provide guidelines for overcoming the problems identified in connection with the development of AI systems.[123] As the Blueprint says:

> These problems are well documented. In America and around the world, systems supposed to help with patient care have proven unsafe, ineffective, or biased. Algorithms used in hiring and credit decisions have been found to reflect and reproduce existing unwanted inequities or embed harmful new bias and discrimination. Unchecked social media data collection has been used to threaten people's opportunities, undermined their privacy, or pervasively tracked their activity—often without their knowledge or consent.

The Blueprint contains five principles that set out policies intended to guide the rational development of AI while making certain that individual rights and democratic values are protected. A summary of these principles is as follows.[124]

– Safe and Effective Systems

The first principle is that people should be protected from unsafe or ineffective AI systems. In order to achieve this goal, the creation of AI systems should be done with consultation from different communities, stakeholders and experts to permit adequate identification of concerns, risks and potential AI system impact.

---

121. *Ibid.*
122. OSTP, "About the Office of Science and Technology Policy," online at: whitehouse.gov, accessed May 11, 2023.
123. OSTP, "Blueprint for an AI Bill of Rights," online at: whitehouse.gov, accessed May 11-12, 2023.
124. *Ibid.* For the full texts of the Principles, and accompanying material, please refer to the Blueprint itself at the website cited.

– Algorithmic Discrimination Protections

Discrimination should not be imposed by systems not equitably designed and used:

> Algorithmic discrimination occurs when automated systems contribute to unjustified different treatment or impacts disfavoring people based on their race, color, ethnicity, sex (including pregnancy, childbirth, and related medical conditions, gender identity, intersex status, and sexual orientation), religion, age, national origin disability, veteran status, genetic information, or any other classification protected by law.

– Data Privacy

System design choices should, by default, make sure that the collection of data complies with reasonable expectations "and that only data strictly necessary for the specific context is collected. ... Any consent requests should be brief, be understandable in plain language, and give you agency over data collection and the specific context of use...."

– Notice and Explanation

> Designers, developers, and deployers of automated systems should provide generally accessible plain language documentation including clear descriptions of the overall system functioning and the role automation plays, notice that sex systems are in use, the individual or organization responsible for the system, and explanations of the outcomes that are clear, timely, and accessible. Search notice should be kept up to date and people impacted by the system should be notified of significant use cases or key functionality changes.

§7.03 HUMAN ALTERNATIVES, CONSIDERATION, AND FALLBACK

When appropriate, users should be able to opt out of an AI system and have the opportunity to choose an efficient and effective human alternative:

> [I]n some cases, a human or other alternative may be required by law.

The instructions on how the Blueprint for an AI Bill of Rights should be applied include the following:[125]

> [T]his framework uses a two-part test to determine when systems are in its scope. This framework applies to (1) automated systems that (2) have the potential to meaningfully impact the American public's rights, opportunities, or access to critical resources or services.

The purpose of the Blueprint is stated to be:[126]

---

125. *Ibid.* For the full text and accompanying material, please refer to the website cited.
126. OSTP, "Blueprint for an AI Bill of Rights," online at: whitehouse.gov, accessed May 11-12, 2023. For the full texts of the Principles, and accompanying material, please refer to the website cited.

> Considered together, the five principles and associated practices of the Blueprint for an AI bill of rights form an overlapping set of backstops against potential harms. This purposefully overlapping framework, when taken as a whole, forms a Blueprint to help protect the public from harm. The measures taken to realize the vision set forward in this framework should be proportionate with the extent and nature of the harm, or risk of harm, to people's rights, opportunities, and access.

§7.04 ANTI-ALGORITHMIC DISCRIMINATION ORDER

In February 2023, President Biden signed an Executive Order requiring federal agencies to eliminate discrimination from new technologies, including AI. The purpose of this Order was to "protect the public from algorithmic discrimination."[127]

In May of that year, the Biden Administration issued a further statement that said:

> "The Biden-Harris Administration is developing a National Artificial Intelligence (AI) Strategy that will chart a path for the United States to harness the benefits and mitigate the risks of AI. This strategy will build on the actions that the Federal Government has already taken to responsibly advance the development and use of AI. To inform the strategy, OSTP (Office of Science and Technology Policy) requests public comments to help update U.S. national priorities and future actions on AI."[128]

§7.05 MAY 2023 MEETING: GOVERNMENT OFFICIALS & TECH CEOs

In early May 2023, the Biden Administration announced that it will introduce policies to address the issues raised by the development of AI. These policies are intended to determine how federal agencies can acquire and use AI systems. These policies are expected to have an impact on the AI market and regulate how Americans can use AI on government websites and in other government and non-government situations. These policies were announced on a day when government officials met with the CEOs of Microsoft, OpenAI,[129] Google and Anthropic.[130]

A number of government officials participated in this meeting, including the Vice-President, the Secretary of Commerce, and officials responsible for science and technology policy, security, domestic policy, and the economy.

The issues that were raised in the meeting included the necessity of reducing the risks that AI potentially posed to individuals, to American society and to international

127. The White House, "FACT SHEET: Biden-Harris Administration Announces New Actions to Promote Responsible AI Innovation that Protects Americans' Rights and Safety," online at: whitehouse.gov, May 4, 2023.
128. A Notice by the Science and Technology Policy Office on 05/26/2023, "Request for Information; National Priorities for Artificial Intelligence," Federal Register, online at: federalregister.gov.
129. The creator of ChatGPT.
130. Brian Fung, "Biden administration unveils an AI plan ahead of meeting with tech CEOs," CNN online, May 05, 2023. Anthropic is an AI safety and research company.

security. The risks that were identified included risks to safety, security, civil rights, human rights, privacy, employment and democratic values.

The CEOs were urged to direct their companies to be models of responsible behavior and to ensure that their companies' actions reflected responsible innovation, necessary safeguards, and protection of the rights and safety of people.

Big Tech companies were told that they needed to be more transparent with both regulators and the public about their AI systems and that it was essential to protect any AI systems they employed against penetration and misuse by malicious attackers and actors.

This meeting was one part of the Biden Administration's policy of engaging with a range of participants and stakeholders in the cyber world to promote responsible innovation and reduction of risks with respect to AI.[131]

§7.06 PROGRESS ON AI REGULATION

As shown in this chapter, AI activity is already subject to significant regulation under the existing regulatory framework of the U.S. federal government. However, there is serious concern that additional regulation by a number of different government agencies and organizations will be necessary in order to focus on the issues of reduction of the risks that may be posed by AI to national security and individual rights, among other things.

There is additional sensitivity to the potential of AI to offer significant improvements to a number of activities, including information, analysis and health protection.

As shown above, several federal government organizations and agencies are giving serious consideration to how AI should be treated. This will undoubtedly result in the development of more specific policies and regulations focused on AI. However, as indicated above, the government is still a considerable distance from determining what these regulations and policies will be and how they should be applied. There will also be additional consideration given to how AI activities should be treated under existing laws and regulations.

Nevertheless, various U.S. officials, including elected officials in the U.S. House of Representatives and the U.S. Senate, have proposed various pieces of legislation to regulate the development, distribution and use of AI systems. Here are some of them.

§7.07 AI IN NUCLEAR PLANTS

In 2022, the U.S. government took a serious look at the role of AI in the operation of nuclear plants with the publication in February of that year of a United States Nuclear

131. White House, "Readout of White House Meeting with CEOs on Advancing Responsible Artificial Intelligence Innovation," online at: whitehouse.gov, May 04, 2023.

Regulatory Commission paper, "Exploring Advanced Computational Tools and Techniques with Artificial Intelligence and Machine Learning in Operating Nuclear Plants[132]."

The paper says:

> The report describes the relationships between statistics and AI/ML, and then introduces the most widely used AI/ML algorithms in both supervised and unsupervised learning. The report reviews the recent applications of advanced computational tools and techniques in various fields of nuclear industry, such as reactor system design and analysis, plant operation and maintenance, and nuclear safety and risk analysis. The report presents the insights from the project on the potential applicability of AI/ML techniques in improving advanced computational capabilities, and how advanced tools and techniques could contribute to the understanding of safety and risk, and what information would be needed to provide meaningful insights to decision makers.[133]

§7.08 AI TRAINING ACT OF 2022

In October 2022, the Artificial Intelligence Training for the Acquisition Workforce Act (AI Training Act) became law.

The AI Training Act requires the Office of Management and Budget (OMB) to provide an AI training program for the acquisition of the workforces of executive agencies (e.g., those responsible for program management or logistics). The purpose of the Act is to make sure that the relevant workforce understands the capabilities and risks of AI. The program must be updated every two years. Participation should be measured, and feedback from participants should be taken into consideration.[134]

§7.09 FEDERAL DIGITAL PLATFORM COMMISSION BILL

In May 2023, Senator Michael Bennett of Colorado proposed a new version of a bill he had previously introduced to set up a Federal Digital Platform Commission to oversee and regulate AI and other digital technology.[135]

Bennet is quoted as saying:

> Technology is moving quicker than Congress could ever hope to keep up with. We need an expert federal agency that can stand up for the American people and ensure that AI tools and digital platforms operate in the public interest.[136]

---

132. United States Nuclear Regulatory Commission, Office of Nuclear Regulatory Research, John Lane, NRC Project Manager, "Exploring Advanced Computational Tools and Techniques with Artificial Intelligence and Machine Learning in Operating Nuclear Plants," published February 2022, online at: inldigitallibrary.inl.gov.
133. *Ibid.*
134. U.S. Public Law No.: 117-207 (10/17/2022), Artificial Intelligence Training for the Acquisition Workforce or the AI Training Act, online at: congress.gov., accessed July 4, 2023.
135. Brian Fung, "US senator introduces bill to create a federal agency to regulate AI," CNN Business, May 18, 2023, online at: edition.cnn.com.
136. *Ibid.*

Sen. Bennet's bill would give the proposed Commission jurisdiction over data systems that use personal data to either create content or make decisions. It would also require "algorithmic audits" and a review of the risks that such systems might cause harm to the public.

The Commission would need to ensure that AI system algorithms are "fair, transparent and safe." The Commission would also be given oversight of online platforms, including social media platforms and search engines. It was suggested that the Commission should also be given responsibility to review the credentials of, and license creators of AI platforms.

This proposal has not been universally met with approval. One critic, Gary Marcus, a professor at New York University, has pointed out that there is a danger that such a commission could fall victim to "regulatory capture." This term describes how industries can gain controlling influence over government agencies set up to regulate them.

Senator Richard Blumenthal of Connecticut has pointed out:

> You can create 10 new agencies, but if you don't give them the resources—and I'm not just talking about dollars, I'm talking about scientific expertise—[industry] will run circles around them.[137]

§7.10 AI DISCLOSURE ACT OF 2023

In June 2023, U.S. Representative Ritchie Torres proposed new legislation requiring all content generated by AI to be accompanied by a disclaimer disclosing its origin. Representative Torres said:

> All generative AI should be required to disclose itself as AI. ... Under the "AI disclosure act of 2023," all material generated by artificial intelligence technology would have to include the following alert—"Disclaimer: this output has been generated by artificial intelligence." It would apply to videos, photos, text, audio, and any other AI generated material. The Federal Trade Commission (FTC) would be responsible for enforcement on violations, which could result in civil penalties.[138]

§7.11 THE FTC INVESTIGATES ChatGPT

One of the most publicized AI projects is the work done by a U.S. company in San Francisco, OpenAI Incorporated, founded in 2015. OpenAI's best-known product is an AI machine called ChatGPT. ChatGPT is in the category of "Generative Artificial Intelligence," that interacts in a conversational way that allows it to conduct a dialogue, follow instructions and produce results, including written documents:

---

137. *Ibid.*
138. U.S. Rep. Ritchie Torres Introduces Federal Legislation Requiring Mandatory Disclaimer for Material Generated by Artificial Intelligence," online at: ritchietorres.house.gov, June 05, 2023.

> Relative to earlier artificial intelligence models, Generative AI models can digest more complex inputs, and can produce human-like output, making Generative AI more versatile and scalable than prior innovations in AI and machine learning.[139]

It has proved controversial because commentators believe it will allow students to instruct ChatGPT to do their homework, and its capabilities are alleged to threaten a number of professions because it is allegedly capable of searching the Internet for information that allows it to answer questions and do tasks that previously only trained human professionals were able to correctly perform.

This has caused something of a panic fueled by "the frankly insane levels of attention paid to ChatGPT since its launch."[140]

In July 2023, it was reported that the FTC had opened a wide-ranging investigation into ChatGPT.[141]

The FTC investigation reportedly concerns issues of whether ChatGPT has violated consumer protection laws by causing risk to personal reputations and personal data.

In commencing its investigation, the FTC sent a 20-page document demand to ChatGPT's parent company, OpenAI, demanding to know how the company deals with risks associated with its AI products. This investigation by a major U.S. federal agency is seen as a serious threat to OpenAI's U.S. business.[142]

The FTC's focus on OpenAI is the result of the huge amount of publicity that ChatGPT has received, citing the potential uses and potential dangers of generative AI systems like ChatGPT. It is reported that ChatGPT, since its release in November 2022, has become one of the fastest-growing consumer apps in history, creating intense interest and concern around the world. Its success has also caused other tech companies to race to produce similar chatbots.

The parallel interest and concern that this product has created has also resulted in calls for governments around the world to introduce regulations to control the potential uses of such AI systems and to protect against the potential misuse they could bring about.

However, the introduction of appropriate and adequate legislation to encourage the positive uses of AI systems and control the potential harms of such systems can be a slow process. For example, the US Senate Majority Leader, Senator Charles E Schumer, is reported as saying that proper AI legislation will take months to introduce.[143]

This lack of new AI-focused legislation has apparently inspired the FTC to issue statements that many existing consumer protection laws already apply to AI products.

139. Andrea L. Eisfeldt, Gregor Shubert, and Miao Ben Zhang, "Generative AI and Firm Values," National Bureau of Economic Research, NBER Working Paper No. 31222, online at: d1e00ek4ebabms.cloudfront.net, May 2023.
140. Robin Wigglesworth, "The ChatGPT market shock," Financial Times, online at ft.com, May 08, 2023.
141. Cat Zakrzewski, "FTC investigates OpenAI over data leak and ChatGPT's inaccuracy," The Washington Post, online at: washingtonpost.com, July 13, 2023.
142. *Ibid.*
143. *Ibid.*

The FTC's investigation of ChatGPT is a practical demonstration of the application of existing law.

It has long been the position of the FTC that many existing Federal laws are applicable to AI and related products.

For example, in April 2020, Andrew Smith, Director of the FTC's Bureau of Consumer Protection, published the following online statement:

> The good news is that, while sophistication of AI and machine learning technology is new, automated decision-making is not, and we at the FTC have long experience in dealing with the challenges presented by the use of data and algorithms to make decisions about consumers. Over the years, the FTC has brought many cases alleging violations of the laws we enforce involving AI and automated decision-making and have investigated numerous companies in this space. For example, the Fair Credit Reporting Act (FCRA), enacted in 1970, and the Equal Credit Opportunity Act (ECOA), enacted in 1974 both address automated decision-making, and financial services companies have been applying these laws to machine-based credit underwriting models for decades. We have also used our FTC Act authority to prohibit unfair and deceptive practices and to address consumer injury arising from the use of AI an automated decision-making.[144]

In June 2023, it was reported that two new pieces of AI-related legislation had been introduced in the U.S. Senate.

§7.12 AI TRANSPARENCY BILL

The first is a bill introduced by the Chairman of the Homeland Security Committee, Senator Gary Peters, along with Senators Mike Braun and James Lankford, that would require U.S. government agencies to tell people when the agencies are using AI to interact with them. People would also be given a way to appeal any decisions being made by AI.[145]

§7.13 TECHNOLOGY COMPETITION BILL

The other bill is aimed at establishing an office to measure whether the United States remains competitive in developing and using the latest technological advances, including advances in AI systems. This has been introduced by Senators Michael Bennett and Mark Warner, along with Senator Todd Young. The bill is aimed at establishing an office of global competition analysis that would identify ways that the U.S. could stay at the forefront in developing AI systems.[146]

144. Andrew Smith, "Using Artificial Intelligence and Algorithms," FTC online at: ftc.gov, April 08, 2020, accessed July 17, 2023.
145. Reuters, "U.S. Congress to consider two new bills on artificial intelligence," online at: reuters.com, June 09, 2023.
146. *Ibid.*

§7.14 RESPONSES OF THE U.S. STATES TO AI

As can be seen, many national governments and international organizations are in the process of deciding what their policy should be with respect to AI and attempting to decide what regulations and laws should be put in place to protect against the potential risks of AI while encouraging the development of those AI systems which may offer significant benefits to things such as healthcare and manufacturing.

Many important regulatory areas in the United States are the province of the federal government, such as intellectual property and national security. However, each of the 50 states has its own system of laws and regulations covering such things as contracts, investments, crime, tax and healthcare.

Each of the states has officials and politicians who are concerned with developing their states' economies to expand job creation and tax revenues.

Consequently, states are making specific efforts to develop AI laws and regulations both to protect their citizens against potential risks and to use the potential benefits of AI to benefit their economies. These efforts will no doubt be in process for some time to come and will undoubtedly change over that time.

To give an idea of how states are developing their responses to AI, some of those efforts are described below. However, it should be kept in mind that at the time that this book is being written, intensive concern about AI and related digital topics (such as robotics and automated decision-making) is so new that many of the legislative bills referred to below were still "pending" rather than "enacted" as state law. Consequently, if any reader wishes to know whether particular legislation has become part of the law of any state, those readers will need to follow up by consulting qualified legal advisers in the states in question.

Of course, the response to AI is developing rapidly everywhere, so it will be necessary to get updates on a regular basis.

For example, the National Conference of State Legislatures (NCSL) published material online in April 2023 commenting on legislation in U.S. States and territories relating to "AI issues generally." However, their posting said:

> Legislation relating solely to specific AI technologies, such as facial recognition or autonomous cars, is being tracked separately.[147]

The U.S. Chamber of Commerce has also published online information about states that are considering legislation to regulate AI. This is done in the form of an interactive map that allows a user to obtain information about the legislation being considered or introduced in 2021.[148]

Please note that at the time this book was being written (primarily in 2023), publicity and concern about AI were expanding rapidly, and most states were in the process of considering the introduction of new laws and regulations to regulate the development and use of AI. The examples given below are by no means a complete

---

147. National Conference of State Legislatures, "Artificial Intelligence 2023 Legislation" updated April 18, 2023, online at: ncsl.org, accessed May 25, 2023.
148. U.S. Chamber of Commerce, "State-by-State Artificial Intelligence Legislation Tracker."

catalog of the measures introduced and implemented by the 50 U.S. states during the writing and following the publication of this book.

[A] Alabama

In 2019, the government of the state of Alabama was tasked with studying AI and reporting on the challenges and opportunities that it presented to the state.

In 2021, Alabama passed a legislative act to create a council on advanced technology and AI which was directed to examine AI and advanced technologies and report to the governor, the legislature and private parties on the uses and applications of those technologies.[149]

In 2022, Alabama passed a law preventing law enforcement agencies from using facial recognition technology in some criminal investigation activities.[150]

[B] Alaska

The University of Alaska, Center for Alaska Native Health Research has published online material relating to "Artificial Intelligence/Machine Learning Prospects for American Indian/Alaska Native Health."[151]

In a somewhat remarkable legislative development, it was reported in April 2023 that a member of the Alaska legislature "used Microsoft Bing AI Copilot to write a bill that would legalize gambling on Alaska ferries."[152]

The legislator said that:

> [H]e submitted the idea for the bill to the legislatures lawyers in January [2023], but they failed to get a draft bill back to him.

[C] Arizona

The Legislature of the State of Arizona has introduced a bill setting requirements for AI.[153] The bill demands that AI algorithms must comply with all federal and state laws.

---

149. Alabama Act No. 2021-344, Passed 27/04/2021. Text online at: arc-sos.state.al.us. *See also* Caroline Kraczon, "The State of State AI Policy (2021-22 Legislative Session)" Electronic Privacy Information Center, online at: epic.org, accessed May 24, 2023.
150. Alabama Act No. 2022-420, Passed April 05, 2021. Text online at: arc-sos.state.al.us. *See also*, Caroline Kraczon, "The State of State AI Policy (2021-22 Legislative Session)" Electronic Privacy Information Center, online at: epic.org, accessed May 24, 2023.
151. University of Alaska, Center for Alaska Native Health Research, online at: canhr.uaf.edu.
152. Jeff Landfield, "Alaska House representative uses artificial intelligence to write bill legalizing gambling on Alaska ferries," *The Alaska Landmine*, online at: alaskalandmine.com, April 13, 2023.
153. Legislature of the State of Arizona, House Bill 2685. "Amending Title 18. Arizona Revised Statutes, By Adding Chapter 7: Relating to Information Technology," online at: azleg.gov, accessed May 25, 2023.

It also requires that artificial intelligence "may not infringe on a human being's constitutional rights."[154]

A state committee on AI was established with a requirement that it review data on AI and submit a report on its findings on or before December 31, 2023.

Arizona has also introduced a bill to regulate the use of AI in ballot processing and adjudication.[155]

[D] Arkansas

A bill has been introduced in the State Legislature, creating requirements for "railroad train defect detectors."

[E] California

California has a number of laws and regulations in the works that affect the use of AI systems.

There is a pending bill that will require the California Department of Technology and other government bodies to inventory all "high risk automated decision systems" that are proposed, used, in development or proposed to be purchased by state agencies.[156]

At the end of January 2023, California introduced more legislation to regulate AI, including Bill 331.[157]

Bill 331 is directed largely at "deployers" and developers" of "an automated decision tool." These terms can include a "local government agency."

Bill 331 includes a number of relevant definitions, including the following:[158]

- "Automated decision tool" is defined as a system or service that uses artificial intelligence and has been specifically developed and marketed to, or specifically modified to, make, or be a controlling factor in making, consequential decisions."
- "Consequential decision" is defined as "a decision or judgment that has a legal, material, or similarly significant effect on an individual's life relating to the impact of, access to, or the cost, terms, or availability, of any of the following [in summary]: ... "employment ... education and vocational training

154. *See* text online, as cited above.
155. Arizona Bill 1565, "Relating to the Conduct of Elections," February 28, 2023, online at: custom.statenet.com.
156. California Assembly Bill 302, "Department of Technology: high risk automated decision systems inventory"(Amended), online at: custom.statenet.com, accessed July 03, 2023.
157. California Legislature, Assembly Bill No. 331, "An act to add Chapter 25 (commencing with Section 22756) to Division 8 of the Business and Professions Code, relating to artificial intelligence.," January 30, 2023, published, as amended, April 19, 2023, corrected as of April 20, 2023, accessed June 28, 2023.
158. *Ibid.*

... housing ... essential utilities ... family planning ... health care ... financial services ... criminal justice ... legal services ... voting."

- "Deployer" is defined as "a person, partnership, state or local government agency, or corporation that uses an automated decision tool to make a consequential decision."
- "Developer" is defined as "a person, partnership, state or local government agency, or corporation that designs, codes, or produces an automated decision tool, or substantially modifies an artificial intelligence system or service for the intended purpose of making, or being a controlling factor in making, consequential decisions, whether for its own use or for use by a third party."

The Bill is to take effect on or before January 1, 2025. After that, all deployers using automated decision tools would have to do an impact assessment on the decision tools that they use. This assessment would have to be documented annually. Those who are subjects of a decision based on an automated decision tool will need to be notified. People would be able to make a request not to be the subject of an automated decision tool. The deployer would need to accommodate that if it's feasible. A governance program would need to be developed by the deployers to incorporate appropriate safeguards.

There are a number of other provisions provided detailing the steps that the deployers would need to take to document their use of automatic decision tools. They would be required to provide certain safeguards and opportunities for subjects to object to the use of such tools, and they would need to make certain information publicly available about their use of such tools. Generally, certain of these provisions will apply to deployers with 25 or more employees.[159]

Pending California Senate Bill 313 requires any state agency that uses AI to communicate with a natural person to provide notice to the person that the communication is being made using AI. Instructions are to be included informing the person how they can communicate with a natural person at the state agency in question.[160]

Pending California Senate Bill 398 provides for a Government Services Advanced Technology Act to develop and implement a comprehensive research plan to study how using advanced technology could improve state and local government services.[161]

Pending California Senate Bill 721 creates a California inter-agency AI Working Group to report to the legislature about AI. Members are required to be Californians with expertise in areas such as computer science, AI and data privacy.[162]

---

159. Chris Mitchell, "AB 331: AI Tools," California Globe, March 23, 2023, online at: californiaglobe.com, accessed June 29, 2023.
160. California Senate Bill 313, "Department of Justice: Advanced Technology Research (Amended), online at: custom.statenet.com, accessed July 03, 2023.
161. California Senate Bill 398, "Department of Technology: high risk automated decision systems inventory"(Amended), online at: custom.statenet.com, accessed July 03, 2023.
162. California Assembly Bill 721, "California Interagency AI Working Group," online at: custom.statenet.com, accessed July 03, 2023.

California Senate Counsel Resolution 17, introduced on January 30, 2023, affirmed the California Legislature's commitment to President Biden's call for safe AI.[163]

[F] Colorado

A legislative bill has been introduced in Colorado restricting the use of facial recognition technology. Certain notices and reports need to be filed to justify the use of this technology.[164]

Colorado has also instituted regulations relating to the use of AI in the insurance business. Essentially, the regulations require life insurance companies to use AI governance measures that are designed to prevent unfair discrimination in the insurance business.[165]

[G] Connecticut

In Connecticut, the Governor and Legislature have undertaken an examination of AI and created an AI bill of rights.

The Connecticut Department of Administrative Services is required to do an inventory of AI systems being used by state agencies. They are to report back on the survey by December 31, 2023.[166]

[H] Delaware

The *Delaware Journal of Corporate Law* published by Delaware Law School has published the following statement about the use of AI in corporate governance in that state:

> Delaware law requires corporate directors to comply with fiduciary duties of loyalty and care. ... These fiduciary duties include acting in the best interest of the corporation and shareholders and being fully informed prior to making decisions on behalf of the company. ... The use of AI in corporate governance can be beneficial by making the board more effective and efficient in its direction, control, and coaching. ... The board can use AI to track overall trends in how business is allocating funds and extract data to align with the goals of business in various departments. ... (Footnotes omitted). ... In sum, the use of AI can be beneficial to Delaware boards of directors in corporate governance. Due to Delaware laws' emphasis on fiduciary duties of loyalty, care, non-delegation, and oversight, it is

163. California Senate Counsel Resolution 17, "Artificial Intelligence," online at: custom.statenet.com, accessed July 03, 2023.
164. Colorado General Assembly, SB22-113, online at: leg.colorado.gov. *See also*, Caroline Kraczon, "The State of State AI Policy (2021-22 Legislative Session)" Electronic Privacy Information Center, online at: epic.org.
165. Colo. Rev. Stat. Section 10-3-1104.9, online at: leg.colorado.gov.
166. *See* the Act signed in aid of these provisions: SB 1103, "An Act Concerning Artificial Intelligence, Automated Decision-Making and Personal Data Privacy," online at: cga.ct.gov.

> unlikely that AI systems will completely replace boards of directors. However, AI systems can potentially be required in corporate governance by Delaware law where the fiduciary duty of loyalty is linked with adopting compliance monitoring systems.[167]

[I] District of Columbia

The Council of the District of Columbia, the jurisdictional location of Washington DC, has introduced a bill to prohibit users of algorithmic decision-making from utilizing algorithmic eligibility determinations in a discriminatory manner, to require corresponding notices to individuals whose personal information is used, and to provide appropriate means of civil enforcement.[168]

[J] Florida

Florida does not, as of May 2023, have any specific regulation focusing on AI. However, lawyers' groups in Florida are keen for the state to remain at the forefront of the technology business. In aid of this, the Florida Bar has organized a study of AI development. It seems likely that, in the future, Florida will have specific legislation relating to AI.[169]

However, as previously pointed out, Florida does have a range of laws and regulations applicable to AI development, distribution and use, including criminal and consumer protection laws which are intended to protect Floridians from fraud, misrepresentation, and other abuses.

[K] Georgia

The legislature of the State of Georgia has established a House Subcommittee on AI. Representative Brad Thomas is the Chair of this Subcommittee and the Vice Chairman of the House Technology and Infrastructure Innovation Committee. Mr. Thomas compares the development of AI to the early days of the steam locomotive. He is quoted as saying:

> That was a new thing, an emerging technology and several of them blew up. The American Society of mechanical engineers came out and set standards for the industry which I think is important. We're not experts in AI so we are going to lean heavily on the industry and the appropriate people to make sure that we're doing the things that make sense.[170]

---

167. Kamia Mc Daniels, "The Future of Using Artificial Intelligence in Delaware Corporate Governance," *Delaware Journal of Corporate Law*, May 16, 2023.
168. District of Columbia Council Bill 302, "Stop Discrimination by Algorithms Act of 2023," online at: custom.statenet.com, accessed July 03, 2023.
169. Florida Bar, online at: floridabar.org.
170. Ross Williams, "Georgia lawmakers poised to study real and imagined threats from artificial intelligence," WABE News (Live radio broadcasts on BBC World Services), July 05, 2023.

[L] Hawaii

A resolution has been passed in the Hawaii Senate in April 2023, urging the U.S. Congress to begin a discussion considering the benefits and risks of AI technologies.[171]

[M] Idaho

To the extent that Idaho has not enacted specific laws dealing with AI systems, there are numerous laws in effect in that state that can affect the way that AI systems can be developed, distributed and used in ways that may affect residents of the state. These include criminal laws, tort laws, privacy laws, commercial laws, etc.

For example, in March 2019, Idaho passed a criminal procedure statute to the effect that "all pretrial risk-assessment tools shall be transparent."[172]

> (1) ...(a) All documents, data, records, and information used by the builder to build or validate the pretrial risk assessment tool and ongoing documents, data, records, and written policies outlining the usage and validation of the pretrial risk-assessment tool shall be open to the public inspection, auditing and testing.
>
> (2) For purposes of this section, "pretrial risk assessment tool" means a pre-trial process that creates or scores particular factors in order to estimate a person's level of risk to fail to appear in court, risk to commit a new crime, or risk posed to the community, in order to make recommendations as to bail or conditions of release based on such risk, whether made on an individualized basis or based on a grid or schedule.[173]

At least one commentator has called this:

> An example for states committed to using algorithms in pre-trial sentencing while retaining the notions of fairness and due process.[174]

Also, in Idaho, a significant amount of work has been done with respect to examining the use of AI and machine learning in operating nuclear plants. Specifically, the authors of the United States Nuclear Regulatory Commission publication "Exploring Advanced Computational Tools and Techniques with Artificial Intelligence and Machine Learning in Operating Nuclear Plants" was written by nuclear experts in Idaho, working at either the Idaho National Laboratory or the University of Idaho, both in Idaho Falls.[175]

---

171. Hawaii Legislature. Senate Concurrent Resolution, "Urging Congress to Begin a Discussion Considering the Benefits and Risks of Artificial Intelligence Technologies," April 28, 2023, online at: custom.statenet.com, accessed July 05, 2023.
172. Idaho Legislature, Title 19, Criminal Procedure 19-1910, "Pretrial Risk Assessment Tools," added 2019, online at: legislature.idaho.gov., accessed July 12, 2023.
173. *Ibid.*
174. Electronic Privacy Information Center, "State Artificial Intelligence Policy, State and Local Laws, Idaho Law" online at: epic.org, accessed July 12, 2023.
175. United States Nuclear Regulatory Commission, Office of Nuclear Regulatory Research, John Lane, NRC Project Manager, "Exploring Advanced Computational Tools and Techniques with

[N] Illinois

In 2021 and 2022, Illinois introduced legislative acts relating to employment and AI.[176]

One is the Illinois Future of Work Act which created in Illinois Future of Work Task Force responsible for assessing new technologies, such as AI, that could affect employment.[177]

Amendment to the Illinois Human Rights Act as also been proposed to provide that an employer that uses "predictive data analytics" in employment decisions may not consider an applicant's race or postal code to reject an applicant in the context of recruiting, hiring, promotion, renewal of employment, selection for training or apprenticeship, discharge, discipline, tenure or terms, privileges, or conditions of employment.[178]

Another is the Artificial Intelligence Interview Act. This requires employers, who are using AI analysis of video interviews in selecting job applicants, to report data on the race and ethnicity of applicants who are not selected for in-person interviews and of those who are hired to the Illinois Department of Commerce and Economic Opportunity.[179]

Illinois also introduced the anti-click gambling data analytics collection act. This is intended to prevent any gambling platform from collecting with the intent of predicting how a gambling participant will bet in a particular gambling situation.[180]

Illinois has had a bill introduced to create an "Innovation and Technology Act." This is intended to have the Illinois Department of Innovation and Technology establish a Generative AI and Natural Language Processing Task Force to report on generative AI and natural language processing systems.[181]

[O] Indiana

To the extent that Indiana has not enacted specific laws dealing with artificial intelligence systems, there are numerous laws in effect in that state that can affect the way that AI systems can be developed, distributed, and used in ways that may affect

---

Artificial Intelligence and Machine Learning in Operating Nuclear Plants," published February 2022, online at: inldigitallibrary.inl.gov.

176. Caroline Kraczon, "The State of State AI Policy (2021-22 Legislative Session)" Electronic Privacy Information Center, online at: epic.org, accessed May 24, 2023.
177. Illinois General Assembly, "Illinois Future of Work Act," Public Act 102-0407, effective date, August 19, 2021, text online at: ilga.gov.
178. General Assembly, State of Illinois, Proposed Amendment to Illinois Human Rights Act, February 17, 2023, regarding use of predictive data analysis in employment decisions, online at: custom.statenet.com, accessed July 05, 2023.
179. General Assembly, State of Illinois, "Artificial Intelligence Video Interview Act" Public Act 101-260, as amended by Public Act 102-47, effective date: January 01, 2022, text online at: ilga.gov.
180. General Assembly, State of Illinois, "Anti-Click Gambling Data Analytics Collection Act," Bill Number H. 2570, Introduced: February 15, 2023, text online at: ilga.gov, accessed July 06, 2023.
181. General Assembly, State of Illinois, "Innovation and Technology Act," Bill Number H. 3563, Introduced: May 18, 2023, text online at: ilga.gov, accessed July 06, 2023.

residents of the state. These include criminal laws, tort laws, privacy laws, commercial laws, etc.

For example, in May 2023, the Governor of Indiana signed into law a comprehensive privacy act that affects the application of AI systems to the personal data of Indiana residents. The law applies to entities that offer products or services to Indiana residents, those entities that come within the law or those that control or process the personal data of 100,000 consumers, or if the entities get more than half their revenue from selling personal data involving 25,000 consumers. The legislation is called the Indiana Consumer Data Protection Act (ICDPA) and is modeled on EU privacy laws and those passed by other U.S. states.[182]

Among other things, the ICDPA:[183]

- prohibits data controllers from processing personal data in ways that violate anti-discrimination laws;
- gives persons rights to correct, delete, and opt out of personal data processing or sale;
- requires processors to have security to protect data;
- requires processors to get consent to process personal data;
- requires processers to provide persons with clear notices about data processing; and
- provides civil penalties for violations.

Processing entities have until January 1, 2026, to come into compliance with the act which will take effect on that date.

Although the law does not expressly deal with AI systems, it undoubtedly affects the way that AI systems can be used when processing the data of Indiana residents.

[P] Iowa

To the extent that Iowa has not enacted specific laws dealing with AI systems, there are numerous laws in effect in Iowa that can affect the way that AI systems can be developed, distributed, and used in ways that may affect residents of the state of Iowa. These include criminal laws, tort laws, privacy laws, commercial laws, etc.

[Q] Kansas

To the extent that Kansas has not enacted specific laws dealing with AI systems, there are numerous laws in effect in Kansas that can affect the way that AI systems can be developed, distributed, and used in ways that may affect residents of the state of Kansas. These include criminal laws, tort laws, privacy laws, commercial laws, etc.

182. Alan L. Friel, Kyle R. Fath, David J. Oberly, "Follow the Leader: Indiana Becomes Latest State to Enact Consumer Privacy Statute," The National Law Review, July 13, 2023.
183. Anokhy Desai, "Indiana governor signs a comprehensive privacy act into law," The Privacy Advisor, International Association of Privacy Professionals (IAPP), online at: iapp.org.

However, there is involvement of at least one Kansas state-supported institution, Kansas State University (KSU), in the research and development of AI systems. This is described on the KSU website as follows.

> The center for artificial intelligence and data science of the Department of Computer Science, Carl R. Ice College of Engineering, Kansas State University, is a consortium of several faculty members and the research labs, undertaking research in applied and theoretical topics in the broad areas of artificial intelligence and/or data science. It brings together researchers from Kansas State University, other universities, and industry in pursuit of knowledge and applications related to artificial intelligence and data science.[184]

This activity may lead to significant interaction between state government officials and legislators in defining specific AI regulations for the state of Kansas in the future.

[R] Kentucky

To the extent that Kentucky has not enacted specific laws dealing with AI systems, there are numerous laws in effect in Kentucky that can affect the way that AI systems can be developed, distributed, and used in ways that may affect residents of the state of Kentucky. These include criminal laws, tort laws, privacy laws, commercial laws, etc.

Joining the rapid expansion of academic research on AI and machine learning, the University of Kentucky received a USD 14 million National Science Foundation (NSF) grant in November 2021 to fund a team of experts from the University of Kentucky's College of Engineering and the College of Arts and Sciences to build a lab that will apply AI solutions in cultural heritage projects.

"Heritage Science" has been practiced at the University of Kentucky for some time in determining the meaning and importance of historical information on how human culture has evolved over the millions of years—"It's the signature on a Bourbon barrel—it's the ancient footprints in Mammoth Cave..." Heritage science involves the interpretation of these and many other artifacts.

The application of AI will help interpret and classify historical clues in putting together a more cohesive explanation of how world culture has developed.[185]

It is undoubtedly the case that serious research conducted with AI systems by a state institution such as the University of Kentucky will help inform government officials and legislators about the advantages and potential problems of AI.

184. Department of Computer Science, Kansas State University, Center for Intelligence and Data Science, website online at: caids.cs.ksu.edu, accessed July 18, 2023.
185. "University of Kentucky Receives $14 Million NSF Grant to Construct World-Class Cultural Heritage Lab," online at: engr.uky.edu, November 05, 2021, accessed July 18, 2023.

[S] Louisiana

To the extent that Louisiana has not enacted specific laws dealing with AI systems, there are numerous laws in effect in Louisiana that can affect the way that AI systems can be developed, distributed, and used in ways that may affect residents of the state of Louisiana. These include criminal laws, tort laws, privacy laws, commercial laws, etc.

According to their websites, both Louisiana State University and the University of New Orleans offer programs in the study of and research on AI and machine learning.[186]

It is undoubtedly the case that serious research conducted with AI systems by educational institutions such as Louisiana State University and the University of New Orleans will help inform government officials and legislators about the advantages and potential problems of AI.

[T] Maine

In June 2023, due to "cyber security risks," the State of Maine banned the use of AI by state agencies for a period of six months.[187]

The ban was imposed by Maine Acting Chief Information Officer, Nick Marquis, of the Maine Information Technology Agency. An email was reportedly sent to all Maine Executive Branch agencies that said:[188]

> Generative AI systems have the capacity to automatically process data and information in a way that resembles intelligent human behavior. The risks that Generative AI poses are both known and unknowable and many of these risks transcend security.

"During this time, Maine IT will comprehensively evaluate generative AI technologies within the current regulatory landscape to ensure our approach and adoption cultivates public trust and responsible use of all AI systems while minimizing its potential negative impact."

The State of Maine Office of Information Technology (OIT), also known as Maine IT, was created by state Executive Order in January 2005.[189] Main IT was created:

> To promote statewide information technology solutions and use of information efficiently across the government. ... It also provides networks support for the Judicial Branch, Secretary of State, Attorney General and it supports Maine

---

186. For information *see*, Louisiana State University, "Artificial Intelligence," online at: lsu.edu; and The University of New Orleans, "Machine Learning & Artificial Intelligence," online at: uno.edu.
187. Edward Tomic, "Maine Bans Artificial Intelligence Use by State Agencies for 6 Months Due to 'Cybersecurity Risks'," Main Wire, online at: the mainewire.com, June 21, 2023.
188. *Ibid.*
189. For information, see: State of Maine Office of Information Technology (OIT, also known as "MaineIT"), website online at: maine.gov.

Citizens through the Maine government web portal, and MSCommNet public safety radio communications networks, among other services.

The Maine IT website contains an extensive list of the state of Maine's cyber-policies.

[U] Maryland

Four bills on AI were introduced for consideration by the Maryland General Assembly (the state legislature), but all failed to become law.

The first was the Artificial Intelligence Implementation Causing Harm Bill (Bill H 996). This was intended to impose strict liability on persons who intentionally designed and created AI software to cause physical injury or death and imposed damages and civil penalties.

The second was the Artificial Intelligence Impact Advisory Board Bill (Bill H 1034). This was intended to create an Artificial Intelligence Impact Advisory Board to study issues relating to AI and report findings and recommendations to the governor and the Maryland General Assembly.

The third was a bill (Bill H 1068) to create a Commission on Responsible Artificial Intelligence to study issues relating to the use and regulation of AI. They were required to report findings and recommendations to the House Health and Government Operations Committee, the House Economic Matters Committee, the Senate Finance Committee, and the Senate Education, Energy and Environment Committees. This bill was reported as "adjourned," presumably for later consideration.

A fourth bill (Bill H 1132) reportedly "failed—adjourned" was intended to establish a technology and science advisory commission to study and make recommendations on science and technology in the state of Maryland.

All this makes it appear as though the legislators of Maryland are having difficulty reaching a consensus on how science and technology, particularly AI systems, should be treated under Maryland state law. As some of these bills, as of this writing, have not become law, some were reported to be "adjourned," so it seems possible that versions of these will be incorporated into Maryland law at some point.[190]

[V] Massachusetts

In Massachusetts, a legislator introduced a bill (S.31) that is entitled, "An Act drafted with the help of ChatGPT to regulate generative artificial intelligence models like ChatGPT."[191]

It is not clear if this became law[192], but Massachusetts has introduced several bills to regulate AI:

---

190. Summaries of these bill are available on the site of the National Conference of State Legislatures at, online at: ncsl.org.
191. Massachusetts Legislative Information online at: malegislature.gov, accessed June 29, 2023.
192. A legal opinion of a qualified Massachusetts legal advisor will need to be sought.

- H.64: an Act establishing a commission to regulate automated decision-making by the state government. February 16, 2023.
- H.1974: an Act regulating the use of AI in providing mental health services. February 16, 2023.
- S.31: an Act drafted with the help of ChatGPT to regulate generative AI models like chat GPT. February 16, 2023.
- S.33: an Act establishing a commission on automated decision-making by the government in Massachusetts.

It does not appear that any of these have been enacted into law as of September 2023.[193]

[W] Michigan

To the extent that Michigan has not enacted specific laws dealing with AI systems, there are numerous laws in effect in Michigan that can affect the way that AI systems can be developed, distributed, and used in ways that may affect residents of the state of Michigan. These include criminal laws, tort laws, privacy laws, labor laws, commercial laws, etc.

Joining the rapid expansion of academic research on AI and machine learning, there are at least 23 colleges and universities in Michigan reported to offer programs in the study of and research on AI and machine learning.[194] Examples are courses offered by the University of Michigan and Michigan State University.

It is undoubtedly the case that serious research conducted with AI systems by educational institutions such as the University of Michigan and Michigan State University will help inform government officials and legislators about the advantages and potential problems of AI.

[X] Minnesota

To the extent that Minnesota has not enacted specific laws dealing with AI systems, there are numerous laws in effect in Minnesota that can affect the way that AI systems can be developed, distributed, and used in ways that may affect residents of the state of Minnesota. These include criminal laws, tort laws, privacy laws, labor laws, commercial laws, etc.

Joining the rapid expansion of academic research on AI and machine learning, there are several colleges and universities in Minnesota that are reported to offer

---

193. *Ibid.*
194. For information *see*, Louisiana State University, "Artificial Intelligence," online at: lsu.edu; and The University of New Orleans, "Machine Learning & Artificial Intelligence," online at: uno.edu.

programs in the study of and research on AI and machine learning.[195] Two of these are the University of Minnesota (Twin Cities) and the Mayo Clinic College of Medicine and Science.

It is undoubtedly the case that serious research conducted with AI systems by such educational institutions will help inform government officials and legislators about the advantages and potential problems of AI.

[Y] Mississippi

In 2021, Mississippi passed legislation directing the state Department of Education to offer a curriculum in computer science that included lessons in machine learning and AI.[196] This legislation is titled the Mississippi Computer Science and Cyber Education Equality Act. This Act took effect on July 01, 2021.[197]

[Z] Missouri

A bill is being considered by the Missouri Legislature (Bill H 311) to establish the Twenty-First Century Technology Innovation Task Force. It is intended that the Task Force will review the conditions of the state's technology platforms and make recommendations about the use of technology and AI to improve the state's management of records and to allow citizens of Missouri to have more efficient electronic communications and access.[198]

[AA] Montana

To the extent that Montana has not enacted specific laws dealing with AI systems, there are numerous laws in effect in Montana that can affect the way that AI systems can be developed, distributed, and used in ways that may affect residents of the state of Montana. These include criminal laws, tort laws, privacy laws, commercial laws, etc.

Joining the rapid expansion of academic research on AI and machine learning, four universities in Montana are reported to offer programs in the study of and research

195. For information *see*, Louisiana State University, "Artificial Intelligence," online at: lsu.edu; and The University of New Orleans, "Machine Learning & Artificial Intelligence," online at: uno.edu.
196. Caroline Kraczon, "The State of State AI Policy (2021-22 Legislative Session)" Electronic Privacy Information Center, online at: epic.org, accessed May 24, 2023.
197. Mississippi House Bill HB633, 2021, "The Mississippi Computer Science and Cyber Education Equality Act," effective date July 01, 2021, text online at LegiScan: legiscan.com, accessed May 24, 2023.
198. The Bill was introduced on April 13, 2023. Text is available online at: custom.statenet.com, under 2023 MO H 311.

on AI and machine learning.[199] They are Montana State University, the University of Montana, Montana Technological University and Montana State University Billings.

It is undoubtedly the case that serious research conducted on AI systems by these educational institutions will help inform government officials and legislators about the advantages and potential problems of AI.[200]

[BB] Nebraska

To the extent that Nebraska has not enacted specific laws dealing with AI systems, there are numerous laws in effect in Nebraska that can affect the way that AI systems can be developed, distributed, and used in ways that may affect residents of the state of Nebraska. These include criminal laws, tort laws, privacy laws, commercial laws, etc.

Joining the rapid expansion of academic research on AI and machine learning, colleges and universities in Nebraska are reported to offer programs in the study of and research on AI and machine learning.[201] They include the University of Nebraska.

It is undoubtedly the case that serious research conducted on AI systems by this educational institution will help inform government officials and legislators about the advantages and potential problems of AI.[202]

In January 2022, a bill was introduced in the Nebraska legislature that proposed to appropriate USD 50 million in federal funds to establish an "Artificial Intelligence, Cybersecurity and High Performance Computing Center" facility at the University of Nebraska, Lincoln, Innovation Campus (NIC). However, the bill appears to have been "indefinitely postponed" in April 2022:[203]

> NIC is designed to facilitate new and in-depth partnerships between the University of Nebraska and private sector businesses.[204]

One project discussed on the NIC website that relates to Artificial Intelligence technology is "an AI enabled precision spraying technology for agricultural applications" by Greeneye Technology.[205] In Nebraska, agriculture is a huge business. This seems to be the kind of AI system project that would be natural for NIC to encourage. It will be interesting to see whether future legislative support for this sort of state-supported educational activity relating to AI will develop in Nebraska.

---

199. For information *see*, Louisiana State University, "Artificial Intelligence," online at: lsu.edu; and The University of New Orleans, "Machine Learning & Artificial Intelligence," online at: uno.edu.
200. EduRank, "4 Best colleges for Artificial Intelligence (AI) in Montana."
201. For information see, Louisiana State University, "Artificial Intelligence," online at: lsu.edu; and The University of New Orleans, "Machine Learning & Artificial Intelligence," online at: uno.edu.
202. EduRank, "4 Best colleges for Artificial Intelligence (AI) in Montana."
203. LegisScan, "Nebraska Legislature Bill 904, NE LB904, 2021-2022, 107th Legislature," online at: legiscan.com, accessed July 21, 2023.
204. Nebraska Innovation Campus, "About," online at: innovate.unl.edu, accessed July 21, 2023.
205. Nebraska Innovation Campus, online at: innovate.unl.edu, accessed July 21, 2023.

[CC] Nevada

A Nevada bill has been introduced creating the Emerging Technologies Task Force within the Department of Business and Industry, and it authorizes the Director to create an Opportunity Center for Emerging Technology Businesses as part of the Office of Business Finance and Planning.[206]

[DD] New Hampshire

In July 2023, a publication called New Hampshire Bulletin published this story online, pointing out that few states have adopted regulations about using AI in hiring and other business activities. Such regulation in New Hampshire is not identified. A Maryland state legislator is quoted as saying:

> Technology always innovates first, and then always seems like a good idea, until it isn't ... That's when legislators step up and try to regulate things as best they can.[207]

To the extent that New Hampshire has not enacted specific laws dealing with AI systems, there are numerous laws in effect in New Hampshire that can affect the way that AI systems can be developed, distributed, and used in ways that may affect residents of the State of New Hampshire. These include criminal laws, tort laws, privacy laws, commercial laws, etc.

Joining the rapid expansion of academic research on AI and machine learning, universities in New Hampshire are reported to offer programs in the study of and research on AI and machine learning.[208] They include the prestigious Ivy League school: Dartmouth College in Hanover, New Hampshire. Indeed, it is claimed that research on Artificial Intelligence originated at Dartmouth:

> In 1956, a small group of scientists gathered for the Dartmouth Summer Research Project on Artificial Intelligence, which was the birth of this field of research.[209]

It is undoubtedly the case that serious research conducted with AI systems by educational institutions such as Dartmouth College and the University of New Hampshire will help inform government officials and legislators about the advantages and potential problems of AI.[210]

---

206. Assembly of the State of Nevada, "Emerging Technologies Task Force," Senate Bill Number 165, February 16, 2023, text online at: custom.statenet.com.
207. Madyson Fitzgerald, "As employers expand artificial intelligence in hiring, few states have rules," *New Hampshire Bulletin*, July 18, 2023 (corrected July 19, 2023), online at: newhampshirebulleting.com.
208. For information *see*, Louisiana State University, "Artificial Intelligence," online at: lsu.edu; and The University of New Orleans, "Machine Learning & Artificial Intelligence," online at: uno.edu.
209. Dartmouth College, "Artificial Intelligence Coined at Dartmouth," website online at: home.dartmouth.edu, accessed July 21, 2023.
210. EduRank, "9 Best colleges for Artificial Intelligence (AI) in New Hampshire."

[EE] New Jersey

A legislative bill has been introduced in New Jersey that requires the Commissioner of Labor and Workforce Development to "conduct a study and issue a report on the impact of artificial intelligence" on the state economy.[211]

A bill has been introduced that requires automobile insurers to provide policy holders with annual documentation demonstrating that there are no discriminatory outcomes created by the insurers' automated underwriting system.[212]

A bill has been introduced that regulates the use of automated tools in hiring decisions to minimize discrimination in employment.[213]

Another bill has previously been introduced, also relating to the use of automated tools in hiring decisions that regulate the use of search tools in order to minimize discrimination in employment.[214]

A bill has been introduced relating to the requirements for the disclosure and processing of "personally identifiable information." It establishes the Office of Data Protection and Responsible Use within the Division of Consumer Affairs.[215]

A bill has been introduced that requires the Department of Labor and Workforce Development to track and maintain information on job losses due to automation.[216]

A bill has been introduced the prohibits certain kinds of discrimination in automated decision-making systems.[217]

Opinions of qualified New Jersey legal advisors will be necessary to determine if any of these bills has been enacted into law.

[FF] New Mexico

To the extent that New Mexico has not enacted specific laws dealing with AI systems, there are numerous laws in effect in New Mexico that can affect the way that AI systems can be developed, distributed, and used in ways that may affect residents of the state of New Mexico. These include criminal laws, tort laws, privacy laws, commercial laws, etc.

---

211. Assembly of the State of New Jersey, "Artificial Intelligence Economic Growth Study," Assembly Number A 168, January 11, 2022, text online at: custom.statenet.com.
212. Assembly of the State of New Jersey, "Automobile Insurers Automated Underwriting System," Assembly Number A 537, January 11, 2022, text online at: custom.statenet.com.
213. Assembly of the State of New Jersey, "Use of Automated Tools in Hiring Decisions," Assembly Number A 4909, April 12, 2022, text online at: custom.statenet.com.
214. Assembly of the State of New Jersey, "Use of Automated Tools in Hiring Decisions," Assembly Number A 1926, 11 March 03, 2022, text online at: custom.statenet.com.
215. Senate of the State of New Jersey, "Personal Identifiable Information Disclosures," Senate Number 3714, March 13, 2023, text online at: custom.statenet.com.
216. Assembly of the State of New Jersey, "Job Loss Due to Automation Information," Assembly Number A 5150, June 02, 2022, text online at: custom.statenet.com.
217. Assembly of the State of New Jersey, "Automated Decision System Discrimination," Assembly Number A 1402, October 02, 2022, text online at: custom.statenet.com.

Joining the rapid expansion of academic research on AI and machine learning, the University of New Mexico (UNM) is reported to offer a Master of Science in Artificial Intelligence and has created a number of on-campus resources on AI.[218]

It is undoubtedly the case that a serious educational program on AI systems by UNM will help inform government officials and legislators about the advantages and potential problems of AI.

[GG] New York

New York City passed Local Law 144, which came into effect on July 5, 2023. Local Law 144:

> prohibits employers and employment agencies from using an automated employment decision tool unless the tool has been subject to a bias audit within one year of the use of the tool, information about the bias audit is publicly available, and certain notices have been provided to employees or job candidates.[219]

New York State has introduced the following bills for consideration.

A bill has been introduced in New York that designates rules for using Automated Employment Decision Tools and creates enforcement criteria for dealing with violations of those rules.[220]

New York has introduced a bill to create a temporary State Commission to Study Artificial Intelligence. The remit of the Commission is to investigate how AI robotics and automation should be regulated.[221]

New York has introduced a bill that requires state government units to use responsible standards when purchasing a product or service that employs algorithmic decision systems. The State Commissioner of Taxation and Finance must adopt appropriate regulations that effectively apply regulations relating to unlawful discriminatory practices to state activities performed through algorithmic decision systems.[222]

[HH] North Carolina

A legislative bill has been introduced in North Carolina to establish a committee to study automation in the workforce.[223]

---

218. Sara Velasquez, "UNM launches AI resources website to highlight campus-wide AI endeavors," UNM Newsroom, online at: news.unm.edu, August 23, 2023.
219. New York City, "Automated Employment and Decision Tools (AEDT)," NYC Consumer and Worker Protection, online at: nyc.gov.
220. Legislature of the State of New York, Assembly Bill A 567, "Use of Automated Employment Decision Tools," January 9, 2023, text online at: custom.statenet.com.
221. Legislature of the State of New York, Assembly Bill A 4969, "State Commission to Study Artificial Intelligence," February 27, 2023, text online at: custom.statenet.com.
222. Legislature of the State of New York, Assembly Bill A 5309, "An Act To Amend the State Finance Law in Relation to the Purchase of Products That Are or Contain an Algorithmic Decision Systems," March 7, 2023, text online at: custom.statenet.com.
223. General Assembly of North Carolina, Senate Bill 460, April 03, 2023, text online at: custom.statenet.com.

[II] North Dakota

A law was enacted in North Dakota relating to the definition of the term "person." Under this statute, the term does not include "environmental elements, artificial intelligence, an animal or an inanimate object."[224]

[JJ] Ohio

To the extent that Ohio has not enacted specific laws dealing with AI systems, there are numerous laws in effect in Ohio that can affect the way that AI systems can be developed, distributed and used in ways that may affect residents of the state of Ohio. These include criminal laws, tort laws, privacy laws, commercial laws, etc.

Joining the rapid expansion of academic research on AI and machine learning, a number of colleges and universities in Ohio are offering academic programs in AI, including Ohio State University.[225]

It is undoubtedly the case that a serious educational program on AI systems by such colleges and universities will help inform government officials and legislators about the advantages and potential problems of AI.

[KK] Oklahoma

To the extent that Oklahoma has not enacted specific laws dealing with AI systems, there are numerous laws in effect in Oklahoma that can affect the way that AI systems can be developed, distributed, and used in ways that may affect residents of the state of Oklahoma. These include criminal laws, tort laws, privacy laws, commercial laws, etc.

Joining the rapid expansion of academic research on AI and machine learning, the University of Oklahoma is reported to offer studies in such disciplines.[226]

It is undoubtedly the case that a serious educational program on AI systems by the University of Oklahoma and other institutions of higher learning in Oklahoma will help inform government officials and legislators about the advantages and potential problems of AI.

[LL] Oregon

In August 2023, the Oregon legislature passed Senate Bill 619, which is a comprehensive consumer privacy law that permits consumers to find out whether a personal data

---

224. Legislative Assembly of North Dakota, House Bill No. 1361, April 11, 2023, text online at: custom.statenet.com.
225. Department of Computer Science and Engineering, "Experiencing AI: Artificial intelligence research is booming at Ohio State, and it's opening doors for students," College of Engineering, online at: cse.ohio-state.edu, October 06, 2021.
226. "Artificial Intelligence and Machine Learning at OU," online at: ou.edu.

controller is processing the consumer's personal information, the categories of data being processed and a list of the third parties to which the comptroller has disclosed the consumer's personal data.[227]

A consumer can choose to refuse to be subject to being profiled by automatic decision-making systems that will analyze and predict things about their behavior when these predictions might have legal or professional consequences. The law becomes effective on January 1, 2024. The Bill also provides for reparations for black Oregon residents who can show a heritage of slavery.[228]

[MM] Pennsylvania

Pennsylvania has introduced a bill creating an Artificial Intelligence Registry. It would amend the state Administrative Code in respect to the powers and duties of the Pennsylvania Department of Data to provide for said Artificial Intelligence Registry.[229]

That Bill became law in March of 2023 by an Act amending P.L. 177, No. 175, of 1929, creating the Artificial Intelligence Registry. The details are set out in a new section 817, added to the Act of April 9, 1929. That amendment was to take effect in May 2023.[230]

There have been additional amendments to the Public Laws of Pennsylvania relating to the use of AI tools, including: Health Care (HB0155); Education (HB0928); Employment (HB0947); Technology (HB0964) and Securities (HB1402), and others.[231]

[NN] Puerto Rico

The U.S. territory of Puerto Rico has reportedly adopted a bill launching an investigation on the use of automated Artificial Intelligence systems that may significantly impact the rights and opportunities of persons and institutions in the territory. The bill calls for recommendations to address any potential problems.[232]

It has also introduced a bill that would create an Artificial Intelligence Officer, and an Artificial Intelligence Council to assist with implementation of AI in Puerto Rico,[233] and a bill creating a registry of companies developing or using AI.[234]

---

227. 2023 Session, "Senate Bill 619," online at gov.oregonlive.com.
228. *Ibid.*
229. The General Assembly of Pennsylvania, House Bill 49, "Artificial Intelligence Registry," July 3, 2023.
230. Pennsylvania General Assembly, Bill Information—History, "House Bill 49, Regular Session 2023-2024," online at: legis.state.pa.us, March 07, 2023.
231. More information at: Pennsylvania General Assembly, Bill Information—History, "More bills from this session under the same topics as House Bill 49, Regular Session 2023-2024," online at: legis.state.pa.us, accessed September 20, 2023.
232. Legislative Assembly of Puerto Rico, Senate Resolution, SR 684 "Artificial Intelligence," text online at: custom.statenet.com.
233. Senado de Puerto Rico, "P. del S. 1179," online at: senado.pr.gov, April 18, 2023.
234. National Conference of State Legislatures, "Puerto Rico SjR 412," online at ncsl.org, accessed September 20, 2023.

[OO] Rhode Island

Rhode Island has introduced a bill that prohibits any algorithms or predictive models that use external consumer data in any way that unfairly discriminates based on race, color, national or ethnic origin, religion, sex, sexual orientation, disability, gender identity, or gender expression by insurers.[235]

Rhode Island has also introduced a bill to establish a commission to monitor the use of AI in state government and to make recommendations suggesting changes in the way that state government uses AI.[236]

Rhode Island has also introduced a bill to prohibit the use of facial recognition technology in betting contexts.[237]

[PP] South Carolina

To the extent that South Carolina has not enacted specific laws dealing with AI systems, there are numerous laws in effect in South Carolina that can affect the way that AI systems can be developed, distributed, and used in ways that may affect residents of the state of South Carolina. These include criminal laws, tort laws, privacy laws, commercial laws, etc.

Joining the rapid expansion of academic research on AI and machine learning, there are a number of colleges and universities in South Carolina reported to offer studies in such disciplines, including the University of South Carolina and Clemson University.[238]

It is undoubtedly the case that serious educational work on AI systems by institutions of higher learning in South Carolina will help inform government officials and legislators about the advantages and potential problems of AI.

[QQ] South Dakota

To the extent that South Dakota has not enacted specific laws dealing with AI systems, there are numerous laws in effect in South Dakota that can affect the way that AI systems can be developed, distributed, and used in ways that may affect residents of the state of South Dakota. These include criminal laws, tort laws, privacy laws, commercial laws, etc.

---

235. The General Assembly of the State of Rhode Island, House Bill 5734. "Business Regulation Regarding Insurance Discrimination," February 21, 2023, text online at: custom.statenet.com.
236. The General Assembly of the State of Rhode Island, Senate Bill 117, "Artificial Intelligence in the Decision-Making Process," February 1, 2023, text online at: custom.statenet.com.
237. The General Assembly of the State of Rhode Island, Senate Bill 146, "Use of Facial and Bio Metric Recognition Technology," February 1, 2023, text online at: custom.statenet.com.
238. EduRank, "Computer Science, Artificial Intelligence(AI)—North America—United States—South Carolina," online at: edurank.org.

Joining the rapid expansion of academic research on AI and machine learning, there are a number of colleges and universities in South Dakota reported to offer studies in such disciplines, including the University of South Dakota.[239]

It is undoubtedly the case that serious educational work on AI systems by institutions of higher learning in South Dakota will help inform government officials and legislators about the advantages and potential problems of AI.

[RR] Tennessee

To the extent that Tennessee has not enacted specific laws dealing with AI systems, there are numerous laws in effect in Tennessee that can affect the way that AI systems can be developed, distributed, and used in ways that may affect residents of the state of Tennessee. These include criminal laws, tort laws, privacy laws, commercial laws, etc.

Joining the rapid expansion of academic research on AI and machine learning, there are a number of colleges and universities in Tennessee reported to offer studies in such disciplines, including Vanderbilt University.[240]

It is undoubtedly the case that serious educational work on AI systems by institutions of higher learning in Tennessee will help inform government officials and legislators about the advantages and potential problems of AI.

[SS] Texas

The State of Texas has introduced a bill to set up an Artificial Intelligence Advisory Council.[241]

Texas has also introduced a bill to establish a program, to be administered by the State Workforce Commission, to train people in skills relating to AI systems.[242]

Texas has also introduced a bill relating to using AI in the provision of mental health services.[243]

[TT] Utah

To the extent that Utah has not enacted specific laws dealing with AI systems, there are numerous laws in effect in Utah that can affect the way that AI systems can be

239. EduRank, "Computer Science, Artificial Intelligence(AI)—North America—United States—South Dakota," online at: edurank.org.
240. EduRank, "Computer Science, Artificial Intelligence(AI)—North America—United States—Tennessee," online at: edurank.org.
241. The Legislature of the State of Texas, House Bill 2060, "Artificial Intelligence Advisory Council," June 13, 2023, text online at: custom.statenet.com.
242. The Legislature of the State of Texas, House Bill 3633, "State Workforce Commission," March 6, 2023, text online at: custom.statenet.com.
243. The Legislature of the State of Texas, House Bill 4695, "Artificial Intelligence Health Services," March 10, 2023, text online at: custom.statenet.com.

developed, distributed, and used in ways that may affect residents of the state of Utah. These include criminal laws, tort laws, privacy laws, commercial laws, etc.

Joining the rapid expansion of academic research on AI and machine learning, there are a number of colleges and universities in Utah reported to offer studies in such disciplines, including the University of Utah.[244]

It is undoubtedly the case that serious educational work on AI systems by institutions of higher learning in Utah will help inform government officials and legislators about the advantages and potential problems of AI.

[UU] Vermont

The State of Vermont has introduced a bill to restrict the monitoring of employment and the use of employment-related automated decision systems.[245]

[VV] Virginia

To the extent that Virginia has not enacted specific laws dealing with AI systems, there are numerous laws in effect in Virginia that can affect the way that AI systems can be developed, distributed, and used in ways that may affect residents of the state of Virginia. These include criminal laws, tort laws, privacy laws, commercial laws, etc.

Joining the rapid expansion of academic research on AI and machine learning, there are a number of colleges and universities in Virginia reported to offer studies in such disciplines, including the University of Virginia.[246]

It is undoubtedly the case that serious educational work on AI systems by institutions of higher learning in Virginia will help inform government officials and legislators about the advantages and potential problems of AI.

[WW] Washington

The State of Washington has introduced a bill relating to the use of "automated decision systems." It is intended to establish guidelines for government procurement and use of automated decision systems. These guidelines are intended to protect consumers, improve transparency and create more market predictability.[247]

---

244. EduRank, "Computer Science, Artificial Intelligence(AI)—North America—United States—Utah," online at: edurank.org.
245. The General Assembly of the State of Vermont, House Bill 114, "Electronic Monitoring," January 25, 2023, text online at: custom.statenet.com.
246. EduRank, "Computer Science, Artificial Intelligence(AI)—North America—United States—Virginia," online at: edurank.org.
247. The Legislature of the State of Washington, Senate Bill 5356, "Use of Automated Decision Systems," January 12, 2023, text online at: custom.statenet.com.

[XX] West Virginia

To the extent that West Virginia has not enacted specific laws dealing with AI systems, there are numerous laws in effect in West Virginia that can affect the way that AI systems can be developed, distributed, and used in ways that may affect residents of the state of West Virginia. These include criminal laws, tort laws, privacy laws, commercial laws, etc.

Joining the rapid expansion of academic research on AI and machine learning, there are a number of colleges and universities in Virginia reported to offer studies in such disciplines, including the University of West Virginia.[248]

It is undoubtedly the case that serious educational work on AI systems by institutions of higher learning in West Virginia will help inform government officials and legislators about the advantages and potential problems of AI.

[YY] Wisconsin

To the extent that Wisconsin has not enacted specific laws dealing with AI systems, there are numerous laws in effect in Wisconsin that can affect the way that AI systems can be developed, distributed, and used in ways that may affect residents of the state of Wisconsin. These include criminal laws, tort laws, privacy laws, commercial laws, etc.

Joining the rapid expansion of academic research on AI and machine learning, there are a number of colleges and universities in Wisconsin reported to offer studies in such disciplines, including the University of Wisconsin.[249]

It is undoubtedly the case that serious educational work on AI systems by institutions of higher learning in Wisconsin will help inform government officials and legislators about the advantages and potential problems of AI.

[ZZ] Wyoming

To the extent that Wyoming has not enacted specific laws dealing with AI systems, there are numerous laws in effect in Wyoming that can affect the way that AI systems can be developed, distributed, and used in ways that may affect residents of the state of Wyoming. These include criminal laws, tort laws, privacy laws, commercial laws, etc.

Joining the rapid expansion of academic research on AI and machine learning, there are colleges and universities in Wyoming reported to offer studies in such disciplines, including the University of Wyoming.[250]

---

248. EduRank, "Computer Science, Artificial Intelligence(AI)—North America—United States—West Virginia," online at: edurank.org.
249. EduRank, "Computer Science, Artificial Intelligence(AI)—North America—United States—South Dakota," online at: edurank.org.
250. EduRank, "Computer Science, Artificial Intelligence(AI)—North America—United States—Wyoming," online at: edurank.org.

It is undoubtedly the case that serious educational work on AI systems by institutions of higher learning in Wyoming will help inform government officials and legislators about the advantages and potential problems of AI.

§7.15 AI HARDWARE

[A] Nvidia Computer Chips

It is the case that AI systems such as the well-known ChatGPT of OpenAI require sophisticated and powerful hardware to perform their functions.

It was reported in May 2023 that a computer chip that has made it possible for AI systems to function at the level they do is made by the California-based computer chip maker Nvidia Corp. This association has led to a significant increase in Nvidia's business:[251]

> Originally known for making the type of computer chips that process graphics, particularly for computer games, Nvidia hardware underpins most AI applications today.

Several super computers use Nvidia chips in their graphics processing units (GPUs). For example, it is reported that ChatGPT used 10,000 Nvidia processing units to train its functionality. Nvidia is reported to have about 95% of the machine learning GPU market. In 2022, the AI business boomed, increasing revenue by about 40% to around USD 15 billion.[252]

A positive effect on Nvidia has been dramatic. Nvidia has raised its production to meet growing demand, and its share price rose almost 30% in May 2023. The AI chips Nvidia sells to data centers can cost about USD 10,000 but it is now producing more powerful chips that sell for much more.[253]

Nvidia was founded in 1993 and initially focused on making better graphics chips for gaming and other sophisticated applications. For important computer tasks such as operating the visual pixels found on a computer screen, GPUs are designed to perform many parallel tasks at the same time.

When it was discovered that such GPUs could dramatically increase the speed of mathematical calculations, the basis of AI was established.[254]

In about 2006, the head of Nvidia focused their technology on creating a way to make its GPUs programmable which meant that they could be used in many functions other than improving graphics performance. This made it possible for consumer-level computers to do much more sophisticated processing than had previously been possible. This was a "breakthrough" which made today's AI possible.

---

251. Zoe Corbyn, "Nvidia: The chip maker that became an AI superpower," BBC News, online, May 26, 2023.
252. *Ibid.*
253. *Ibid.*
254. *Ibid.*

By about 2012, it was possible to use Nvidia GPUs to "train" AI systems to produce more sophisticated results. This started computer scientists and computer businesses buying such GPUs to massively speed up the processing needed for the operations they were seeking to do.

By 2021, the capabilities of such GPUs produced not only positive outcomes but also made it possible to produce negative and potentially damaging outcomes such as "deep fakes" such as photographic, video and audio simulations that could appear to be real productions by actual people, such as movie stars and others.[255] This reportedly led to a statement by Harrison Ford in 2023 that "I could be dead and I'm still working."[256]

It is obvious that there are risks to the expansion of AI systems that will, hopefully, be sensibly dealt with by appropriate laws and regulations.

It is true that, at present, Nvidia dominates the GPU market for sophisticated computer applications such as AI systems. However, competitors such as AMD and Intel are trying to catch up. One industry analyst reportedly said:

> Nvidia is the one with the target on its back that everybody is trying to take down.[257]

So far, Nvidia has managed to stay ahead of the competition in the race to provide sophisticated GPUs to cutting-edge digital creators. In May 2023, it was reported that Nvidia was on track to become "the first chip company with a $1 trillion market value."[258] When its role in the AI market became more widely known, increases in the price of its stock made Nvidia the most valuable chip company in the world and the fifth most valuable company in the United States. In 2023, Nvidia, a company founded in 1993, saw its market value more than double.

§7.16 U.S. LEGAL PROFESSION VIEWS

There is no doubt that the growing expansion of the use of AI will significantly impact both law and law practice. This has been an expanding topic of discussion by practicing lawyers and professional organizations in the United States.

Many U.S. law firms have published their views on AI developments and offered to advise on the impact of AI systems. Their views are often stated as publications on their websites.

Professional associations of lawyers have collectively published a number of opinions about the development and impact of AI systems. For example, the American Bar Association (ABA), which is a nationwide voluntary association of lawyers, has

255. *Ibid.*
256. Mary MacNamara, "Why does this movie exist? Harrison Ford explains reprising 'Indiana Jones' at 80," *Los Angeles Times*, online, May 19, 2023.
257. Zoe Corbyn, May 26, 2023, as cited above, quoting industry analyst, Kevin Krewell.
258. Alex Ralph, "Nvidia on track to be the first trillion-dollar chip company," *The Times*, online, May 25, 2023.

issued a number of publications on its website[259] about issues relating to AI, including the following:

- AI and robotics (accessed May 15, 2023)
- AI and the practice of law (April 11, 2023)
- AI: legal, industry, and regulatory highlights (April 4, 2023)

In February 2023, the ABA House of Delegates adopted a resolution setting up three guidelines to improve the use of AI:[260]

- Developers of AI should ensure that their products, services, systems and capabilities are subject to human authority, oversight and control.
- Organizations should be accountable for consequences related to their use of AI, including any legally cognizable injury or harm caused by their actions, unless they have taken reasonable steps to prevent harm or injury.
- Developers should ensure the transparency and traceability of their AI and protect related intellectual property by documenting key decisions made regarding the design and risk of data sets, procedures and outcomes underlying their AI.[261]

These are clearly good guidelines for developers and users of AI to aspire to. They are also descriptions of goals that legal and regulatory systems should incorporate.

They are not terribly different than guidelines that have been suggested by other commentators, both private and those related to regulatory organizations.

It is hoped that such requirements are included as fundamental regulations in legal systems around the world and in the mission aspirations of both developers and users of AI.

§7.17 SOME U.S. AI CASES

[A] ChatGPT Gets It Wrong

In late May 2023, it was reported that a New York lawyer employed ChatGPT help with legal research used in a legal brief submitted to a Federal Court in Manhattan in a lawsuit against an airline.[262] Unfortunately, the brief cited a number of supporting court decisions that did not exist and had been invented by ChatGPT.

The lawyer who submitted the citations admitted his mistake and "threw himself on the mercy of the court." He said that he had queried the chatbot whether its citations existed and were correct and accurate. The chatbot replied that the citations were authentic, which was false.

259. American Bar Association (ABA), online at: americanbar.org.
260. *Ibid.*
261. *Ibid.*
262. Benjamin Weiser, "Here's What Happens When Your Lawyer Uses ChatGPT," *The New York Times*, online, May 27, 2023.

It appears that ChatGPT may not only provide false information, but it may also "lie" about its authenticity.

However, the judge, saying that the brief contained "bogus judicial decisions, with bogus quotes and bogus internal citations," ordered a hearing to consider whether to impose sanctions.[263]

Clients hire lawyers and pay them large fees because they believe their attorneys have the legal knowledge and experience to provide them with arguments on their behalf that are the product of careful professional analysis by those lawyers. Clients are not paying to be represented by chatbots or other AI systems. They are paying for highly educated, well-qualified and appropriately experienced human legal minds.

It should be clear that no lawyer should rely on chatbots to provide legal research. Chatbots did not study for years to earn a law degree, passed no bar exams, and have no ethical obligation to be truthful.

It may be true that in some jobs, AI can be helpful, but in legal representation, actual intelligence is much more important.

The recent expansion of the creation and use of AI-related systems means that there is no long history of litigation and court decisions on issues raised by AI. However, that is changing both in the United States and elsewhere.[264]

In 2023, the U.S. news organization CNBC published a story outlining some of the cases that were being brought because of issues relating to the creation and use of AI systems.[265]

The article said:

> As companies including Microsoft, Google and open AI launch generative AI to the general public, lawsuits are piling up from the creative industries about copyright work co-opted or used by AI.

As examples of the kinds of cases that are being brought to resolve AI related issues, there are the following examples.

[1] Bev Standing v. TikTok[266]

In September 2021, TikTok reportedly settled a lawsuit brought by the actress Bev Standing.

263. *Ibid.*
264. *See*, for example, the United Kingdom case referred to in an earlier chapter in which a scientist named Stephen Thaler tried to have patents issued in the UK to an artificial intelligence system Thaler created. Thaler claimed that certain inventions were independently "created," without human intervention by his AI system.
265. Ellen Sheng, "In generative AI legal Wild West, the courtroom battles are just getting started," CNBC online at: cnbc.com, April 03, 2023.
266. Jacob Kastrenakes, "TikTok Settles lawsuit with actress over its original text-to-speech voice/ She said TikTok never had permission to use her voice," The Verge, online at: theverge.com, September 29, 2021.

Ms. Standing reportedly alleged that TikTok was using her voice without permission. An electronic version of what Ms. Standing alleged sounded like her voice was used to speak over videos on the TikTok website.

Lawyers for the parties said the lawsuit had been settled amicably and that TikTok would license Ms. Standing's voice.

[2] Butterick v. GitHub

In November of 2022, a class action lawsuit was filed in the U.S. District Court for the Northern District of California against defendants, including GitHub Inc., Microsoft Corporation, and OpenAI Inc.

Among other things, the Complaint says:

> 8. In June 2021, GitHub and OpenAI launched Copilot, an AI based product that promises to assist software coders by providing or filling in blocks of code using AI. GitHub charges Copilot users $10 per month or $100 per year for the service. Copilot ignores, violates and removes the Licenses offered by thousands—possibly millions—of software developers, thereby accomplishing software piracy on an unprecedented scale.
>
> 35. Plaintiffs do not know the exact number of class members, because such information is in the exclusive control of defendants. Plaintiffs are informed and believe that there are thousands of class members geographically dispersed throughout the United States section of joinder of all class members in the prosecution of this action is impractical.[267]

One commentator has said:

> This case is only at its earliest stages but could have a huge effect on the broader world of AI, where companies are making fortunes training software on copyright-protected data.[268]

Matthew Butterick, one of the attorneys who filed the lawsuit, is quoted as saying:

> As far as we know, this is the first class-action case in the US challenging the training and output of AI systems. It will not be the last.[269]

Another online tech commentator has written:

> The current legal cases against generative AI are just the beginning: AI that can generate art, text and more is in for a reckoning.[270]

267. Complaint filed on November 03, 2022, available online at: githubcopilotlitigation.com.
268. James Vincent, "The lawsuit that could rewrite the rules of AI copyright," The Verge, online at: theverge.com, November 08, 2022.
269. *Ibid.*
270. Kyle Wiggers, "The current legal cases against generative AI are just the beginning: AI that can generate art, text and more is in for a reckoning," TechCrunch online at: techcrunch.com, January 27, 2023.

There is little doubt that the resolution of this case will have a significant impact on intellectual property protection law in the United States and perhaps far beyond.

[3] Getty Images v. Stability AI

In February 2023, a similar case was filed by Getty Images US Inc. in the United States District Court for the District of Delaware against Stability AI, Inc., also based on an infringement of intellectual property claim.

The Complaint says:

> 1. This case arises from Stability AI's brazen infringement of Getty Images' intellectual property on a staggering scale. On information and belief, Stability AI has copied more than 12 million photographs from Getty Images collection, along with the associated captions and meta data, without permission from or compensation to Getty Images, as part of its efforts to build a competing business. As part of its unlawful scheme, Stability AI has removed or altered Getty Images' copyright management information, provided false copyright management information, and infringed Getty Images' famous trademarks.

This case and similar cases are very serious matters for Stability AI and other makers of generative AI systems that produce written, audio or visual output.

If it is necessary for such generative AI systems to be "trained" by reviewing and using protected intellectual property found on the Internet (or elsewhere), and court decisions that hold such "training" is a violation of the legal rights of the owners of such IP, then generative AI creators may be required to pay large damages for their usage of such IP and, if they decide to create such output in the future, may be required to pay large licensing fees in order to be able to do so.

Rulings that are unfavorable to the "training" procedures of generative AI systems may make some uses of search generative AI tools economically difficult or impossible.

§7.18 PRISMA LABS

In March 2023, a Chicago law firm filed a class action lawsuit against Prisma Labs Inc. Prisma marketed an AI-powered photo editing app called Lensa Ai. It is claimed that Prisma:

> Violated the Illinois biometric information and privacy act (BIPA) by collecting users facial geometry without their permission, using it to train/develop Prisma's artificial intelligence (AI) to see neural networks, and illegally storing the data.[271]

It is alleged that:

271. Christopher Yasiejko, "Prisma Labs Sued Over Lensa AI App's Biometric Data Harvesting.

> Prisma Labs Inc. trained ... Lensa Ai by harvesting biometric data from billions of photographs it "covertly scraped" from the Internet, including facial images of thousands of Illinois residents, ...[272]

Unlike the previous AI lawsuits mentioned above, this involved as much an invasion of privacy violation as a theft of intellectual property claim.[273]

However, both flow from the "training" procedures involved in providing functionality to an AI system.

It seems that although AI tools might be usable in a variety of crimes and civil law violations, a substantial number of the claims brought in lawsuits against AI systems will flow from the setting-up and "training" of AI tools as much as from violations created by their subsequent operations.

§7.19 *STEPHEN THALER* CASE

On April 24, 2023, it was reported that the U.S. Supreme Court refused to hear a challenge brought by a computer scientist named Stephen Thaler to the refusal by the U.S. Patent and Trademark Office to issue patents to his AI system for inventions Thaler claims were created by his AI system:

> The justices turned away Thaler's appeal of a lower court's ruling that patents can be issued only to human inventors and that his AI system could not be considered the legal creator of two inventions that he said it had generated.[274]

As shown in another chapter, Thaler also tried to get registrations for his AI system in England as well but was rejected there for the same reasons.

272. Jeremy Gray, "Lawsuit Alleges Lensa.ai App Illegally Took Users' Biometric Data" PetaPixel, online at: petapixel.com.
273. Although intellectual property issues may be involved depending on how the photographs were made and posted and who owned them.
274. Blake Brittain, "US Supreme Court rejects computer scientist's lawsuit over AI-generated inventions," Reuters' online April 24, 2023.

CHAPTER 8
UK Law

§8.01 DISCUSSIONS OF REGULATION

Since the release of ChatGPT, there have been numerous discussions in all types of media about the need to regulate AI. Most of these have consisted of general discussions outlining what the author believes to be the risks that AI systems will present to the human race, usually ending with a call for government regulation of AI. Few of these articles have given specific details of what the author believes the regulation should be. One important exception to this is the proposed European Artificial Intelligence Law.[275]

§8.02 UK/U.S. SUMMIT ON AI REGULATION

The UK has a reputation for leading expertise on AI that should be enhanced by its organization of the first international summit to discuss the development of AI. This is intended to propose international regulations for its safe development and control. The agenda of this summit was agreed in a June 2023 meeting between the Prime Minister of the UK and the President of the United States. One of the key purposes of the summit is to protect international cyber infrastructure against compromise by anti-western nations such as China and others.[276]

The UK government published an online statement about the proposed summit as follows:[277]

---

275. *See* Chapter 5 above on EU Law.
276. Mark Sellman, June 10, 2023, as cited above; Chris Smyth, "US will join Rishi Sunak summit to rein in 'existential' AI risk," *The Times*, online, June 08, 2023.
277. Prime Minister's Office, 10 Downing Street and The Rt Hon Rishi Sunak MP, "UK to host first global summit on Artificial Intelligence," Press release, online, June 07, 2023.

- As the world grapples with the challenges and opportunities presented by the rapid advancement of AI, the UK will host the first major global summit on AI safety.
- This summit will bring together key countries, leading tech companies and researchers to agree safety measures to evaluate and monitor the most significant risks from AI.
- The PM and President Biden "will take a coordinated approach to the opportunities and the challenges of emerging tech" that were discussed in their meeting in the United States on June 7, 2023.
- Global companies are expanding their work in the UK as the PM confirms new university scholarships to further UK/US Tech leadership.

The press release states that the summit is being arranged because the UK has "a global duty" to make certain that AI is developed and used safely and responsibly.

The summit was scheduled for November 1-2, 2023.[278]

The UK is said to be "a world leader" in AI, ranking third behind the U.S. in China. The AI sector is said to employ 50,000 people in the UK and contribute more than GBP 3.5 billion to the UK economy. The UK's departure from the EU is said to allow the UK to act "more quickly and agilely" with respect to the AI market.[279]

Prior to organizing this AI summit, the UK had been engaging in wide-ranging international discussions about cooperation with respect to AI. It has discussed the issues raised by AI development with the members of the G7 at the Hiroshima summit in May 2023.

§8.03 PRE-EXISTING REGULATION

Prior to the time that the UK considered it necessary to legislate specific AI legislation, the UK considered its legislation to be largely "technology neutral."

However, there were in existence a number of laws and regulations which affected both the development and application of AI. A summary review of these is found in the "white paper" published in March 2023.[280]

In the United Kingdom, at the beginning of June, Sajid Javid, a former Chancellor and Home Secretary of the UK, published a long comment in t giving his view of regulation in the UK should be approached.[281]

In his comment, Javid talks about both the positive and negative potential of AI. His particular concern is that AI may prove to be dangerously influential in politics:

> I am especially worried that the UK and US elections next year will become testing grounds for some of the most harmful capabilities.

278. William James, "Britain Invites China to its global AI Summit," Reuters online, September 19, 2023.
279. Prime Minister's Office, press release, June 07, 2023, as cited above.
280. Department for Science, Innovation & Technology, "A pro-innovation approach to AI regulation," online at: assets.publishing.service.gov.uk, March 2023, accessed May 16, 2023. See, Part Two: The current regulatory environment, pp. 14-19.
281. Sajid Javid, "On election day, I fear we'll see how harmful AI can be," Comment, *The Sunday Times*, online, June 4, 2023.

> But the heart of the debate about AI is it's "dual use" potential to enable dangerous and disruptive capabilities. These are particularly troubling when their evolution can be hard to forecast, even by their creators. In the wrong hands, future AI will be able to conduct offensive cyber operations to enable mass fraud, manipulate and generate content to undermine trust and democracy, and initiate deep and personal relationships to facilitate abuse. As former home secretary it is also easy to see the capabilities AI brings to serious crime and hostile state activity.[282]

Mr. Javid urges the policymakers in the UK to follow a framework that balances the need for caution with the need to promote innovative technology. He suggests that there should be three parts to this framework. First, he proposes that there be a "system of accountability for AI developers" to allow support, transparent data sharing and increased AI safety resources. Second, there should be an "ethical framework" to protect society. Third, there should be "incentives" that encourage that encourage adherence to "shared global objectives."

There is nothing wrong with these objectives, but they beg the question of whether they will be strong enough to both control the risks of AI and encourage the development of its positive aspects. Ethics and incentives are all very good, but given the seriousness of the risks that are being discussed with respect to AI development and its potential abuse, it seems that enforceable laws and regulations will be needed to deter and punish the abuse of AI systems, and effectively encourage the development of helpful AI systems.

One thing that isn't emphasized enough in discussions about the need for regulation of AI is the fact that much behavior relating to AI development is already heavily regulated by existing systems of law and regulation. As the originating "home" of the Common Law system, shared to one degree or another in former English colonies, including the U.S., Australia, Canada, and many other now independent nations, it is useful to review how existing UK laws and regulations impact AI development.

§8.04 EQUALITY ACT OF 2010

This requires data processing systems, such as AI systems, to fairly process data. If AI systems produce data that includes unfair discrimination or bias, that could violate the Act. *See*, for example, Article (5)(1)(a) of the Act concerning personal data processing. The Act protects against unfair discrimination relating to age, disability, gender reassignment, marriage and civil partnership, race, religion or belief, sex, and sexual orientation.[283]

---

282. *Ibid.*
283. Department for Science, Innovation & Technology, March 2023, cited above, footnotes 54 and 55.

§8.05 PRODUCT SAFETY LAWS

These require that goods that are manufactured and sold are safe to use.

There are specific laws and regulations requiring safety for electric and electronic goods, such as the Electrical Equipment (Safety) Regulations, HM Government, 2016.[284]

Safety with respect to medical devices is covered by the Medical Devices Regulation, HM Government 2002.[285]

Toys are required to be safe by the toys (safety) regulations, HM Government 2011.[286]

§8.06 CONTRACT LAW AND CONSUMER RIGHTS

In cases where AI-related systems or services are provided under contracts, consumer rights laws and regulations may apply, such as the Consumer Rights Act of 2015 and the Consumer Protection from Unfair Trading Regulations (HM Government, 2008).[287]

Contract terms include a variety of duties on the contracting parties that they are required to meet. For example, the terms of the contract may require that goods be of a certain quality, that they are fit for a described purpose, or that they match other descriptions in the contract.[288]

Failure to comply with those terms may constitute a "breach of contract" that may give rise to rights to seek remedies such as monetary damages or relief from performance obligations for innocent parties.[289] The requirements of contract law will be likely to apply to providers of AI systems as much as to any other business transactions.

It is important to remember that under many systems of law, including English Common Law, it is possible that contracts can be found to exist from oral agreement, behavior, custom or implication, as well as from written documentation.[290]

§8.07 LAW OF TORTS

A "tort" is a civil wrong (as distinguished from a criminal act). A person injured by a tort may have a right to seek monetary damages or an injunction (to require performance or to restrain from the performance of a particular act or acts) as

284. *Ibid.*, footnote 56.
285. *Ibid.*, footnote 57.
286. *Ibid.*, footnote 58.
287. *Ibid.*, footnote 59.
288. *Ibid.*, cited above.
289. *See*, Peter Shears and Graham Stephenson, *James's Introduction to English Law*, 13th edition (London, Butterworths, 1966), pp. 219-285.
290. For examples, *see* G.H. Treitel, *The Law of Contract*, 15th ed., (London: Sweet & Maxwell, 2020).

compensation for their injury and/or to demonstrate to the guilty party the impropriety of their injurious behavior.[291]

Under tort law, it is certainly the case that those who believe themselves to be damaged by negligence or other harm caused by AI systems may be able to seek compensation or redress under—depending on the circumstances of their interaction with the AI system in question.

§8.08 CRIMINAL LAW

Criminal law deals with offenses against the State. It is applicable to many types of behavior considered serious and/or dangerous enough to merit intervention by the State to investigate and/or prosecute the authors of such behavior.

Some behaviors can violate both civil and criminal law, such as in some cases where damage or harm is caused.

Creators, sellers and users of AI systems are subject to the restrictions of criminal law as much as any other persons.

§8.09 FINANCIAL SERVICES LAW

In many situations where a third party is given authority to decide how another's financial or other assets are to be deployed, that third party may be subject to financial services law and regulation.

That may also be true of any person conducting business relating to AI who may seek others to help fund or promote their business.

In the UK, financial services business is generally subject to the Financial Services and Markets Act 2000, as amended, and the regulations thereunder.

§8.10 HEALTH LAW

The medical and health fields are areas where there has been a great deal of discussion about the potential usefulness of AI. However, it has been recognized that there may be potential risks arising from deploying AI in these critical sectors.

Consequently, the UK government has paid special attention to the use of cyber-related services in the health sector. There has been established within the UK National Health Service (NHS), an AI and Digital Regulations Service for health and social care. This has been funded by the NHS AI lab in the NHS Transformation Directorate.[292] Overseeing these efforts are three government agencies in the UK:

- The Medicines & Healthcare Products Regulatory Agency;
- The Care Quality Commission; and

291. Department for Science, Innovation & Technology, March 2023. *See also*, Peter Shears and Graham Stephenson, *James's Introduction to English Law*, p. 303.
292. *See* information online at: digitalregulaltions.innovation.nhs.uk.

- The NHS Health Research Authority.

Their overall goals are to gain benefits to health and social care while ensuring that safety standards are maintained.

§8.11 THE UK APPROACH TO AI REGULATION

The legal areas discussed above are just a few of the legal and regulatory provisions already in existence that may be applicable to the creation, distribution and use of AI. There are undoubtedly many others, including intellectual property law, which is treated in a separate chapter of this book. Others may be cited in other places in this book.

§8.12 AI IS NOT "UNREGULATED"

It is of no benefit for anyone to assume that AI is somehow "unregulated."

Like most other areas of human activity, it will be subject to legal scrutiny by many existing laws and regulations.

The UK government is certainly aware of the potential benefits and risks of AI systems. It is certainly aware that AI businesses, like other businesses that offer both benefits and risks, need regulation. The UK remains sensitive to the fact that additional regulation may be needed:

> While AIA is currently regulated through existing legal frameworks like financial services regulation, some AI risks arise across, or in the gaps between, existing regulatory remits. The industry has told us that conflicting or uncoordinated requirements from regulators create unnecessary burdens and that regulatory gaps may leave risks unmitigated, harming public trust and slowing AI adoption. ... Regulatory coordination will support businesses to invest confidently in AI innovation and build public trust by ensuring real risks are effectively addressed.[293]

§8.13 A PRO-INNOVATION WHITE PAPER

At the end of March 2023, through the Department for Science, Innovation and Technology and the Office for Artificial Intelligence, the UK government published a "white paper" that indicated that a goal for the UK was to become an AI "superpower."[294]

In a "Ministerial Foreword" from Michelle Donelan, the Secretary of State for Science, Innovation and Technology, she said:

---

293. Department for Science, Innovation & Technology, March 2023, cited above, p. 14.
294. *Ibid.*, p. 2.

> To ensure we become an AI superpower, though, it is crucial that we do all we can to create the right environment to harness the benefits of AI and remain at the forefront of technological developments. This includes getting regulation right so that innovators can thrive, and the risks posed by AI can be addressed.[295]

§8.14 COMPETITION AND MARKETS AUTHORITY REVIEW

In early May 2023, the UK Competition and Market Regulation Authority (CMA) announced that it was undertaking an initial review of how the development and use of AI would impact competition and consumer protection.[296]

The CMA reports that the purpose of this inquiry is:

> To ensure that innovation in AI continues in a way that benefits consumers, businesses and the UK economy, the government has asked regulators, including the Competition and Markets Authority (CMA), to think about how the innovative development and deployment of AI can be supported against five over-arching principles: safety, security and robustness; appropriate transparency and explainability; fairness; accountability and governance; and contestability and redress.

The CMA intends to review how "generative AI" could evolve, to look at risks that might affect competition and consumer protection, and publish guidelines that would protect both competition and consumers, but which would allow AI to productively develop.

The CMA has requested AI-related businesses to provide both their views and other evidence about generative AI development by the beginning of June 2023 and indicated they would publish a report and CMA findings in September 2023.[297]

§8.15 REPORT AND PRINCIPLES

On September 18, 2023, the CMA did issue a Report entitled "AI Foundation Models" (FMs).[298]

The FM that they are referring to are the "large, machine learning models trained on vast amounts of data... The first public FM was released by open AI in 2018 and since then it is estimated that around 180 FMs have been developed and released."[299]

The view of the CMA is that:

> To ensure that people, businesses, and the wider economy benefit from innovation AI can bring, businesses must comply with the existing consumer and competition law. Alongside this, to ensure that competition and consumer protection remains

---

295. *Ibid.*, p. 2.
296. Competition and Markets Authority, Press release, "CMA launches initial review of artificial intelligence models," CMA online at: www.gov.uk, May 04, 2023.
297. CMA online at: www.gov.uk, May 04, 2023, as cited above.
298. The FMs Report and other documents and comments relating to it are found online at: https://assets.publishing.service.gov.uk/. Artificial Intelligence.
299. *Ibid.*

an effective driving force as the development and deployment of FMs evolves, we propose the following guiding principles.

§8.16 CMA INITIAL REPORT PRINCIPLES FOR FMs

- Access: Ongoing ready access to key inputs.
- Diversity: Sustained diversity of business models, including both open and closed.
- Choice: Sufficient choice for businesses so they can decide how to use FMs.
- Flexibility: Flexibility to switch or use multiple FMs according to need.
- Fair Dealing: no anti-competitive conduct, including anti-competitive self-preferencing, tying or bundling.
- Transparency: Consumers and businesses are given information about the risks and limitations of FM-generated content so they can make informed choices.

§8.17 NOVEMBER 2023 BLETCHLEY PARK AI SAFETY SUMMIT

In response to concerns about AI, the UK Prime Minister arranged and hosted an AI safety summit on November 1 and 2, 2023:

> The summit will bring together international governments, leading AI companies, civil society groups and experts in research to consider the risks of AI, especially at the frontier of development, and discuss how they can be mitigated through internationally coordinated action.[300]

300. "The UK Prime Minister will host the AI Safety Summit 2023 on the 1 and 2 November at Bletchley Park, Buckinghamshire." Information online at: gov.uk.

CHAPTER 9
French Law

Because France is a prominent member of the EU, France is among the principal authors of the proposed EU AIA. There was a little doubt that France would adopt and follow the requirements of the final version of the AIA and the regulations thereunder.[301]

French legislators have clearly been additionally concerned about developments in AI and their implications in the legal field.

For example, in June of 2019, France added a section to Article 33 of the Justice Reform Act, which is reported to require that:

> The identity data of magistrates and members of the judiciary cannot be reused with the purpose or effect of evaluating, analyzing, comparing or predicting their actual or alleged professional practices.[302]

This ban was reportedly added because of concern about the work of an organization called Ravel Law.

Ravel Law states that it has supported the Harvard Law School Library in its work to digitize 40,000 printed volumes of law cases, including over 40 million pages of court decisions dating as far back as the 17th century, which has been included in a "Public Case Law Access site."[303]

> Members of the public now have access to one of the largest collections of published case law available online. The site offers robust search and filter functionality, as well as links to PDF images that resulted from the scanning project. ... The public case access contains all US court cases published in official reports from 1658 to 2018. The collection includes over 8 million cases from state courts, federal courts, and territorial courts for American Samoa, Dakota Territory,

301. *See* EU AI regulation in Chapter 5, above.
302. Ian Connett, "France Resists Judicial AI Revolution: France bans predictive analysis of case law. Does this protect or impede universal justice?," Above the Law, online at: abovethelaw.com, June 10, 2019.
303. Ravel Law, "Public Case Access," online at: ravel.com, accessed September 27, 2023.

> Guam, native American courts, Navajo Nation, and the Northern Mariana Islands.[304]

The concern of the French legislators, magistrates, and judges apparently had to do with the fact that digitization of legal decisions, such as accomplished with the support of Ravel Law, may give parties the power to "model the decision—making tendencies of judicial decision makers with relative ease … ."[305]

Article 33 reportedly bans law firms from assembling an overall review of judicial decisions, with offenders being subject to a five-year prison term.

Although the French judiciary apparently does not agree, it has been argued that Article 33 interferes with the creation of a fairer judicial system:

> Since publication of French court decisions, there have been studies confirming the bias of French judges. AI is now blowing the whistle, alerting us that unbiased judging is not as universal as we once believed.[306]

Ravel was purchased by Lexis/Nexis in June of 2017:[307]

> Ravel is a legal search, analytics, and visualization platform. At a time when the amount of legal information is rapidly growing in scale and complexity, Ravel provides insight into what's important, why it's important, and how to use it. We make research radically easier and more insightful.[308]

France, like other countries and legal jurisdictions, discussed in other chapters, has in existence many laws and regulations that will bear on the creation, distribution and use of AI systems without specifically referring to AI.

However, recent reports indicate that France believes that the proper way to regulate AI is through international cooperation and regulation.

France has certainly shown that through its support of the EU AIA legislation.

Going beyond that, it is reported:

> France's top politicians have told CNBC[309] they see the beginnings of global regulation on artificial intelligence coming by the end of this year, with French president Emmanuel Macron saying the country wants to work with the US on rules around fast growing technology. … France has looked to position itself as the European hub for AI development … .[310]

It is quite clear that France's goal is to be one of the leading creators of international AI regulation. They are certainly making efforts within the EU and internationally to achieve that:

304. *Ibid.*
305. Ian Connett, June 10, 2019, as cited above.
306. *Ibid.*
307. LinkedIn, "Ravel Law (acquired by LexisNexis)—LinkedIn," LinkedIn, online at: fr.linkedin.com, accessed September 27, 2023.
308. *Ibid.*
309. A U.S. news and entertainment network.
310. Arjun Kharpal, "France sees global A.I. regulation ideas by the end of this year, wants to work with U.S. on tech laws," CNBC, online at: cnbc.com, June 15, 2023.

> But there is no global consensus on how AI should be managed and controlled with the US, China and the European Union taking different approaches to rules around the tech. Any global regulatory framework would be a huge feat.[311]

France's efforts to shape international AI regulation will require participation in a long process. How successful they will be and how they will affect French domestic law will only be revealed over time.

311. *Ibid.*

CHAPTER 10
Chinese Law

Chinese regulators have been concerned about the development of AI products for some time.

In 2018, an Artificial Intelligence Standardization White Paper (AI White Paper) was published that was generally positive about the benefits that could be gained from the applications of AI.

As of March 2022, China has introduced new comprehensive regulations for AI-related businesses and products.

Part of those regulations focused on forbidding the use of algorithms that use personal information to set different prices for the products and services offered to different customers. The rules apply to algorithms that set prices, control search results, recommend videos, and filter content. The regulations also impose restrictions on ride-hailing, e-commerce, streaming, and social media companies.[312]

These regulations are imposed by the Cyberspace Administration of China and are entitled the Internet Information Service Algorithmic Recommendation Management Provisions (Provisions).

Punishment for violations of the Provisions can include fines, forbidding enrollment of new customers, cancellation of business licenses, or deletion of websites and apps.[313]

There are also regulations on "synthetic content." These apply to fake news, AI-created audio, and "deep fake" pictures and videos. Creators of AI-generated content must label it as "synthetic," give their real names and clearly label any "deep fake" content.[314]

Since that time, Chinese regulators have introduced a variety of new laws and regulations affecting the use of AI-related products.

---

312. Jennifer Conrad and Will Knight, "China Is About to Regulate AI—and the World is Watching," *Wired*, online at: wired.com, February 22, 2022.
313. *Ibid.*
314. *Ibid.*

Updated laws on data protection, cyber security and personal information have all included provisions that affect AI-related products.

Also, local regulations have been adopted in Shenzhen and Shanghai to both encourage and regulate the development of AI systems in those areas. Both generally follow the ideas set out in the AI White Paper.

In April 2023, the Cyberspace Administration published proposed measures focused on regulating Generative AI Services:

- These apply to both online and offline generative AI products.
- The creation of discriminative content is forbidden.
- They also bar "training" that violates IP protections and uses personal data without consent.

- Security assessments need to be provided to the relevant Internet Information Services before generative AI services can be published.

Many of the Chinese regulations mirror regulations either introduced or proposed in major competing market centers such as the United States and the EU. However, others are more locally focused on China. It is not clear yet whether China will cooperate in agreeing to global international treaties regulating AI. However, it is clear that China is focused on establishing comprehensive regulations for AI within China.

Anyone doing business there should be aware that many such regulations exist and are being constantly expanded. Consequently, it is sensible for anyone doing business in China to obtain up-to-date local advice from qualified persons to assist them in offering any AI-related products there.

CHAPTER 11
Indian Law

§11.01 LAWS AGAINST CYBERCRIME

The principal Indian law regulating electronic commerce and defending against cybercrime is The Information Technology Act 2000 (ITA) that came into force on October 17, 2000, and has been amended since then.

Although there is considerable concern about the use of AI-related systems providing tools in the commission of cybercrimes, India is currently relying on laws already in place to protect against and punish such violations.

These offenses are prohibited by the Copyright Act of 1957.[315]

An express definition of "cybercrime" is not found in either the ITA 2000 or the National Cyber Security Policy 2013.

There is no specific regulation prohibiting "cybercrime" as such in India.

Cybercrime is brought within the scope of criminal behavior by being recognized as a crime prohibited by criminal legislation in combination with the use of digital technology.

India's laws that can be applied to situations where cybercrime is found are those laws that deal with such things as electronic signatures, intellectual property, or privacy and data protection.

As a practical law enforcement matter in India, cybercrime is recognized as any crime done with the assistance of telecommunication or computer technology or any crime where computers or digital technology is either used in the crime or is the target of the crime. This means that there is really no crime that will not be considered cybercrime if it involves digital or telephonic technology.[316]

The above is an indication that any violations that involve AI tools may be considered criminal under Indian law.

---

315. Indian Copyright Act, 1957, sections 63 to 65A.
316. Vinit Verma, "Importance of Cyber Law in India," Legal Service India, online, retrieved September 09, 2020.

§11.02 AI CRIME REPORTS IN INDIA

Unfortunately, there are already instances of reports where AI tools have been used to commit crimes in India.

One disgusting example involved an Indian journalist who had been critical of India's ruling party. She was attacked by a vicious online hatred campaign in 2018 that included a deepfake porn video of her. The video went viral, and she was bombarded with online threats of rape and death. Since this happened, the journalist said, "I have not been the same person."[317]

§11.03 INDIAN REGULATION OF AI

India has been rather cautious in adopting regulations specifically targeting AI.

India's Communications and IT minister, Ashwini Vaishnaw, is reported to have said in May 2023 that a number of developed economies were considering what should be the appropriate framework for the regulation of the rapidly expanding field of AI. He is quoted as saying:

> The whole world is looking at what should be the framework, and what should be the regulatory set up. In the G7, all digital ministers (of G7 countries) are seriously concerned about what should be the regulatory framework. So, this is a global thing. This is not one country issue. This has to be looked at from the international perspective.[318]

India is not rushing into regulating AI. Its attitude towards the subject has been evolving over the last few years.

At the end of July 2023, it was reported that working groups had been set up by the government to study and report on AI, but reports were not yet available.

However, a Digital Personal Data Protection Bill 2023 has been drafted. Information about that draft has suggested that it may include protections against personal data being used to "train" AI systems like ChatGPT.[319]

317. *Ibid.*
318. "India for international framework to regulate AI platforms like ChatGPT" *The Times of India*, online at: timesofindia.indiatimes.com, May 17, 2023, accessed September 07, 2023.
319. "Why India can afford to wait and watch before regulating AI," ET Government, online at: government.economictimes.indiatimes.com, July 31, 2023.

CHAPTER 12

Japanese Law

In April and May of 2023, Japan chaired G7 meetings that discussed how AI should be regulated and what agreements the G7 might be able to reach on such regulation.

Japan is reported to be in favor of the sensible development of AI and has been supportive of the adoption of "reasonable AI uses" by both the public and industry in Japan.[320]

At the G7 meeting in April of 2023, Japan's goal reportedly was to seek G7 agreement on providing "flexible" regulation for AI rather than a specific overarching regulation on all types of AI technology, according to reported statements by Japan's Industry Minister Yasutoshi Nishimura.[321]

Japanese Prime Minister Fumio Kishida discussed proposed AI regulation with other world leaders when Japan hosted the G7 summit in May of 2023.[322]

It is reported that Japan has been working toward adopting more liberal regulations for AI than are included in the proposed EU regulation.

Japan, like many other countries, wishes to profit from the potential benefits of AI. It is believed that this wish will bring Japanese regulation closer to US regulation than the EU's AIA. Nevertheless, EU industry official, Thierry Breton, was reported to have visited Tokyo in July 2023 to promote the EU approach to AI regulation. It is not reported that Mr. Breton's efforts are likely to make any difference to Japan's reaction to the EU proposals:[323]

> The chair of the government's AI strategy council, the University of Tokyo's Prof. Yutaka Matsuo, called the EU's rules a "little too strict ... .

320. Kantaro Komiya, "G7 should adopt 'risk-based' AI regulation, ministers say," Reuters, online, May 01, 2023.
321. *Ibid.*
322. *Ibid.*
323. Sam Nussey and Tim Kelly, "Japan leaning toward softer AI rules than EU, official close to deliberations says," Reuters, online at: reuters.com, July 03, 2023, accessed September 29, 2023.

Matsuo, who also chairs the Japan Deep Learning Association and is a non-executive director of the Softbank Group, is reported to have said:

> With the EU, the issue is less about how to promote innovation and more about making already large companies take responsibility.

However, officials who are working on the formulation of Japan's AI regulation system have said they are not allowed to talk to the media.

CHAPTER 13
South Korean Law

It is reported that South Korea is seeking to become one of the leading nations in the fields of developing, manufacturing and using AI. One significant advantage that will benefit South Korea in this area is its dominating position in the manufacture of memory chips—a key component of AI systems.

AI systems require a great deal of digital memory. South Korean firms Samsung Electronics and SK Hynix are reported to produce about 70% of the world's digital memory chips.

South Korea is hoping to become the third largest producer of AI systems after the U.S. and China.

South Korea's Minister for Science, Information and Communications is quoted as saying:

> South Korea seeks to emerge as a prominent player in rapidly growing and promising areas such as AI semiconductors. ... [South Korea] aims to maintain its leading position in memory semiconductor field.[324]

§13.01 LEGAL ENCOURAGEMENT OF AI DEVELOPMENT

In order to help fulfill South Korea's AI ambitions, the South Korean Parliament as reportedly approved a new set of AI regulations that are reported to be less restrictive than other regulations, such as those of the EU.

For example, in February 2023, a committee of the South Korean parliament approved a draft law guaranteeing "freedom" to market AI products and services. If

324. Sheila Chiang, "South Korea wants to be a top A.I. hub—its memory chip dominance could be an advantage," CNBC, online at: cnbc.com, July 05, 2023.

this law comes into effect as drafted, AI systems will only be restricted if they are found to harm the lives, safety or the rights of people.[325]

In order to provide industry guidance on AI, the South Korean Personal Information Protection Commission (PIPC) published an English version of its "draft guidance" for AI in July 2021.[326]

The PIPC is the "national data protection authority" of South Korea. It was designated as an "independent regulatory agency in 2020." It has powers to investigate data privacy violations and to adjudicate disputes involving personal data. Under the Personal Information Protection Act of 2011 (PIPA), PIPC can impose fines for data violations. It consists of nine Commissioners, and its Chairperson has the status of a government minister.[327]

This checklist (Checklist) was created by PIPC for "Developers and Operators." It states:

> This self-checklist was prepared for the purpose of not only complying with the obligations regarding personal information protection, but also providing information on matters necessary for implementing and checking autonomous personal information protection suitable for its technology and service environment in consideration of the fact that AI technology and service are continuously developing and changing... As it includes guidelines pursuant to the Personal Information Protection Act, personal information controllers in areas other than AI service can also use the checklist.[328]
>
> The PIPC Checklist emphasizes the important connection between data privacy and the operation of artificial intelligence systems. It states that there are six principles of AI personal information protection that need to be complied with: "legitimacy, safety, transparency, participation, responsibility and fairness.[329]

The Checklist provides detailed additional information about the following eight phases of AI development and operation, where personal information protection requirements need to be considered and implemented by AI developers and operators. These eight phases are:[330]

(1) Planning and design
(2) Collection of personal information
(3) Use and provision of personal information
(4) Storage and destruction of personal information
(5) AI service management and supervision
(6) AI service user protection and damage relief
(7) Autonomous personal information protection activities

---

325. Joyce Lee and Heekyong Yang, "Open AI CEO encourages South Korea to supply chips in AI boom," Reuters, online at reuters.com, June 09, 2023.
326. PIPC, "Artificial Intelligence (AI) Personal Information Protection Self-Checklist (May 31, 2021)."
327. The English version of the PIPC website is online at: pipc.go.kr.
328. PIPC, "Artificial Intelligence (AI) Personal Information Protection Self-Checklist" (Checklist), p. 2.
329. *Ibid.*, p. 5.
330. *Ibid.*, pp. 9-35.

(8) Checking AI ethics.

Each of the above includes several things to check when considering that category.

In particular, with respect to number 8 above, checking AI ethics includes in its Appendix, a review of "Major domestic and overseas ethical principles."[331] The clear implication of this is that AI developers and operators need to consider both with respect to the development and operation of their AI system. This Appendix includes a list of ethical standards developed both by international organizations and a number of national governments. It includes ethical standards published by South Korea itself, as well as those published by the OECD and the G20, and standards published by Singapore, the United States, the European Union, Canada, Germany, France, the United Kingdom, Australia, China, Japan, and Hong Kong.

In addition to the list of ethical standard publications provided in the first part of the ethical material in the Appendix, there is additionally a second part that provides "People-centric Artificial Intelligence (AI) ethical standards," published in December 2020 by the South Korean Ministry of Science and Information and Communications Technology (ICT).

This section comprises: "Artificial intelligence standards: 3 basic principles and 10 key requirements."[332]

The three basic principles are the following:

(1) The principle of human dignity;
(2) The principle of the public good of society; and
(3) The principle of the purposiveness of technology.

All three include more detail about their definition and application.

In addition, there are "10 key requirements—detailed requirements for realizing the basic principles." These 10 detailed requirements are headlined as follows:

(1) Human Rights Guarantee
(2) Privacy protection
(3) Respect for diversity
(4) Prohibition of infringement
(5) Public interests
(6) Solidarity
(7) Data management
(8) Responsibility
(9) Safety
(10) Transparency.

331. *Ibid.*, pp. 38 and 39.
332. *Ibid.*, pp. 39-41.

Each of the 10 contains more detail about their meaning and application.

The Checklist also cites the following additional assistance as being available:

> For consultation on the sales license checklist and inquiries on personal information protection laws, please contact the "Personal Information Infringement Report Center" (privacy.kisa.or.kr or call 118).[333]

It is clear from the detail provided in the PIPC Checklist and from public statements by officials in Korea that Korea is very serious about becoming a major creator and operator of AI systems and is equally serious about playing a prominent role in developing international standards and regulations to promote the advantages of AI systems and to control the risks they may present.

§13.02 INDUSTRY SUPPORT FOR KOREAN AI DEVELOPMENT

It isn't only from the political community that Korea is receiving support for expanding its AI business. South Korea is receiving strong support from the major industry players as well. For example:

> ChatGPT-maker OpenAI's CEO Sam Altman, who met with South Korean president Yoon Suk Yeol ..., urged South Korea to play a leading role in creating international AI standards as well as focusing on making the chips needed for the technology.[334]

Among the suggestions made by Altman were that South Korea should produce semiconductors and the memory needed for AI, that they should encourage AI projects by modifying corporate regulations, and that they should participate actively in setting international AI standards.[335]

Altman also said that he had met with about a hundred newly created South Korean digital industry companies.[336]

§13.03 SOUTH KOREAN AI COMPANIES

South Korea has also been one of the leading countries in developing its own AI-technology-related companies. These include Naver, Kakao and LG.

South Korea is reportedly seeking to expand its AI businesses in areas not already dominated by US and Chinese firms. For example, Kyunghoon Bae, the head of LG AI Research, is quoted as saying:

333. *Ibid.*, p. 2.
334. Joyce Lee and Heekyong Yang, "Open AI CEO encourages South Korea to supply chips in AI boom," Reuters, online at reuters.com, June 09, 2023.
335. *Ibid.*
336. *Ibid.*

> In order for Korean companies to have strength in the global AI ecosystem, each company must first secure specialized technology for vertical AI ... . [or AI for specific uses].[337]

Korean AI companies are also reportedly trying to develop AI products that cater to cultural sensitivities in areas like the Middle East and meet the needs of non-English speaking countries in the Far East.[338]

Two prominent Korean AI companies, Naver and Kakao, are also making efforts to shape AI regulation by publishing their own statements on what constitutes good ethical behavior in developing and operating AI systems. These two statements are taken seriously by the PIPC and are cited in its Checklist Appendix.[339] It is the case that in South Korea, most of the AI used in commerce is produced by big Korean tech companies such as Naver and Kakao.[340]

It is reported that in South Korea, major companies in many industries, such as Hyundai Motor, LG, Samsung and Doosan, are hard at work implementing AI and robot technologies.[341]

Kakao is a South Korean digital media company founded in 1995 and employing about four thousand people. It offers products in the fields of communication, media, content, games, lifestyle, fintech, and search.[342] Starting in 2018, Kakao introduced an Algorithm Ethics Charter[343] and educated its employees in ethics for AI and algorithms.[344]

Naver describes itself as a global tech company offering South Korea's leading search portal, "Neighbor." It also has subsidiaries and affiliates that provide a variety of information technology-related products.[345]

Naver produced its "Naver Artificial Intelligence (AI) Ethics Rules" in February 2021.

337. *Ibid.*
338. *Ibid.*
339. PIPC Checklist, p. 38.
340. AI Network, "How can Korean Big tech like Naver and Kakao keep AI ethics?," online at: ai-network.medium.com, February 18, 2021.
341. *Ibid.*
342. Profile: "Kakao," Forbes, online at: forbes.com, accessed July 28, 2023.
343. This Charter was updated in 2019 and 2020. PIPC Checklist, p. 38.
344. AI Network, "How can Korean Big tech like Naver and Kakao keep AI ethics?," online at: ai-network.medium.com, February 18, 2021.
345. For information, *see* Naver website at: navercorp.com.

CHAPTER 14
Singapore AI Law

The government, legal institutions and legal practitioners in Singapore are certainly aware of the international development and expansion of advanced technology, including AI and machine learning. They are well aware that significant changes will need to be made to the body of Singapore law and regulations in order to take a proper account of the effect of these things.

However, Singapore's legal community is still in the process of evolving legal and regulatory changes to both control the risks of AI systems and to realize the benefits that they may offer to the small but vibrant nation.

The Singapore Personal Data Protection Commission (PDPC) has issued an online guide to Singapore's approach to AI governance.[346] The PDPC says:

> As Singapore develops its digital economy, a trusted ecosystem is key—one where organizations can benefit from tech innovations while consumers are confident to adopt and use AI. In the global discourse on AI ethics and governance, Singapore believes that its balanced approach can facilitate innovation, safeguard consumer interests, and serve as a common global reference point.

Singapore, like the European Union, is apparently hoping that its approach to AI regulation will be copied around the globe.

The rest of the world, when considering the effectiveness of those two sets of regulations, will need to wait until those legal systems have completed their policies on AI regulation before they will be able to judge which, if either, would be worth emulating.

In Singapore, the PDPC has taken the lead in formulating a policy for AI regulation.

Another institution that has been at the forefront of determining how AI should be regulated in Singapore is the Infocom Media Development Authority (IMDA).

346. The PDPC website is online at: pdpc.gov.sg.

The IMDA is a statutory board of the Singapore government. They are tasked with developing and regulating the information communications (Infocom) and media sectors. The goal of IMDA is to encourage dynamic Infocom and media sectors that encourage innovation and business development. They have established a number of programs to assist the digital sector, along with other media sectors.[347]

To assist in providing an effective system of AI oversight, the IMDA has published a program called "AI Verify." It consists of a framework to test AI regulation and a software tool kit to assist in using the framework:

> The testing framework consists of 11 AI ethics principles which jurisdictions around the world coalesce around and are consistent with internationally recognized AI frameworks such as those from the EU, OECD and Singapore's model AI governance framework. AI Verify helps organizations validate the performance of their AI systems against those principles through standardized tests.

The 11 "ethics principles" referred to are:

(1) Transparency
(2) Explainability
(3) Repeatability/Reproducibility
(4) Safety
(5) Security
(6) Robustness
(7) Fairness
(8) Data Governance
(9) Accountability
(10) Human Agency and Oversight
(11) Inclusive Growth, Societal and Environmental Well-Being.

There is a little question that it is worth considering issues that fall into those categories when reviewing and regulating AI systems. However, it is clear that all of these can be subject to very different standards of interpretation. It seems unlikely that any nation would have any significant objections to any of these principles, but recognition of them will not automatically guarantee a consistent international standard of law and regulation.

With respect to the application of AI Verify in Singapore itself, it will take some time to know precisely how these "ethical principles" will be applied as AI systems are developed and used in that nation. For example, will they be part of legislatively established laws and regulations relating to AI or will they simply be left as "ethical" standards that may be interpreted significantly differently by AI developers, users and regulators?

Of course, there is not only government interest in the development of AI systems in Singapore. The private legal sector is also keenly interested in understanding how AI should be both controlled and encouraged through law and regulation.

347. The IMDA online website is at: imda.gov.sg.

§14.01 PDPC GUIDES

In addition to providing a model AI governance framework, the Singapore PDPC also provides several guides to the implementation and use of AI.

As a supplement to the Model Framework described above, the PDPC provides an Implementation and Self-assessment Guide for Organizations (ISAGO). This guide was developed in consultation with the World Economic Forum Center for the Fourth Industrial Revolution and with over 60 industry organizations.[348] It provides a list of industry examples and practices to guide organizations in the adaptation and use of AI systems.

To supplement the Model Framework and ISAGO, a Compendium of Use Cases is provided. This Compendium shows how Singapore and international organizations in different sectors can implement and align their AI practices with the Model Framework. The compendium comprises two volumes. Volume One includes use cases from a selection of major banks and organizations around the Asia Pacific region, such as HSBC and Visa Asia Pacific. Volume Two provides cases from the city of Darwin in Australia and from major companies such as Google and Microsoft. It also has a section on how Singapore implemented its AI Framework in "100 Experiments" projects with organizations such as IBM.

§14.02 JOB REDESIGN FOR AI AGE

Singapore has also constituted an Advisory Council of the Ethical Use of AI and Data (AI Advisory Council) to advise the government on how to respond to the effects of the development of AI systems on employment.

For several years, there has been concern around the world about how the introduction of AI systems will affect many jobs and professions.

The government of Singapore has been aware that the expansion of AI may affect the job market there. Consequently, the AI advisory Council, the PDPC, the IMDA and the Singapore University of Technology and Design published a Guide in December 2020 that is intended to assist companies in dealing with the impact of AI on employees and how, otherwise, to adapt themselves to the electronic future.[349]

§14.03 COPYRIGHT PROTECTION OF AI PRODUCTS

The Singapore Copyright Act 2021 does appear to have some implications for AI systems. Under section 13(3)(b), the Act is stated to apply to a "computer program," which is said to be protected as a "literary work." However, a literary work is only protected under Singapore copyright law if it has a human author(s).

This would seem to exclude claims that are made by some AI scientists that AI systems, because they are regarded as possessing a form of "intelligence" that may

348. *See*, the PDPC website online at: pdpc.gov.sg.
349. *See*, *ibid*.

produce results unexpected by its human creator, should have legal recognition as "Creators" of unexpectedly resulting works. This position has been rejected by courts that have considered that issue in Singapore, as well as in the United Kingdom and the United States.[350]

In the case of *Asia Pacific (Publishers) Pte Ltd v. Pioneers & Leaders (Publishers) Pte Ltd* [2011] SGC 837, the Court of Appeal in Singapore ruled that copyright protection will be granted only to works created by humans.[351]

§14.04 SINGAPORE ACADEMY OF LAW

The Singapore Academy of Law (SAL) is a statutorily established organization that characterizes itself as a "promotion and development agency for Singapore's legal industry. Our vision is to make Singapore the legal hub of Asia":[352]

> Our mandates are to build the intellectual capital of the legal profession by enhancing legal knowledge, raise the international profile of Singapore law, promote Singapore as a center for dispute resolution, and improve the standards and efficiency of legal practice through continuing professional development and use of technology.

The SAL provides a "knowledge hub for the legal community." The SAL provides a significant amount of information about Singapore legal cases and legislative developments in private law and practice and also provides online access to international legal developments. As such, the SAL provides a significant amount of information and insight about developments touching on the world of AI.

In its capacity as a legal knowledge center, the SAL, as of the time of this writing in mid-2023, was providing information about the following AI-related developments in Singapore:[353]

- An SAL innovation program for lawyers and others about how technology is changing the practice of law through machine learning and automation.
- A special issue of the SAL Journal 2021 on law and technology, including a discussion of the "limitations in machine learning."
- A program on Data Protection Law in Singapore reviewing issues relating to AI and machine learning on the local, regional and international level.

350. Such as the Thaler cases discussed in other chapters.
351. Similar copyright cases in the United Kingdom and the United States are discussed in Chapters X & Y above.
352. The SAL website is online at: sal.org.sg.
353. SAL online at sal.org.sg.

CHAPTER 15
AI Health and Safety

Although there are undoubted benefits that AI systems can offer in the area of health and safety, there are also some questions about their accuracy and dependability. Consequently, it will be necessary for AI tools employed to facilitate health and safety to be carefully created and carefully controlled.

In any nation, there are usually numerous laws and regulations in place to protect the health and safety of its citizens. There are also international standards and agreements.

There is no question that AI tools being created to be used with respect to health and safety are already subject to the health and safety regulations already in existence. However, their novelty will undoubtedly require careful thinking about how they can be most effectively and safely employed, and conclusions about that may lead to a necessary introduction of additional laws and regulations to control health and safety-related AI systems, and AI systems that may not operate specifically in the areas of health and safety but the use of which has an impact on health and safety.

§15.01 THE PROMISE OF AI

It is unquestionably true the employment of AI in certain areas related to health and safety offers opportunities to make those things more effective and more efficient.

When it comes to a concentrated analysis of data relating to health and safety, there will be many instances where an AI system can perform those tasks more quickly and more efficiently than human operators. This will increasingly be true as the use of hyper-fast quantum computers becomes more developed and more widely available to be employed by people and institutions.

AI tools are already making remarkable strides in the treatment of medical conditions which have been extremely difficult to treat effectively.

§15.02 THE PROBLEMS

Despite its ability to act independently once it is set in motion, an AI system still requires human intervention. It needs programming and training to perform the tasks expected of it, it needs operators to oversee its performance, and it needs to be checked to make certain that the results it produces are accurate and effective.

Although AI systems are labeled as "intelligent," their awareness of their impact on the human recipients of their production is limited by the completeness of their programming. It is sometimes going to be impossible for their creators and operators to know in advance whether the performance of an AI system will create danger or false understanding.

There have been reported cases where AI systems have got things badly wrong and even "lied" about the accuracy of their results.

These things may not be critical when asking an AI system to write certain documents, but they are critical when AI systems are directing or suggesting paths for the health and safety of human beings which, if the bot has got it wrong, can result in injury or death.

This makes it certain that the deployment of AI systems in many, if not all, situations where they affect health and safety will require careful regulation of the creators and operators of AI systems and of the AI tools themselves.

§15.03 POTENTIAL CURATIVE POWERS OF AI

The possible benefits of AI tools can affect people in both physical and situational ways. They can make a significant difference in the well-being of individuals and larger populations. It is obvious that the application of AI tools in these ways is both wide-ranging and complex. Consequently, it is important to understand what these possibilities are and what regulations will be necessary to assure that the use of such tools remains effective and safe.

There have already been encouraging reports about the positive effects that AI tools can have on difficult-to-treat health problems. Some examples are as follows.

§15.04 STROKE RECOVERY WITH AI

In August 2023, it was reported that a 30-year-old woman who had been paralyzed and unable to talk as the result of a stroke was having her ability to talk restored through the use of AI:

> The brain activity of a paralyzed woman is being translated into words spoken by an avatar. This milestone could help others who have lost speech.

> In a milestone of neuroscience and artificial intelligence, implanted electrodes decoded Mrs. Johnson's brain signals as she silently tried to say sentences. Technology converted her brain signals into written and vocalized language, and

> enabled an avatar on a computer screen to speak the words and display smiles, pursed lips and other expressions.

Synthesizing spoken words and facial expressions from brain signals has never been possible before. The patient from Regina, Canada, chose an avatar that looked something like her, and the AI programmers used a recording of a speech she had given at her wedding to train the voice of her avatar.[354]

§15.05 PARALYSIS OVERCOME WITH AI

In August 2023, there was a story published about a Dutch man who, with the help of Swiss scientists using AI tools, was able to overcome his paralysis and walk again.[355]

He was reportedly paralyzed in an accident in 2011. Scientists have come up with a computer program that "decodes electrical signals in his brain and sends instructions to nerves in his spinal cord." This means that his intention to take a step results in his ability to take a step.

When he was paralyzed in Beijing in a traffic accident on his bicycle, he was told that he would never be able to walk again. He was returned to the Netherlands but was told there that he would be in a wheelchair for the rest of his life. He was told that he had no chance of walking again.

However, over a decade, a group of Swiss scientists created an AI system that was able to decode signals in his brain and translate them to his legs as instructions to move. The result is that Mr. Oskam is now able to take steps with the assistance of a walker.

A surgical team in Lausanne put implants in his skull to interpret brain activity related to walking. Using an AI system, signals from the brain are decoded. The resulting information is sent to another device implanted in his lower back. This stimulates the spinal cord to instruct his legs to take steps:

> The system that allows him to walk includes two sets of electrodes, each enclosed in a circular titanium case about 5 cm wide, which [a neurosurgeon] placed in the top of his skull. They sit on the surface of his brain and monitor tens of thousands of nerve cells as they crackled with electrical activity. An AI system decodes that activity. In a sense, it reads his mind: it can recognize when Mr. Oskam, who is now 40, is thinking about taking a step. It translates that intention into a series of signals that are sent—wirelessly, every 300 ms—to another set of electrodes. These are placed on the surface of his spinal cord—the bundle of nerves that should relay messages from the brain to the body—at the base of his back. When different points of the cord are stimulated by the electrodes, different muscles—in his hips, thighs and ankles—are activated.[356]

354. Pam Belluck. "A Stroke Stole Her Ability to Speak at 30. A.I. is Helping to Restore It Years Later," *The Times* online, August 23, 2023.
355. Rhys Blakely, "How AI helped me to walk again," Interview with Gert-Jan Oskam, *The Times* online, August 15, 2023.
356. *Ibid.*

As these examples demonstrate, AI systems have the potential to develop tools that can make a dramatic difference in the quality of life of people who have suffered otherwise catastrophic physical disabilities.

The advances that have been described above have taken many years to develop. It seems that with further developments occurring over decades in the future, the possibilities for overcoming serious injuries may be significantly improved, producing faster and better results than are shown in the examples given.

However, there is no question that such treatments are serious intrusions into the physical and neurological systems of the patients. Although they are being shown to offer dramatic improvements in the lives of the patients who are being treated, they need to be extremely carefully applied and may have effects that are difficult or impossible to foresee. Consequently, the need for detailed regulation of how such things are used is critical. In the cases described above, it seems that a great deal of care was taken in treating those patients. That is as it should be.

With respect to any medical practice, there are strict regulations relating to who can practice medical interventions in all legal jurisdictions. Certainly, the laws and regulations relating to medicine already in existence will apply to any treatments resulting or modified by the use of AI. However, the novelty and dramatic possibilities presented by AI may well require specific regulations addressing the specific ways that AI intervenes in medical treatments.

With respect to the jurisdictions discussed in this book, it is not clear whether any have introduced regulations specific to AI and its uses in medicine. In many cases, these are already being considered. But because there are cases where medical solutions are already being driven or modified by AI tools, it seems that AI is way ahead of the lawmakers. This needs to be corrected. Failure to do so may have dramatic and possibly negative, unforeseen consequences.

§15.06 THE ELON MUSK EXPERIMENTS

However, there is one expected Internet access tool that will require a significant amount of new and stringent regulation in the future. This is the insertion of electronic devices into the human body.

Elon Musk is sponsoring research that goes beyond the AI treatments described above.

In August of 2020, an article appeared in The Times that described how Elon Musk had arranged for a small Computer chip to be planted in the brain of a pig that was supposed to be able to interact with the nervous system to cure dementia, Parkinson's disease, and paralysis. This procedure was reported to be "a prototype of the first brain-to-machine interface." According to Mr. Musk, this procedure is the start of "a new era of superhuman cognition."[357]

357. Charlie Mitchell, "Elon Musk wires up a pig 'to cure dementia'," *The Times*, Monday, August 31, 2020, online, accessed August 31, 2020. https://www.thetimes.co.uk/article/elon-musk-wires-up-a-pig-to-cure-dementia-55vqpgzkx?shareToken=c9c8b45dcf950cc6e0f81f213e829e81.

All of the results of Mr. Musk's experiments have not yet been published as of this writing, but if the procedure is successful, the potential implications are enormous. If such implantations become more widely done with human beings, that will make enormous differences in the ways that society and life generally are conducted.

It was reported in April 2021 that Musk's company, Neuralink, released a film showing a monkey playing the primitive computer game "Pong" by communicating with a computer through a chip planted in the monkey's brain. The commands are apparently sent wirelessly through the skin.[358]

On 30 January 2024, it was reported by Kieran Southern in *The Times* that Musk had received FDA approval to conduct tests on humans. Musk says that Neuralink has made a brain implant in a human and that so far the results are "promising."

It is probably impossible to imagine all the ways that such a development would affect us.

For example, if it were possible to safely implant communicative tools in the human brain, we would not need external physical devices to receive much of the information we get from computers and mobile devices. We may be able to receive telephone calls and written, oral or even pictorial messages without an external device. We may be able to access websites without the need for a physical device. We might be able to access reference sources such as dictionaries, encyclopedias books, or articles just by thinking about it to activate a chip.

Our ability to speak foreign languages without intensive training might be enhanced or even perfected. Speeches would not require paper or electronic notes. The possibilities are endless.

However, there are many negative possibilities—perhaps too many to permit this kind of thing to be done to humans.

If this technology becomes widespread and effective, it might be impossible to stop criminal or politically hostile groups from using it to their advantage.

It becomes obvious that the strictest and most thoughtful legal controls must be imposed on the use of such technology.

[A] Medical Issues

First, there are the medical issues. How safe is this technology? Medical regulatory and professional ethical authorities will need to carefully control such things as:

- What specifications and limitations will need to be applied to the electronic or chemical implantations?
- Who will be permitted to manufacture, sell, install and service such devices?
- Who will be allowed to have such devices implanted?
- Are there circumstances in which such devices can be implanted in a person without their consent?

358. Tom Knowles, "For Musk's next trick ... monkeys playing mind games," *The Times*, April 10, 2021, online, accessed April 10, 2021.

- What ethical standards will need to be complied with?
- What signals or information can be transmitted to and from such devices?
- What third parties, if any, will be allowed to communicate with the possessor of such a device?

These are only some of the questions that will have to be asked and answered.

One is reminded of reports and even criminal cases where it is alleged that individuals or their parents paid large sums to have clever test-takers take professional or educational evaluation exams in place of the persons who were registered to take the exams.

If this technology develops to a sufficient level, paying third-party substitutes for exam takers may no longer be necessary. The original registrants could have correct answers fed directly to their brains as they sit there taking the tests. Alternatively, they may be able to access the internet to get helpful information while they are taking the exam. It's hard to imagine how invigilators could stop this. The nature of the relevant examinations would have to be completely changed.[359]

[B] Third Party Brain Access

Beyond asking the question of what the possessor of such implants might be able to access with these devices, there is the perhaps more worrying question of what access such devices would give third parties to the body and brain of others.

We are facing a world that becomes like the plot of a Christopher Nolan movie, whereby third parties will be able to communicate with the electronic chips implanted in peoples' brains and implant ideas, thoughts, desires, and instructions that the possessors of the chips will believe they thought of themselves. Will such "inceptions" be put into practice in the physical world?[360]

The sinister implications of having such power are too broad and too inhuman to fully imagine.

Significant legislation needs to be promulgated throughout the world to limit and control such activities. Otherwise, the negative possibilities are too awful to think of.

---

359. Joey Garrison, "NY attorney sentenced to 1 month in prison for paying $75K to have daughter's ACT answers fixed" *USA Today*, December 15, 2019, online, accessed September 02, 2020. https://eu.usatoday.com/story/news/nation/2019/10/03/college-admissions-scam-lawyer-gordon-caplan-faces-prison-paying-cheat-test/3828754002/; Josie Ensor, "Donald Trump cheated on exams to get into university, claims his niece in new 'tell-all' book," *The Telegraph*, July 8, 2020, online, accessed September 02, 2020.
360. In 2010, the writer and film director, Christopher Nolan released a "science fiction" film called "Inception," in which persons are hired to implant an idea into the mind of a businessman that will be profitable for other businesspeople. The implanters are required to do this in such a way the person receiving the implanted idea believes the idea to be his own. This implanted idea is an "Inception" as opposed to a "conception." https://www.imdb.com/title/tt1375666/, online, retrieved September 03, 2020.

[C] Cybercrime and Cyberwar Enhanced

This kind of voluntary or even involuntary third party brain access may be the ultimate cybercrime and the ultimate weapon of cyberwar. The potential consequences could be far more deadly and long-lasting than a nuclear strike.

For example, following the "Inception" theme, the consequences could be devastating for business and the financial markets.

Financial analysts frequently fail to accurately predict the direction of financial market moves. But they are generally thought to be relying on their own judgment and analysis when they take positions in the markets. Of course, there have been too many instances where investors have taken a position based on inside information that gives them a better view of the future of prices than those who do not have this information.

However, such conduct is illegal and can be punished with large fines, banning from the market, and even imprisonment.

But what happens when market participants are guided not by their own judgment and analysis but by ideas implanted in their brains by others intending to profit from the execution of those ideas, which the receiving persons may even believe to be their own? Will there ever be a level playing field in the financial markets again? How will regulators be able to prevent or even investigate such communications?

[D] Chile: "Inception Law"

In response to the problems that the above scenario presents, there are already attempts to put into place laws to protect people from digital manipulation of their brains.

Chile is apparently seeking to become the first country to pass legislation to protect its citizens from having their brains digitally controlled. This is being called the "inception law" in the press.[361]

The purpose of the law is said to be to protect the "neuro-rights" of Chilean citizens by covering them with statutory legal protection.

Going beyond that, Chilean legislators say that the nation's constitution should be revised to protect all things connected to "fundamental human autonomy."

It is reported that the members of the Chilean parliament unanimously support the passage of this law and are considering making a part of it a proposed constitutional revision.

[E] Health Benefits

However, there is another side to this mind manipulation debate. Apparently, there have been significant technological advances in using digital brain manipulation to

361. Stephen Gibbs, "'Inception' law aims to stop mind control." *The Times*, online, May 07, 2021, accessed May 08, 2021.

diminish the effects of Parkinson's disease and epilepsy. These successes are apparently dependent on accessing and manipulating the brain.[362]

There has even been a program in the United States, supported by the Obama Administration, seeking to learn more about the causes and cures of brain diseases. This program is itself called "Brain," which stands for brain research through advanced innovative neuro-technologies.

As discussed above, Elon Musk and others are involved in experiments to plant electrodes in the brains of animals and humans. The nature of these experiments is worrying, but one positive aspect of them is that there is an intention that the knowledge gained from such experiments may be useful for helping people suffering from paralysis to be able to use computers or telephones or even disabled parts of their bodies by controlling them directly with signals electronically transferred from their brains. It is hard to know how far this can go or how long it will take.[363]

[F] Mind/Computer Interface Developments

Despite legitimate concerns about the impact of interface between the brain and digital machines, the mind/computer interface is developing rapidly.

One of the positive effects of the research that is being done is that there is help for people with paralysis in some of these developments. The formal name for this type of technology is brain machine interface technology (BMI). It is a small field of technology currently, but some of the research being done in the field already provides the types of dramatic results described above.

Important large tech companies are investing a great deal of money in BMI. There has been, in addition to the examples described above, U.S. human recipients of BMI technology that promises to improve their lives.

A U.S. man broke his neck in a car accident and was left quadriplegic. He now takes part in BMI lab experiments that implant his brain with electronic sensors that allow him to control certain devices with his thoughts. He says, "I can control a robotic arm and hand or a computer cursor or I've played some games that use a computer emulator."[364]

A story in The New York Times told of another man who had been paralyzed in a car accident at the age of 20 and had not been able to speak for nearly 20 years. Now, electrodes have been planted in the speech areas of his brain which allow his brain to transmit signals to a computer that shows the words he wants to say on a screen.

Clearly, this is a use of computer science and AI in coordination with human biology of a type that does need to be encouraged and nurtured in the future.

However, an important element in this situation is that AI allows patients to express their own decisions and does not direct them to carry out tasks formulated by

362. *Ibid.*
363. *Ibid.*
364. Antony Funnell, "The Potential of Brain-Machine Interface technology has Silicon Valley excited, and ethicists worried," ABC News, online May 11, 2021, accessed May 27, 2021.

a third person who may have the best interests of the subject of the implantation at heart.[365]

[G] Safer Surgery

In one positive development, AI is being harnessed to make brain surgery easier and safer.

It is certainly the case that brain surgery entails significant risks to the patient. Tinkering with the control center of a human being is a dangerous business.

But now AI and computers are progressing to the point where the risks of brain surgery can be reduced by providing surgeons with an AI tool that creates a computer representation of a brain on which the surgeons will be working.

In the United Kingdom, the system was first employed in 2021. In its favor, it is believed the system will reduce the stress that surgeons feel during these delicate operations, save lives and reduce the costs of this kind of complicated surgery.

This "virtual brain" is a product of a British business called Oxford Heartbeat.

The system is employed by taking a scan of the patient's brain from which a 3-D computer model is produced. This model can be used to test the effect of certain procedures (such as the insertion of stents into blood vessels) when applied to the brain of the patient. This eliminates the "hit and miss" trials that are often necessary during the insertion of stents into brain vessels to treat brain aneurysms.

It is believed that this system and other computer modeling systems that can be developed for different kinds of surgery using AI will benefit a huge number of patients in the future.[366]

There are those who worry that BMI technology will allow big businesses to enslave consumers by controlling their minds.[367]

This may be a legitimate concern, but it should be possible to harvest the benefits of such technology while controlling potential abuses through carefully thought-out regulations, laws, and treaties. There will no doubt be a need for careful international cooperation and regulation to use the positive results of this technology and prevent cross-border abuse of BMI.

§15.07 LICENSING AND LIABILITIES

Any intervention into the health of a human being (whether physical or psychological) raises questions of liability, responsibility and accountability. The responses to these questions are often determined by established legal statutes and regulations regarding by whom and under what circumstances such interventions are permitted, but

365. Pam Belluck, "Tapping Into the Brain to Help a Paralyzed Man Speak," *The New York Times*, online, July 15, 2021. *See also*, "Neuroprothesis for Decoding Speech in a Paralyzed Person with Anarthria," *The New England Journal of Medicine*, 2021: 385: 217-227.
366. "Artificial intelligence gives surgeons a practice run on virtual brains," *The Times*, online, September 06, 2021, accessed September 07, 2021.
367. Funnell, ABC News, May 11, 2021.

otherwise, particularly in cases where damage is alleged, they may be determined by courts or other designated tribunals.

Many of the questions relating to liability and accountability for the use of AI tools in relation to human health problems may already be answered by existing laws and regulations relating to medical practice, licensing, and distribution of health aides such as drugs and other things, and by general tort law.

However, the expanding international nature of the digital world means that AI tools developed in one jurisdiction may quickly be widely available or copied throughout the world. This makes an urgent need to establish international standards for the creation, distribution and application of AI tools relating to human health and safety.

Those working in the fields of health and safety are already demanding clearer guidance as to the liability and accountability of their professional activities. Clearer guidance needs to be established internationally so that there is an adequate understanding of the limits and requirements of AI in health. For example:

> Traditionally, medicine was a biological science. For two decades the health field has been infiltrated by the legal establishment changing the nature of healing art into a legal act. The legal interest in medicine was attracted by the still inaccurate knowledge of life itself and the margin of error in all human acts. This change forced in unprecedented personal accountability on health practitioners ... We would expect that accountability and liability would be defined by law—for example, who can provide narcotics or who can sign the death certificate. The liability crisis has no such characteristics of an orderly legal process. It was shaped in court rooms, by judges and attorneys without specific statutes ... Organized medicine should strive for an orderly constitutional process where the perimeters of accountability and liability are stated by law ... .[368]

The letter from which the above quotes are taken was written by a doctor in the US state of Illinois to a medical journal in 1983. However, its concerns are even more applicable to the uncertain status of the intervention by AI tools in health and safety. It will clearly not be enough for local laws and regulations to protect against the abuse or misapplication of such tools when intervening in human health and safety. International treaties and conventions establishing clear standards and regulations for their application are urgently needed.

368. James Scott, MD, "The Legal Requirements of Medical Practice," *Western Journal of Medicine*, Correspondence, August 1983, 139(2), p. 229.

CHAPTER 16

AI & Intellectual Property Law

As pointed out throughout this book, the creation, sale and use of AI systems is a fact by numerous legal issues that also apply to the creation, use and sale of any other creation.

Among these are intellectual property issues.

For example, generative AI, such as ChatGPT, which produces linguistic responses (orally or in writing) to the requests of users, is reported to construct its requests from surveying data found on the Internet from which it fashions its response. It is difficult or impossible to know the extent to which a generative intelligence system copies, in whole or in part, data provided on the internet by others.

It is reported that the AI generative systems currently known do not provide adequate source references. Indeed, it has been reported that there is at least one case where the sources provided were entirely made up by the chatbot used.

There is also a question as to how accurate or truthful a chatbot can be when fashioning its response.

These are worrying general issues. However, in the sphere of pure intellectual property law, there are two fundamental issues that are raised by generative AI. These are:

(1) Does a generative chatbot's use of data created by others to prepare its responses constitute a violation of the copyrights of the creators of the data used by the bot?
(2) To what extent, if any, does the generative bot's use of that data constitute plagiarism?

§16.01 PROTECTION OF AI INTELLECTUAL PROPERTY

Aside from the legal issues discussed above, legally created AI intelligence products can benefit from the same type of national and international protections available to other human creations.

An emphasis here must be made on "human creations." There have been at least two legal cases to date, one in the U.S. and one in the United Kingdom that have ruled that one must be human to benefit from the protections of intellectual property rights. Such rights have been held not to be available to AI systems themselves.

To give a brief summary, the following are the intellectual property legal protections that may be available to AI systems.

§16.02 INTERNATIONAL INTERNET LAW

The following constitute important international treaties and conventions, regulations and legal instruments that affect governance of the Internet.[369]

[A] United Nations Declaration on Human Rights (UDHR)

The Universal Declaration of Human Rights promulgated by the UN in 1948 asserts the fundamental rights that all human beings are entitled to simply by being human.[370]

Particularly relevant for Internet law is the second paragraph of the Preamble which states that "... human beings shall enjoy the freedom of speech and belief...." Also, the statement in the third paragraph that "... human rights should be protected by the rule of law....." Furthermore:

> Member States have pledged themselves to achieve, in cooperation with the United Nations, the promotion of universal respect for and observance of human rights and fundamental freedoms.

There is also Article 12 that asserts protection of privacy, stating:

> No one shall be subjected arbitrary interference with his privacy, family, home or correspondence nor to attacks upon his honor and reputation. Everyone has the right to the protection of the law against such interference or attacks.

Article 19 is particularly relevant to Internet usage stating:

> Everyone has the right to freedom of opinion and expression; this right includes freedom to hold opinions without interference and to seek, receive and impart information and ideas through any media and regardless of the frontiers.

369. UNESCO, Internet Governance Glossary, section 7, 7.1, 7.2, 7.3; https://en.unesco.org/glossaries/igg/groups/7.4%20Conventions%20and%20treaties%2C%20regulations%20and%20legal%20instruments, retrieved August 11, 2020.

370. *Ibid*, section 7.4.1.

It is certainly true that the Internet has the potential to fulfill and enhance the right to cultural life asserted in Article 1, which states:

> 1. Everyone has the right to participate in the cultural life of the community, to enjoy the arts and to share in scientific advancement and its benefits.

Although this Universal Declaration of Human Rights is not legally binding, 192 members of the UN have agreed to it because acceptance of its principles is an intrinsic requirement for membership to the UN.

In addition, 150 countries have ratified and signed the International Bill of Human Rights (OHCHR), which consists of the Universal Declaration of Human Rights and two other international treaties:

(1) The International Covenant on Civil and Political Rights (ICCPR, 1966); and
(2) The International Covenant on Economic, Social and Cultural Rights (ICESR, 1966).

[1] Internet Communication as A Human Right

The United Nations has tried to extend internationally recognized human rights onto the Internet.

In June 2012, it proposed a resolution on human rights on the Internet. The resolution sought to promote the protection and exercise of human rights on the Internet through Article 19 of the Universal Declaration of Human Rights.

However, it is not certain that this resolution (which remains in draft) has any significant legal impact because several countries have reservations about it, and it has not yet been approved.

[2] Resistance to the UDHR

Although 150 countries have ratified the UN conventions protecting human rights discussed above, there is a significant group of countries that are opposed to some of their protections.

Saudi Arabia has not signed UDHR, claiming that it violates Islamic law and fails to account for the religious and cultural backgrounds of non-Western countries. All Saudi citizens are required to be Muslims, and there are restrictions on women's rights.

An Iranian representative to the UN has also said that it is impossible to comply with the UDHR without violating Islamic law.[371]

In response to the concerns of Muslim countries, 45 countries belonging to the Organization of the Islamic Conference agreed to adopt the Cairo Declaration of Human Rights in Islam (CDHRI) in 1990. However, the CDHRI does not conform to the UDHR

371. Dania Akkad, "The Universal Declaration vs. The Cairo Declaration," online, blogs.lse.ac.uk, December 10, 2012, accessed November 13, 2021.

and "undermines many of the rights the UDHR is supposed to guarantee." For example, it allows for the establishment of different rights for men and women.[372]

The CDHRI has the effect of restricting freedom of expression in a number of ways that would limit the use of the Internet to express certain ideas. Article 22 of the CDHRI says:

> Everyone shall have the right to express his opinion freely in such manner as would not be contrary to the principles of the Shari'ah.[373]

Since 1990, there have been several proposals to expand interpretations of human rights under Islamic law, but so far, they have not met with significant success.[374]

It is likely that, although many countries respect the breadth of human rights guaranteed under the UDHR, and their application in relation to the Internet may be limited by some countries that, for religious and political reasons, will be unwilling to extend those rights to all their citizens.

[B] International Telecommunication Regulations (ITR)

The International Telecommunication Regulations (ITR) came into force in 1998 through the International Telecommunication Union (ITU). Its purpose was to promote international liberalization of pricing and Internet services and to permit new functions of basic services with respect to the Internet. This involved such things as leased lines and helped the rapid growth of the Internet by the 1990s. The principal international organizations responsible for the international regulation of telecommunications are the World Trade Organization and the ITU.[375]

[C] Basic Telecommunication Agreement (BTA)

The formal name of this agreement is the Fourth Protocol to the General Agreement on Trade in Services. This came into force in 1998. Under this agreement, over a hundred countries have opened their telecommunication markets to promote the development of new communication services, including Internet services.[376]

372. *Ibid.*
373. Alan Sears, "Protecting Freedom of Expression over the Internet: An International Approach," *Notre Dame Journal of International & Comparative Law,* Volume 5 (2015), online, accessed November 13, 2021.
374. *See,* Konstantinos Magliveras and Gino Nardi, The Arab Court of Human Rights: A Study in Impotence, The Quebec Journal of International Law, Volume 29, Number 2, pp. 1 to 342, 2016, online, accessed November 13, 2021.
375. UNESCO Glossary 7.4.2.
376. UNESCO Glossary 7.4.3.

[D] UNCITRAL Model Law on Electronic Commerce

This was issued by UNCITRAL in 1996. It is not a legally binding instrument, but it provides a model for legislation and also assists Internet users in drafting their contracts.[377]

[E] Berne Convention for the Protection of Literary and Artistic Works (Berne Convention)

This is an international convention with a long history. It was first adopted in 1886. The signers of this agreement are required to recognize the copyright of authors from other signing countries in the same way that they recognize the copyrights of their own citizens. Signatories to this agreement are known as the Bern Union.

The agreement also requires signatories to provide minimum standards in their copyright law.[378]

[F] WIPO Copyright Treaty (WCT)

This treaty was agreed by the Member States of the World Intellectual Property Organization in 1996. It was created as an enhancement to existing copyright treaties because of advances in digital information and Internet technology.[379]

[G] Agreement on Trade-Related Aspects of Intellectual Property Rights (TRIPS)

The TRIPS is an International intellectual property agreement administered by the World Trade Organization. It establishes standards for applying intellectual property regulations to nationals of other countries that also happen to be World Trade Organization members.[380]

[H] Budapest Convention on Cybercrime (Budapest Convention)

The Budapest convention was entered into in July 2004. It was the first treaty trying to deal with Internet and other computer crimes. The goals of the treaty are to align the Internet laws and regulations of the signatory countries, to update and improve their

377. UNESCO Glossary 7.4.4.
378. UNESCO Glossary 7.4.5.
379. UNESCO Glossary 7.4.6.
380. UNESCO Glossary 7.4.7. For additional information how about these and other agreements regulating intellectual property on the Internet, please *see* Chapter 14 on Intellectual Property Law and the Internet.

methods of investigation, and to get them to cooperate more in preventing international cybercrime.[381]

[1] Convention on the Recognition and Enforcement of Foreign Arbitral Awards (New York Convention)

This is a convention that has been in existence for some time. It was created in 1958, long before the Internet rose to prominence. Its purpose has been and remains the regulation of the terms under which the national courts of signatories are obliged to enforce arbitration awards regardless of where the arbitration awards are made. It is commonly called "the New York Convention."

About 24 countries are signatories that allow their national courts to enforce the arbitration awards of other signatories under the terms of the Convention.[382]

[2] UNCITRAL Model Law on International Commercial Arbitration

This is a template that nations can use to create their own commercial arbitration law. The Model Law itself is not legally binding, but it is something that countries can make part of their own national law if they wish. It was introduced in 2006.[383]

[3] W3C Web Accessibility Initiative Web Content Accessibility Guidelines (WCAG)

The World Wide Web Consortium has issued a series of guidelines on web accessibility that were published by the Web Accessibility Initiative (WAI) of W3C.

They are a collection of ways to make the web accessible for users who may be disabled or who are using mobile devices such as phones. The latest version was published in 2008, and a related standard from the International Organization for Standardization (ISO) was issued in 2012.[384]

[I] United Nations Convention on the Use of Electronic Communications in International Contracts (Electronic Communications Convention)

The United Nations Convention on the use of Electronic Communications in International Contracts (Electronic Communications Convention) was initially adopted in 2005.[385] However, since then, it has been adopted by only 18 countries. The only major country being the Russian Federation. It only entered into force for those signatories in

381. UNESCO, Internet Governance Glossary, 7.4.8.
382. UNESCO Glossary 7.4.9.
383. UNESCO Glossary 7.4.10.
384. UNESCO Glossary 7.4.11.
385. Vienna Convention, Introduction, 2, online at uncitral.org, accessed August 18, 2020.

2013. However, the importance of this Convention goes beyond those countries. A number of countries have adopted parts of this Convention as provisions in their own national legislation. Others have indicated some interest in adopting the Convention or preparing legislation to include provisions like those of the convention. That interest has been expressed by several major countries, including the United States.

In fact, the Convention was based on the already existing laws of the United States and Canada (American Uniform Electronic Transactions Act) and Canada (Canadian Uniform Electronic Transactions Act).[386]

The purpose of this Convention is to provide a treaty that removes the formal obstacles that separate electronic from written contracts. It is aimed at providing an opportunity for countries involved in international commerce, whether signatories or not, to adopt similar legislation governing the creation of contracts in electronics commerce. This would make international trade easier by harmonizing the different national regulations that govern electronic commerce.[387]

If this convention is more widely adopted by major legal jurisdictions such as the U.S., the EU, China, India and the European Union, it is thought that its provisions could have a significant impact on trading areas such as energy, shipping, technology and financial services.[388]

President Obama sent the Convention to the U.S. Senate along with a recommendation of ratification on February 10, 2016.[389] However, the U.S. Senate has not yet agreed to ratify the Convention. In the Senate, issues have been raised that may delay or prevent ratification of the Convention. The first is that provisions of the convention are like provisions already existing in U.S. law, such as the Uniform Commercial Code. It is the thought that many U.S. legal practitioners would prefer to operate under established law rather than a new treaty that may make small variations to the law that may be confusing. The second is that the Convention is not self-executing and would, therefore, require further legislation to implement provisions into U.S. law. Consequently, there does not seem to be a strong likelihood that the Convention will be ratified by the U.S. any time soon.

[J] Internet Corporation for Assigned Names and Numbers (ICANN)

ICANN was established in 1998. It is an international organization overseen by the U.S. government.[390] ICANN is responsible for the administration of three kinds of Internet identifier systems. These are:

(1) domain names;

386. J. Benjamin Lambert, "The U.N. Convention on Electronic Contracting: Back From the Dead?," *Michigan State International Law Review*, Vol. 25.1. pp. 32-75, online at Digital Commons Network, accessed August 18, 2020.
387. UN Commission on International Trade Law, online, accessed at uncitral.un.org, August 18, 2020.
388. Lambert, p. 34.
389. *Ibid.*
390. *See* the discussion of U.S. domain name regulation in Chapter 4.

(2) numerical Internet protocol addresses (IP); and
(3) a code that identifies port and parameter numbers.

The Internet community can participate in determining the policy of ICANN through the Non-commercial Users Constituency (NCUC)[391] and/or the At-Large Advisory Committee (ALAC).[392]

[K] Internet Assigned Names and Numbers Authority (IANA)

The IANA is the department of ICANN. It was established in 1988 to execute policy with respect to IP number allocations and some administrative functions for the Internet Engineering Task Force (IETF) and ICANN.[393]

[L] Number Resource Organization (NRO)

This is an unincorporated group formed in 2003 to coordinate the Regional Internet Registries (RIRs), of which there are five regional RIRs around the world. Those five RIRs are:

(1) APNIC, covering India, the Far East, and the Antipodes;
(2) ARIN, covering North America;
(3) LACNIC, covering Latin America;
(4) RIPE NCC, covering Europe, the Middle East, and the Russian Federation; and
(5) AFRNIC, covering Africa.

The NRO's goal is to provide a coordinating body for the registrations of domain names through the RIRs.[394]

The NRO doesn't do domain name registration. Rather, it functions as a central registry and communication point for the RIRs with respect to such things as statistical reports, Internet governance efforts and policy coordination. To help do that, it supports coordinating groups on common issues such as communications, registration services, engineering, and administrative leadership. The aim of these groups is to help promote security, stability, and cooperation in global domain name registration.

§16.03 NATIONAL IP PROTECTION

In addition to the extensive attention that is being paid to international protection of various categories of intellectual property, which would be applicable to AI products, nations also have statutes and regulations to protect intellectual property. Learning

391. http://ncdnhc.org/.
392. http://www.allarge.icann.org/.
393. *Ibid.*
394. NRO website, nro.net, retrieved September 07, 2020.

about them in detail with respect to any particular situation would require consultation with qualified expert advisers in the jurisdictions in question.

However, to give a general idea of the approaches in some of the major market nations, some examples are as follows.

[A] National Law Protecting Internet IP

[1] United States

In 1998, the U.S. a new copyright statute called the Digital Millennium Copyright Act (DMCA). The purpose of the Act was to deal with the changes that digital commerce was making to trade, domestic and international.

One of its purposes was to implement the WIPO 1996 Internet treaties discussed above.

Among its provisions were sections criminalizing:

(a) The production and distribution of any works that violated copyrights.
(b) Any actions to circumvent systems that control access to copyrighted material.
    (i) Such as Digital Rights Management (DRM) systems.
        - Even if the copyright itself is not breached.

Some exemptions were provided to the DMCA, principally for internet service providers or other intermediaries. For example, ISPs were protected from direct or indirect liability for any copyright violations by the ISP's users who posted copyright-violating material.

§16.04 THE "TRAINING" CASES

One issue that has become prominent through legal actions in the U.S. and is likely to receive similar attention in the courts of other countries as time goes on and generative AI becomes more widely available is the issue of generative chatbots, such as ChatGPT, being trained in language use through "scraping" written material from the World Wide Web to learn examples of how language is used and how topics of interest are treated in written material.[395]

A powerful objection to this training process that has risen from the community of authors and other creators worldwide is that many have become aware that their copyrighted material which exists on the Internet in electronic form is, or maybe, used in such training.

395. Winston Cho, "Top Authors Join Lawsuit Against Open AI Over 'Mass Scale Copyright Infringement" of Novels" *The Hollywood Reporter*, online at: hollywoodreporter.com, September 20, 2023.

One association of authors filed a proposed "class action" lawsuit on behalf of authors in a New York federal court against OpenAI, alleging that the creator of ChatGPT was engaging "in a systemic course of mass-scale copyright infringement."[396]

Other lawsuits have reportedly been filed by creators against AI art-generating companies, including Meta, Stability AI, Midjourney and Deviant Art, alleging copyright infringement.[397]

It is reported that AI companies have been obtaining material to train their generative AI products from online collections of books held in "shadow libraries," such as Library Genesis, Z-Library and Bibliotik.[398]

The displeasure of authors and creators of copyrighted material is reported to be growing. There be great interest in the resolution of the lawsuits that have been filed to date, and many others may be filed in jurisdictions around the world.

AI products that are instructed to create content (music, writings, videos, etc.) that reflect the qualities necessary to qualify, in the views of human judges, as usable content such as music, writings, videos, etc.) may use material copied or sampled from databases as the raw material for their content production. A legal problem arises when they acquire material to use from copyrighted sources without "consent, credit or compensation."[399]

AI products such as OpenAI's ChatGPT are sophisticated machines operating according to complex instructions. One function they perform is the acquisition of data from existing sources, some of which may be copyrighted. If the purpose of this acquisition is to use copyrighted material to compete with human artists in the creation of media (which would not exist if the AI machine did not have access to copyrighted material), this would appear to fail the "fair use" tests if copyrighted material was not obtained with consent, credit or compensation.

Perhaps the gravest threat to intellectual property is that its production will be curtailed because the hacking and theft of intellectually created material on the Internet will become so extensive that those who produce it will lose interest in doing this kind of work because their ability to earn a profit from this work will be greatly reduced or indeed lost altogether.

An example of how this threat can affect academia is founding a website called the sci-hub website which is a digital database that supposedly has copies of 70 million academic and scientific papers. This is a huge percentage of the number of academic papers that have been produced. It is estimated that this represents around 80% of the existing total. Apparently, this collection has been assembled by hacking into the libraries and databases of universities around the world. 42 British universities are alleged to be victims.[400]

396. *Ibid.*
397. *Ibid.*
398. I was surprised to find a copy of my copyrighted book, "Internet Law" (Kluwer International, 2022) offered online by Z-Library!
399. Schumpeter, "Napster revisited," *The Economist*, March 18, 2023, p. 62.
400. David Brown, "Hacking Fear over Pirated Research Site Sci-Hub," *The Times*, March 21, 2021, online, accessed March 21, 2021.

The theft of academic research presents, of course, exactly the same problem as the theft of other kinds of intellectually produced media, such as songs, films and books. The people who produce such work do so because it is their job from which they expect to earn money and sometimes as their sole source of income. Much, if not all, of the papers on sci-hub are works for which it is expected that in order to gain access to them, one will have to pay a purchase price or subscription fee. Nevertheless, a young woman named Alexandra Elbakyan from Kazakhstan boasts that she has put together this vast academic library on the basis of her skills as an expert computer data miner without violating the intellectual property rights of the owners or authors. Not surprisingly, law enforcement authorities in a number of countries have found this hard to believe. For example, Ms. Elbakyan is currently under investigation by U.S. law enforcement authorities because they suspect her of using her hacking skills on behalf of Russian intelligence to access databases that contain sensitive U.S. military data.[401]

§16.05 INTELLECTUAL PROPERTY: AI CREATED CONTENT

Another legal issue that came up in March 2023 Was the legitimacy of using AI to copy or "sample" parts of existing copyrighted musical compositions and to use that information to create "new" musical compositions.

This rests on the fundamental copyright law issue of "fair use." Fair use permits the legal use of copyrighted work when the use:

Serves a valuable social purpose;
The source material is transformed from the original; and
It does not affect the copyright owner's core market.

In this case, the use of AI to Hoover up copyrighted material from publicly available sources and use it to transform that material into "original" compositions by an artificially intelligent machine fail both the first and third tests. With respect to the third test, the person directing the artificially intelligent machine to perform these searches to create material which competes with the original copyright owner, and with respect to the first, this does not appear to be a valuable social purpose.

Some Intellectual Property Cases—U.S.

(i) From Beach Boys v. Chuck Berry
- *"Surfin U.S.A." v. "Sweet Little Sixteen."*
- Settled 1966: Publishing rights to Berry's publisher

(ii) To *Lana Del Ray v. Radiohead*
- *"Get Free" v. "Creep"*
- March 2018: Del Ray says resolution reached.

(iii) https://www.rollingstone.com/politics/politics-lists/songs-on-trial-12-landmark-music-copyright-cases-166396/robin-thicke-vs-marvin-gaye-2014-60709/

401. *Ibid.*

Sampling

(i) Started in 1956 ("The Flying Saucer")
  - Writers cut borrowed sound copyright holders in on royalties

(ii) 1990s and Beyond
  - Computers & internet allowed electronic "borrowing" of parts of songs
  - Many artists have been sued: 50 Cent ("In Da Club"), Kayne West ("Gold Digger"), Snoop Dog & Warzone ("Flashbaccs"), Jay Z ("Run This Town"), Mark Ronson ("Uptown Funk").

(iii) Don't Get Sued: Artists must get pre-approval for sampling
  RIAA v. Napster (1999). Music Sharing
  Google Trademark Words (2009)
  David Slater/Naruto case (2011)

Jamie Thomas-Rasset case (8th Cir. Fed. CA). Minnesota woman fined USD 222,000 for illegally downloading 24 Rolling Stones songs. USD 8,250 per song.

Alice Corp v. CLS Banking Int'l (2014). U.S. Supreme Court. Business methods can't be patented. Abstract ideas cannot be patented. Electronic escrow service cannot be patented just because it is executed on the computer.

- *Katz v. Chevaldina* (2015). Use of unflattering headshot on a blog.
- *Garcia v. Google* (2015). Misuse of copyrighted dance performance for anti-Muslim post
- *MTM v. Amazon* (2015). Watch search on Amazon

TV Piracy

(i) 21% of U.S. consumers pirate TV shows

(ii) Game of Thrones
  - Most pirated TV show ever

Film Piracy

(i) 24% of U.S. consumers pirate movies
  - While movies are still in theaters

Books

A lawsuit has been filed against an organization named Internet Archive (Archive). Archive is a non-profit organization being sued by publishing companies about archives lending of Ebooks.[402] Lila Baily, attorney for Archive, says, "We think the future of libraries hangs in the balance here."

402. Jeff John Roberts, "As Libraries Fight for Access to E-books, a New Copyright Champion Emerges," *Fortune*, online, November 28, 2020, accessed May 07, 2021.

The case concerns the creation of a "National Emergency Library" by Archive. This was set up during the COVID-19 pandemic to allow people to borrow e-books. The publishing industry claimed that Archive was handing out e-books without permission and brought suit. An article in the magazine, The Nation, said the publishing industry was "taking the internet to court."[403]

Archive's attorney subscribes to the view that internet law should align with public interest rather than simply create barriers to accessing digital information. She claims that Archive is a digital version of the libraries we are used to as lenders of physical books. Archive lends out digital versions of books that it owns. Publishers are demanding injunctive relief that would require Archive to destroy the approximately 4 million digital books it has assembled in its collection.[404] The case was set for trial in 2021, but it is possible that a settlement will be reached without the necessity of completing the litigation.[405]

***Bouchat v. Baltimore Ravens and NFL.*, et al.**

This 2013 ruling by the U.S. Court of Appeals for the Fourth Circuit was on the issue of "fair use." The plaintiff was a graphic artist who drew and proposed a team logo for the Baltimore Ravens. The ravens did not adopt his particular design but used a similar design between 1996 and 1998. The plaintiff sued, and in 2000 the Fourth Circuit ruled that the ravens had violated the shots copyright. In 2012, Bouchard started another suit against the Ravens and other NFL-related organizations, claiming that the defendants had again used his logo by showing it in a Storico video about the history of the Ravens. In the district court case, the defendants claimed that their use of this historical logo was protected as a "fair use." Shot appealed to the Fourth Circuit. The Fourth Circuit ruled that the use of the logo in these circumstances was a protected "fair use" because the logo only appeared in "fleeting" instances in videos that were focused on the Ravens history. The court ruled that it was used in a video that was designed to preserve the Ravens history, and the appearance of the logo was only an "incidental" component of the exhibits in question. The court did not find any market harm to the plaintiff, and its overall view was that the plaintiff's arguments did not overcome the substantial weight of the factors in favor of a finding of "fair use."[406]

§16.06 SOME INTELLECTUAL PROPERTY CASES: EUROPE

(1) *Ashby Donald and others v. France.* European Court judgment on publication of photos on the internet. (January 10, 2013).
(2) eDate Advertising. ECJ judgment of October 25, 2011—C-509/09 and C-161/10—eDate Advertising; Conflict of laws Personality rights. A German national, convicted of murdering a well-known actor in 1993 was released on

403. *Ibid.*
404. *Ibid.*
405. *Ibid.*
406. *Bouchat v. Balt. Ravens Ltd. P'ship*, 737 F. 3rd 932 (4th Cir. 2013).

parole in 2008. He complained, in German court, of violation of his personality rights. An Austrian website (eDate Advertising) published his name, conviction, and the fact that he was appealing. Where publication is made in a Member State different from the one in which the claimant has brought his case, can the court try and enforce personality rights claims? Relevant regulations: Article 3(1) and 3(2) of the Directive on, Directive 2000/31/EC. Is there an established jurisdiction rule on the application of law to a service provider? A person who considers his rights infringed can bring an action either in his own Member State or in the Member State where the publication was made. Publication online could expose publishers to legal action outside their own country of operation.

(3) Wintersteiger. ECJ judgment of April 19, 2012—C-523/10—*Wintersteiger AG v. Products 4U Sondermaschinenbau GMBH*. Infringement of trademark by internet registration. Wintersteiger holds an Austrian trademark on its name. It is a maker of ski and snowboard servicing tools. A competitor registered "Wintersteiger" on the internet in Germany as a Google AdWord. Each time a "Wintersteiger" is entered, an advert for the competitor would appear. Wintersteiger sues in an Austrian court. Article 5(3) of Regulation (EC) No. 44/2001. On jurisdiction and the recognition and enforcement of judgments in civil and commercial matters. What is balance between national trademark and international issues created by infringement on the internet? Person domiciled in a Member State may be sued in the state where the harmful event occurred. The defendant's actions in Germany caused infringement of a trademark registered in Austria. Where conduct on the internet is liable to infringe a national trademark registered in a Member State, that will attribute jurisdiction to the courts of the Member State where the trademark is registered.

(4) Pinckney. ECJ judgment of October 3, 2013—C-170/12—*Peter Pinckney v. KDG Mediatech AG*. Placing dematerialized copyrighted songs on the internet and offering CDs of the songs. French resident author of 12 copyrighted song,. sues Austrian company for offering CDs of songs on the internet. CDs marketed by two UK companies on a number of websites. Accessible in the complainant's hometown: Toulouse. Complainant sues in Toulouse. Territoriality of copyright: All regimes of the EU are required to protect copyrighted work in parallel. What court has jurisdiction where there has been a copyright violation on the internet? In proceedings relating to a claimed infringement of the exclusive distribution right by the online sale of material reproducing content protected by copyright, the person harmed may bring proceedings either before the courts of the place of establishment of the persons who sold the compact discs (CDs) online or placed the content online in order to seek

compensation for all the damage suffered or before the courts of the Member State at which the website in question aims its activity. In this case, Austria or UK.

(5) *Swisscom* case (2019). Federal Supreme Court held that internet service providers are not liable for websites and portals that illegally make movies available for streaming and are not required to block access to such sites.

(6) Swisscom refused to block access after being requested by film producer and distributor of the movies being illegally streamed. Those who steam for their own use are not violating Swiss copyright law. Parties providing illegal streams are.

(7) In July 2021, Google was fined EUR 500 million by the French competition regulator because the regulator found that Google had not negotiated "in good faith" with News companies about the use of the content published by those news companies. In 2020, the French regulation authority had ordered Google to negotiate with news companies in good faith about Google's use of content from those news organizations and from other content providers. The fine was imposed in 2021 because the French competition regulator believed that Google had not negotiated in good faith. In 2019, France had adopted the new EU digital copyright directive which contained a provision directing compensation for publishers and news organizations for the use of their content. This is the so-called neighboring rights provision. This is the law under which the French competition authority sought to compel Google to provide good faith compensation to contact providers and which it found Google had failed to comply.[407] It remains to be seen whether other tech companies will suffer similar punishment with regard to their use of the content or extracts of the content provided by third parties.

[A] China

China has recently been representing that it is making efforts to encourage protection for and respect for IP.

In January 2017, China publicly announced a plan to improve cooperation with other nations on IP protection.

One of its steps was to set up a new Internet court to review cases of alleged improper use of protected IPOs. To date, that court has accepted about 30,000 cases. More than 80% of those cases are Internet cases.

In 2021, China announced a supplementary plan to improve IP protection.[408]

One of the important goals of both plans is to improve China's international reputation for IP protection.

407. Rory O'Neill, "China's New Five-Year Plan Targets 'Hi-Tech' IP, World Intellectual Property Review," online, worldipreview.com, April 27, 2021.
408. *Ibid.*

[B] France

[1] France Enforces EU Neighboring Right

In 2019, France had adopted the new EU Digital Copyright Directive which contained a provision directing compensation for publishers and news organizations for the use of their content. This is the so-called neighboring rights provision.

This is the law under which the French competition authority sought to compel Google to provide good faith compensation to contact providers and which it found Google had failed to comply with.[409]

It remains to be seen whether other tech companies will suffer similar punishment about their use of the content or extracts of the content provided by third parties.

This may also affect generative AI creators who are "training" their generative AI systems with materials created by third parties.

[C] The Threat of Internet Piracy

"Internet Piracy" constitutes illegal accessing, using, copying, or sharing of IP via the Internet without permission of the IP owner.

Internet IP piracy is a huge problem:[410]

- There are around 220 billion views of pirated videos annually.
- Pirate streaming sites are responsible for more than 75% of online piracy worldwide.
- Internet video piracy may cost the U.S. economy as much as USD 60 billion in losses annually.
- 126.7 billion viewings worth of U.S.-produced TV episodes are pirated every year.
- More than 50,000 U.S. jobs are lost a year because of music piracy.
- Around the world, the movie industry loses as much as USD 75 billion a year from Internet piracy.
- Nearly a quarter of global Internet bandwidth is used to download copyrighted media.

In 2017, in the U.S. alone, there were more than 17 billion visits to Internet piracy sites.

In China, where cheap copies of protected IP products are common, there is even a special name for them, "Shanzhai." There has been significant theft and imitation of popular brands:

409. *Ibid.*
410. Damjan Jugovic Spajic, "Piracy Is Back: Statistics for 2021," *DataProt*, online, March 19, 2021.

> This is a society where, if you open a fake Apple Store, people start writing articles about how innovative and creative you are.[411]

An example of how this threat can affect academia is found on the website, described above, called the Sci-Hub website, created by a woman in Almaty, Kazakhstan, by the name of Alexandra Elbakyan.

Perhaps the gravest threat to intellectual property is that its production will be curtailed because the hacking and theft of intellectually created material on the Internet will become so extensive that those who produce it will lose interest in doing this kind of work because their ability to earn a profit from this work will be greatly reduced or indeed lost altogether.

[1] Danger from the Internet of Things

The problems that the Internet presents in protecting IP or private data are only growing.

In recent years, we have moved beyond accessing information on the Internet to allowing the Internet access to our growing list of "connected devices," often without our intervention or even without our knowledge:

> A new study has found that most Internet of things devices routinely deliver an ocean of sensitive data to partners around the world frequently without making these data transfers secure or transparent to the end-user.[412]

A joint collaboration between Northeastern University and Imperial College London looked at 81 popular smart TVs, streaming dongles, smart speakers and video doorbells made by Google, Roku, Amazon, etc.

In 34,000 experiments, they found that 72 of the devices made contact with someone other than the manufacturer.[413]

§16.07 PROTECTION OF IP

What positive steps can be taken to protect IP and oneself from illegal internet intrusion and theft? There are several.

Basic protections include the following:

- Be careful on public networks because others may be able to listen to you and/or get access to your data;
- Make sure that cyber systems are up to date. New threats are constantly coming online;

411. Kenneth Rapoza, *Forbes Magazine*, online, July 22, 2012.
412. Karl Bode, "The Internet of Things Is Still a Privacy Dumpster Fire, Study Finds," *Vice*, online, September 19, 2019.
413. *Ibid.*

- Make sure all software and cyber-security protections are current and are allowed to accept automatic updates;
- Use complex passwords. Make sure all users use complex passwords all the time and change them regularly;
- Backup and encrypt key data.

It is also important to get detailed information about the state of legal IP protection in the countries where one does business. There are many online sources of information about this, but the detailed report published online by the U.S. Representative is very useful.[414]

In it, there is an extensive description of the protection and enforcement of IP Rights around the world. It describes the laws, policies, and practices of the world's countries in their treatment of IP.

The report also includes a "Priority Watch List" of the countries that the U.S. considers to have the weakest record in IP protection. Those include Algeria, Argentina, Chile, China, India, Indonesia, Kuwait, Russia, Saudi Arabia, Ukraine and Venezuela.

There is a "Watch List" of countries that cause the U.S. concern about the strength of their IP protection. Those include Bolivia, Brazil, Canada, Columbia, Costa Rica, Dominican Republic, Ecuador, Egypt, Greece, Guatemala, Jamaica, Lebanon, Mexico, Pakistan, Paraguay, Peru, Romania, Switzerland, Thailand, Turkey, Turkmenistan, UAE, Uzbekistan, and Vietnam.

One may not agree with the conclusions of the Report about the IP protections provided by certain countries, but if one is doing business in those countries or internationally, it does provide things to consider.

It also offers the following strategies for business IP protection:

- Does your business understand the most influential tech changers? Are you investing in any? Are you paying attention to the opportunities they provide you and your competitors?
- Does your company have a board-level presence and a business culture that fosters understanding of your IP at every level? Does your head of IP have the ear of the top decision-makers?
- Does your IP strategy match the pace of change in your market by planning for the short, medium and long term?

414. https://ustr.gov/sites/default/files/2019_Special_301_Report.pdf.

CHAPTER 17
AI and Competition Law

AI is expanding both in application and public awareness at a time when competition regulators around the world are already taking a careful look at the competitive influence of large tech companies in the cyber world.

This raises questions as to how the presence of AI systems will change the competitive position of tech companies and how it will change the ways in which competition regulation authorities will evaluate the competitive positions of tech companies in the cyber markets.

§17.01 COMPETITION CONCERNS WITH BIG TECH

As the sizes of the major Internet companies such as Google, Facebook, Amazon, Apple, and Microsoft (collectively, Big Tech) have grown, there has been growing concern about their power, and, in particular, the power to limit or eliminate competitors.

Consequently, there has risen significant concern in the U.S., the EU and in other countries that large Internet companies are in danger of violating or actually violating legal and regulatory prohibitions against anti-competitive behavior.

This concern is partly due to regulators' perceptions about the difficulty of competing with companies so large and so wealthy, but it is also a result of the fact that big Internet companies have been buying up related companies to increase their reach in their business areas and to eliminate potential competitors.

§17.02 COVID-19 PANDEMIC

Another powerful impetus to their growth and wealth has been the COVID-19 Pandemic.

Because the response of many countries has been to put their populations under lockdown, severely limiting their ability to leave their dwellings to shop in person, many people turned to the Internet to order goods and to communicate with friends and relatives.

People have also been working from home to a significant degree, which has increased their need to use the Internet and to have efficient, up-to-date computer equipment and systems.

Among the greatest beneficiaries of the Pandemic, although accidental, have been the Big Tech companies, including Apple, Amazon, Meta (Facebook), Microsoft and Google. The results of the Pandemic increased usage of their services and products, made them more essential worldwide, and increased their wealth, making it easier to consolidate and expand their businesses.

These giants have recently made key purchases or commenced business projects that have given competition regulators around the world serious cause for concern.

As The Economist asked in an August 2023 article:[415] "Can anything stop big tech?"

§17.03 COMPETITION LAW

The philosophy behind anti-competition laws is that the public benefits from having competition in commerce allows the public more choice and may offer better prices for goods and services.

This is a view that has been adopted by the governments of many countries around the world, particularly those countries with market economies. To preserve those benefits, many countries have adopted laws and regulations to prevent any commercial operation from being so powerful that it is in the position to exclude competitors from the markets in question and/or dictate prices and/or terms of service that are detrimental to the public.

The basic goal of competition law is to prevent any one person or company, or any cooperating group, from becoming so powerful or influential in a market that they can exclude competitors, prevent new competitors from entering the market, and/or abuse their market power as the only remaining choice in a market to demand excessive compensation for their goods and services.

There are different ways that commercial organizations can seek to gain such market power. One way is to conspire with others to exclude new potential competitors from the marketplace. Another way is to purchase other similar companies in the market to reduce the number of competitors or eliminate competitors altogether. Another way is to temporarily make one's prices and/or terms of service much more favorable than those of competitors, for example, by offering goods and services below cost that competitors who are less financially strong are unable to compete and may be forced to leave the market.

Engaging in actions to try and achieve such market power is called anti-competitive behavior, and most developed countries have laws and regulations to

415. The Economist, "Can Big Tech Keep Getting Bigger in the Age of AI?, online at: economist.com, August 02, 2023.

protect their markets and to encourage the discovery of reasonable prices for goods and services in markets.

Failure to obey these laws and regulations against anti-competitive behavior can result in violators being penalized with civil suits, fines, criminal prosecution and possibly being barred from the markets in question.

The competition laws in various countries may differ somewhat, but their essential goals are usually the ones described above.

[A] AI and Competition

The market for AI products is a submarket of the overall market for cyber products and services. As will be seen in the following parts of this chapter, competition regulators are already paying serious attention to the market power of Big Tech companies such as Google, Facebook, Apple, Microsoft, and others.

The regulatory examinations of the competitive positions and behavior of some Big Tech companies have resulted, in some cases, in fines and injunctions to punish and modify what has come to be regarded as anti-competitive behavior.

The injection of AI systems into markets adds a different aspect to the issue of market power. This is due to the following facts:

- AI systems may attract market participants who have not previously been seriously active in cyber markets. That can expand and change the definitions of relevant cyber markets.
- Companies that have not previously dominated important segments of the cyber markets may significantly increase their market power because of their involvement in the creation, marketing and operation of AI systems, products and related services.
- Some big tech companies that have already been dominant in various parts of the cyber market may be able to expand their market power because of their involvement in the expansion of AI systems and services.
- There is also a concern that certain companies, already more advanced in the development of AI systems, that are usually competitors, may be tempted to join together to use their advances in AI to collectively dominate markets, fix prices and/or exclude competition.

§17.04 COMPETITION THREAT OF BIG TECH

Although the so-called Big Tech companies, Amazon, Apple, Alphabet (Google), Mehta (Facebook) and Microsoft, are beginning to be prominently mentioned participants in the "AI Gold Rush." There is little question that their size, penetration of the cyber markets, and financial power gives them advantages that may, over time, permit them to dominate the rapidly growing market for AI products.

It was reported that their economic performance in mid-2023 continues to be spectacular. At the end of July of that year, it was reported that Alphabet, Meta, and Microsoft collectively gained USD 106 billion in operating profits between January and June 2023, more than USD 9 billion above the collective profits for the same period in 2022. In the second quarter of 2023, Apple reported its highest earnings ever.[416]

An article in The Economist commented:

> ... [I]nvestors expect the tech giants, with their deep technological insights and even deeper pockets, to capture the spoils of artificial intelligence ...
>
> When ExxonMobil and GE were the titans of America Inc. in the 1990s and 2000s, their revenues were rising at an average annual rate of 5 to 6% and their net profits at 5 to 10% or so. The tech giants have been growing at 16% and 13%, respectively, for a decade or more.[417]

This raises the question as to how much of a threat the economic power and digital experience of the tech giants will be to fair competition in the new field of AI and how determined competition regulators will be in protecting a "level playing field" for the participants in the market for AI-related products? Can the expanding market power of the tech giants be controlled for the sake of competition?

Some doubt is being expressed as to whether competition regulators are up to the job:

> Do not look to regulators to stop their march. Last month a court threw out an effort by America's trustbusters to block Microsoft's acquisition of Activision Blizzard, a games developer. The markets have shrugged off other fitful efforts to reign in the tech giants, such as the EU's new rules for digital markets.[418]

It has been suggested that "their size" could be a brake on the ability of Big Tech to continue to grow in power. The argument is that they simply cannot keep up the speed of their expansion indefinitely.[419] That remains to be seen.

§17.05 BIG TECH CAN GROW WITH AI

One way for the Big Tech companies to keep growing is to expand into new markets. The Big Tech companies give every sign of enthusiastically expanding into providing AI systems and related products.

Microsoft is already offering AI tools as an addition to Microsoft 365. Meta and Google will be providing AI assistance for their advertising customers.[420]

Microsoft has been the backer of the generative AI system created by OpenAI.

416. Vincent Kilbride, "A giant conundrum. Can big tech keep getting bigger in the age of AI?," *The Economist*, online, August 02, 2023.
417. *Ibid.*
418. *Ibid.*
419. *Ibid.*
420. *Ibid.*

[A] ChatGPT

This chatbot has received the most attention and has been the most widely used since it became well-known in late 2022. Microsoft shows no signs of slowing down its pursuit of AI expansion.

The other tech giants are keeping pace:

> [In late July of 2023], Apple indicated it was building its expertise in the area. Tim Cook, the chief executive, called AI and machine learning "core, fundamental technologies that are integral to virtually every product that we build."
>
> Every division of Amazon is said to be working on generative AI projects.[421]

§17.06 OTHER FORMS OF MARKET DOMINATION

[A] Education Market

[1] Google

There is another area that is causing concern because of perceived market domination. It has been argued that Google is becoming too dominant in the education sector through Chromebook laptops and Google's Chrome operating system.[422]

During the pandemic, the Chrome system expanded its reach because so much education was moved online. Google appears to have sprung into action to take advantage of this.

During this time, Google has promoted a number of its free Google education apps, the use of which has given Google an enormous amount of data about students and their schools:

They have introduced 40 new models of Chromebook laptops, many upgrades of its education products and AI tools that allow students to have, in effect, conversations with the Internet through their laptops.

While much of this appears to offer significant benefits to educational institutions and their students, and in many respects probably does offer important benefits, it also raises important privacy and ethical issues.

Among the important ones is the fact that the adoption of the hardware and software of a particular supplier, such as Google, makes an educational system worryingly dependent on that company and provides an enormous amount of concern about how educational institutions and their individual students use the Internet system.[423]

---

421. Katie Prescott, "Soaring Cost of Chips Will Hit Use of AI, Warns Slack Chief Lidiane Jones," *The Times*, online, August 07, 2023.
422. Vista Point Advisors, "The Implications for EdTech of Google's Market Share in Education," online at: vistapointadvisors.com, July 29, 2021.
423. Jawad Iqbal, "Tech Giants Have Gained Too Much Power in Schools," *The Times*, online June 07, 2021.

In 2023, Google expanded its offerings to include AI tools and systems.[424]

The question that arises is whether any legislative steps should be taken to limit the amount of penetration that any tech company can be allowed to have into a system influencing the thoughts and behavior of generations of students.

However, the trade-off that must be considered is whether the benefits of the educational tools provided by any particular tech giant outweigh the dangers that their participation raises? Exploration of this issue needs to be done by educational authorities and other government officials.

[2] Microsoft

However, it is hard to ignore the parallel between Google's actions and the penetration of Microsoft systems software and Internet tools into many aspects of the private and business lives of people all over the world. As the importance of computers grew, Microsoft grew with it, providing tools to operate personal computers and communicate with the Internet. Consequently, Microsoft has obtained, whether intentionally or by accident, a huge amount of knowledge and data about how the computing and Internet worlds work and how Microsoft customers interact with them.

Although Google has a significant amount of power in the world of computing systems and is apparently making efforts to expand that power, there is little doubt that they are dwarfed by Microsoft in the areas of education, business, and communications. Microsoft is now using AI products to expand in all these areas.[425]

However, there needs to be more examination of the harm this may be doing and whether it makes sense to legally limit Microsoft to a greater degree than existing legislation permits.

[3] Apple

There are similar issues with Apple products.

These days it is possible for a university professor to look out over a classroom of their students and be facing a wall of silver-colored laptops with the Apple logo.

Although other companies may have been more subtle about their approach to gaining influence in the educational sector, Apple never has.

They have always made open and public efforts to attract students and educational institutions to their products by providing tools and operating systems, often with student discounts, that were compatible with what they believed were the interests and aims of the educational community, as well as the artistic community.

424. Product Announcements: "A New Era for AI and Google Workspace" online at: workspace.google.com, March 14, 2023.
425. "AI Platform, Tools and Services," online at: microsoft.com, accessed November 01, 2023.

In 2023, Apple was reported to be making extensive efforts to develop AI products.[426]

§17.07 OTHER BIG TECH EXPANSION MOVES

The Big Tech companies are engaging in other expansions.

[A] Amazon

Amazon has hired 175,000 people since March 2020, has acquired more airplanes for delivery and has been in talks to acquire a driverless vehicle company.

[B] Microsoft

Microsoft has bought three more cloud computing companies.

In January 2023, Microsoft said it was going to acquire the gaming company, Activision Blizzard. This has met with a mixed reception from competition authorities around the world. For example, the EU has permitted the acquisition, but the U.S. and the UK initially blocked it. The purchase was characterized as the "world's largest gaming acquisition."

In the field of AI, Microsoft is already promoting itself as one of the leaders in the field with a range of programs and controls to permit the development of AI systems.

For example, Microsoft is already promoting its "Azure AI platform, services and solutions" as tools to "Innovate and accelerate with powerful tools and services that bring artificial intelligence to every developer."[427]

Microsoft also offers an "AI School."

In its online "AI platform video," a narrator says that with Microsoft AI tools: "... [Y]ou can find your own use case and how you want to change the world."

This appears to be a promotion of universal and unlimited ambition in the field of AI that Microsoft is pitching to "every developer."

If Microsoft is successful in persuading "every developer" of AI, or a significant percentage of the AI developer population, to adopt the Azure AI "framework,"[428] it remains to be seen whether the competition authorities in different jurisdictions will find that a regulatory response is necessary.

[C] Apple

Apple has bought at least four other companies during 2020.

---

426. Jake Piazza, "Apple, Caught by Surprise in Generative AI Boom, to Spend $1 Billion per Year to Catch Up," online at cnbc.com, October 23, 2023.
427. Microsoft, "Azure AI platform, services and solutions," online at: microsoft.com, accessed August 04, 2023.
428. *Ibid.*

The accidental boost these Big Tech companies got from the unfortunate COVID-19 Pandemic has not only increased their business but has also made them more essential to more people.[429]

This extraordinary increase in the reach and the power of the Big Tech companies has concentrated the minds of competition regulators throughout the developed world. The reactions of governments and regulators have not been concluded yet.

§17.08 GPUs

Another problem for competition may come from the increasing cost of the sophisticated chips needed to power AI.

By mid-2023, the rapid increase in the interest in creating and using AI systems led to a shortage in the specialized components needed for AI.[430] The share price of NVIDIA, the best-known maker of the powerful GPUs necessary to power AI systems, has risen dramatically since late 2022. The growing demand for these kinds of GPUs has led to shortages and price increases.

In November of 2023, NVIDIA announced the launch of "its most advanced super-chip to date, with greater memory, and the ability to train AI models more quickly."[431]

This may mean that access to the tools necessary to build AI-related products will be limited to those competitors that can buy more and pay more for them. It is hard to imagine that in the cost battle, there are many that can compete with Google (Alphabet), Apple, Facebook (Meta) and/or Microsoft.

In summary, the power and potential of AI systems and services may cause dramatic changes in the distribution of market power in cyber-related businesses and activities.

This may cause market competition regulators throughout the world to scrutinize the cyber-related markets more closely and cause those regulators to feel a need to be even tougher when judging whether behavior in those markets has the potential to damage competition or the quality of life of the public generally.

For purposes of this book, prominent jurisdictions where governments are seeking to enforce tough anti-competition laws are the United States and the EU, although some others will be discussed in the context of particular situations.

§17.09 REGULATORY RESPONSES

[A] U.S.

The U.S. has a strong history of anti-trust enforcement dating from the end of the nineteenth century when Congress took action against the gigantic and powerful oil company called Standard Oil that was owned by John D. Rockefeller.

429. Isaac, June 15, 2020.
430. Katie Prescott, August 07, 2023, as cited above.
431. Katie Prescott, "Nvidia's new H200 chip takes AI to next level," *The Times* online, November 14, 2023.

The legislation that resulted from this effort is known as the Sherman Antitrust Act of 1890. (Sherman Act).[432]

The Sherman Act focuses on preventing two types of anti-competitive behavior. The first is preventing powerful market participants from achieving a "monopoly" in their market where they are virtually, or actually, the only company offering particular goods or services to the public. This provision was specifically aimed at Standard Oil which had achieved the position of being so large and powerful in the oil business that no other company could effectively compete with it.

The second is to prevent "combinations and conspiracies in restraint of trade," where business organizations conspire with one or more competitors to fix prices or terms of service to disadvantage other competitors and or to reduce the choices of the public when purchasing goods or services in the markets in question.

From these basic principles, a very large body of anti-trust laws, regulations and interpretive court cases has developed. This is not the place to detail all of those. With respect to questions about any particular matter, qualified expert advisors will need to be consulted.

However, because the Internet is a system that operates throughout the world, it is important to remember that many activities will probably involve transactions with U.S. citizens or U.S. residents. That may bring non-U.S. persons and businesses using the Internet within the jurisdiction of U.S. courts.

U.S. courts will often take jurisdiction over "foreign" activities that directly or indirectly affect the domestic or foreign commerce of the United States. A U.S. court may find that a market that is not "exclusively" a foreign market is part of U.S. commerce.[433]

Also, in U.S. antitrust cases, litigants can request jury trials and treble damages can be awarded.

[1] U.S. Antitrust Action

Amazon, Apple, Facebook, and Google are all under U.S. government investigation about the issue of whether they are restricting competition, particularly when they are also acting as a "gate keeper" through which competing companies get access to potential customers.

In June 2019, the U.S. Justice Department opened an antitrust investigation of major technology firms. It was reported that the Justice Department will be looking into whether Big Tech's online activities have injured competition, interfered with innovation, or harmed consumers.

The Justice Department and the FTC are examining possible anticompetitive practices by Amazon, Apple, and Facebook and have already begun a suit against Google.

432. 26 Stat. 209, 15 U.S.C. Sections 1-7.

433. *Transnor (Bermuda) v. BP North America Petroleum*, 738 F. Supp. 1472 (S.D.N.Y. 1990).

[2] U.S. Dept. of Justice Sues "Monopolist" Google

On October 20, 2020, the U.S. Department of Justice (DOJ) published a notice online entitled, "Justice Department Sue's Monopolist Google for Violating Antitrust Laws."[434]

The Department stated that its goal was to restore competition in the search and search advertising markets.

It was reportedly the largest anti-trust action brought by the DOJ in about 20 years. The department was joined in this action by the state Attorneys General of Arkansas, Florida, Georgia, Indiana, Kentucky, Louisiana, Mississippi, Missouri, Montana, South Carolina and Texas.

The regulators reportedly will also investigate how Google has used its dominance of Internet searches to move into other areas of Internet business, including video, emails, maps, cloud computing, quantum computing and AI.[435]

§17.10 HARM TO CONSUMERS

A principal question raised by such an action will be establishing how consumers have been harmed.

Obviously, it is convenient for many Internet users to search for information using Google, and that basic service is provided by Google without payment. Nevertheless, Google has allegedly used its market power and the vast amounts of money it has earned from its search engine to pay other major Internet companies, such as Apple, to make the Google search app the default search platform on the devices Apple sells, such as MacBooks, iPads and iPhones.[436]

§17.11 FEDERAL TRADE COMMISSION

The DOJ of the U.S. has the power and the track record for bringing anti-competition cases in the U.S. that are related to anti-competitive behavior. However, the principal "regulator" of competition-related matters is the U.S. FTC.

It is certainly the case that both the DOJ and the FTC have access to criminal and administrative law sanctions that will be applicable to cases involving AI in the same way that they are applicable to many other kinds of market-related cases.

In addition, the U.S. government has generally been concerned with AI-related developments, and those particular agencies have expressed views on how they may respond to problems relating to AI.

---

434. Justice.gov.
435. As of November 2023, this suit is ongoing as *United States v. Google LLC (2020)*.
436. Simon Duke, "If the tech giants can't be tamed by new laws, then they should be broken up," *The Times*, October 01, 2020, online, retrieved October 01, 2020. https://www.thetimes.co.uk/article/breaking-up-big-tech-may-be-the-least-worst-choice-dftfn22jd?shareToken=bb1b6d237a194cb9557e94095918e201.

In April 2023, officials of the FTC and the DOJ, along with other federal agencies, released a "Joint Statement on AI."[437]

"FTC chair Lina M. Khan and officials from three other federal agencies jointly pledged today to uphold America's commitment to the core principles of fairness, equality, and justice as emerging automated systems, including those sometimes marketed as "artificial intelligence" or "AI," become increasingly common in our daily lives—impacting civil rights, fair competition, consumer protection, and equal opportunity."

§17.12 U.S. DOJ

The DOJ has considered how to respond to the penetration of AI into the international cyber world. In December 2020, the DOJ published a 13-page document entitled "Artificial Intelligence Strategy for the U.S. Department of Justice."[438] This set out how the DOJ intended to deal with AI, how it would structure its workforce to respond to the challenges, and what were considered its goals to be at that time:

> "This strategy is the result of a department-wide effort led by our Chief Technology Officer and provides a foundational framework that will provide a coordinated approach to AI".[439]

At that time, the DOJ Strategy emphasized familiarizing its workforce with developments in AI and adopting AI solutions where they would help the DOJ in carrying out its missions.[440]

To assist in its responsibilities related to AI, the DOJ uses the National Institute of Justice (NIJ), which is "the research, development and evaluation agency" of the DOJ, "dedicated to improving knowledge and understanding of crime and justice issues through science."[441]

As early as 2018, the NIJ focused on using AI to deal with criminal cases.[442]

In an article in 2018, Christopher Rigano pointed out:

> Even public safety and criminal justice are benefitting from AI. For example, traffic safety systems identify violations and enforce the rules of the road, and crime forecasts allow for more efficient allocation of policing resources. AI is also helping to identify the potential for an individual under criminal justice supervision to reoffend. ... Research supported by NIJ is helping to lead the way in applying AI to

437. Federal Trade Commission, "FTC Chair Khan and Officials from DOJ, CFPB (Consumer Financial Protection Bureau, and the EEOC (Equal Employment Opportunities Commission), Release Joint Statement on AI," online at: ftc.gov, April 25, 2023.
438. Office of the Chief Information Officer, U.S. Department of Justice, "Artificial Intelligence Strategy for the U.S. Department of Justice," (DOJ Strategy) online at: justice.gov.
439. Melinda Rogers, Deputy Assistant Attorney General, Chief Information Officer, Chief Data Officer, DOJ, DOJ Strategy, p. 3.
440. DOJ Strategy, p. 4.
441. National Institute of Justice, "About the National Institute of Justice" online at: nij.ojp.gov., May 02, 2022.
442. Christopher Rigano, "Using Artificial Intelligence to Address Criminal Justice Needs," NIJ, online October 08, 2018, accessed August 09, 2023.

address criminal justice needs, such as identifying individuals and their actions in videos relating to criminal activity or public safety, DNA analysis, gunshot detection and crime forecasting.[443]

§17.13 A SELECTION OF DOJ AND FTC AI-RELATED CASES

[A] *Haitao Xiang Algorithm Theft* Case (November 21, 2019) (DOJ)

Haitao Xaing, 42, formerly of Chesterfield, Missouri, was indicted today by a federal grand jury on one count of conspiracy to commit economic espionage, three counts of economic espionage, one count of conspiracy to commit theft of trade secrets, and three counts of theft of trade secrets. ... Monsanto and The Climate Corporation developed a digital, on-line farming software platform that was used by farmers to collect, store and visualize critical agricultural field data and increase and improve agricultural productivity for farmers. ... Xiang promoted himself to the Chinese government based on his experience at Monsanto. Within a year of being selected as a Talent Plan recruit, he quit his job, bought a one-way ticket to China, and was caught at the airport with a copy of the company's proprietary algorithm before he could spirit it away.[444]

[B] *Meta Platforms Inc. Advertising* Case (June 21, 2022)

The Department of Justice announced today that it has obtained a settlement agreement resolving allegations that Meta-Platforms Inc., formerly known as Facebook Inc., has engaged in discriminatory advertising in violation of the fair housing act (FHA). The proposed agreement resolved in the lawsuit was filed today in the US District Court for the Southern District of New York alleging that Meta's housing advertising system discriminates against Facebook users based on their race, color, religion, sex, disability, familial status and national origin. ... Among other things, the complaint alleges that Meta uses algorithms in determining which Facebook users receive housing ads, and that those algorithms rely, in part, on characteristics protected under the FHA. This is the department's first case challenging algorithmic bias under the Fair Housing Act.[445]

[C] *Amazon: Child Privacy* Case

Proposed order to pay $25 million and delete children's data, geolocation data and other voice recordings.

The Federal Trade Commission and the Department of Justice will require Amazon to overhaul its deletion practices and implement stringent privacy safeguards to settle charges the company violated the Children's Online Privacy

443. *Ibid.*
444. Department of Justice, Press Release, "Chinese National Who Worked at Monsanto Indicted on Economic Espionage Charges," online at: justice.gov, November 21, 2019.
445. Department of Justice, Press Release, "Justice Department Secures Groundbreaking Settlement Agreement with Meta Platforms, Formerly Known as Facebook, to Resolve Allegations of Discriminatory Advertising," online at: justice.gov, June 21, 2022.

Protection Act Rule (COPPA Rule) and deceived parents and users of the Alexa voice assistant service about its data deletion practices. According to the complaint filed by the Department of Justice on behalf of the FTC, Amazon prevented parents from exercising their deletion rights under the COPPA Rule, kept sensitive voice and geolocation data for years and used it for its own purposes while putting data at risk of harm from unnecessary access.[446]

§17.14 PRIVATE SUITS

It is not only government regulatory investigations which are examining are concerned with the anti-competitive behavior of Big Tech. There will almost certainly be a large number of private antitrust suits in the future.

[A] *EPIC Suit v. Apple*

For example, the digital games developer Epic Games, creator of the popular Fortnite game, has reportedly brought a lawsuit in U.S. federal court against Apple, alleging that the commissions that Apple collects on in-app sales by developers using the App Store are "extortionate."[447]

Fortnite reportedly provoked a battle with Apple by creating its own in-app payment system, independent of Apple. When Apple learned of this, it banished Fortnite from its App Store. Fortnite claimed that Apple's behavior made it unfairly difficult for Fortnite and other developers to sell their products. Allegedly, Apple's rules were intended to give Apple a virtual "Monopoly" over the sale of developers' products by severely limiting the options they could choose as a place to market their products.[448]

In September 2021, it was reported that the federal court published a decision in *Epic* case saying that although the court could not declare Apple to be a monopoly, Apple was behaving in an anti-competitive manner by refusing to permit app creators that sold their products through Apple's App Store to purchase the products through their own purchase systems rather than exclusively through the App Store.[449]

The judge in the *Epic* case said that although Apple did control approximately 55% of the market, that did not, in itself, constitute a monopoly. The judge wrote, "Success is not illegal."[450]

---

446. Federal Trade Commission, "FTC and DOJ Charge Amazon with Violating Children's Privacy Law by Keeping Kids' Voice Recordings Forever and Undermining Parents' Deletion Requests," online at: ftc.gov, May 21, 2023.
447. James Clayton, "Apple faces Epic Games in court," BBC News, online, May 03, 2021.
448. *Ibid.*
449. Andrew Ross Sorkin, Jason Karaian, Sarah Kessler, Stephen Gandell, Lauren Hirsch, Ephrat Livini, and Anna Schaverien, "Why Apple Didn't Lose in the Epic Games Ruling: A judge's split decision in the lawsuit mostly went in favor of Big Tech," *The New York Times*, "Dealbook Newsletter," online, September 13, 2021.
450. *Ibid.*

Although they achieved one of their major goals—getting the right to sell their app through their own payment system rather than exclusively through Apple's system, Epic was reportedly still unhappy with the decision, and shortly after it was issued, Epic filed an appeal with the Ninth Circuit Court of Appeal, which ruled in Apple's favor, upholding the lower court decision that Apple was not a monopoly.[451]

§17.15 EU

[A] EU Anti-competition Law

EU anti-competition law has essentially the same goals as U.S. antitrust law. The European Commission says:

> Competition encourages companies to offer consumers goods and services on the most favorable terms. It encourages efficiency and innovation and reduces prices. To be effective competition requires companies to act independently of each other, but subject to the pressure exerted by their competitors.[452]

The basic EU anti-competition legislation is set out in Articles 101 and 102 of the Treaty on the Functioning of the European Union[453] (TFEU).

TFEU Article 101 prohibits anti-competitive agreements between two or more independent market operators.

TFEU Article 102 prohibits abusive behavior by companies holding a dominant position in any given market.

[B] EU Actions

[1] Google Fined

In June 2019, Google was fined USD 1.7 billion by European competition regulators for requiring online advertisers to sign exclusivity agreements that were found to be unfair to competing online advertising companies.[454]

[2] EU v. Amazon

In June 2020, the EU began preparing anti-competition charges against Amazon. The basis of their complaint is that Amazon abused its dominant market position in online commerce by attempting to block out less powerful rivals.[455]

451. *Ibid.*
452. European Commission, Competition Policy, Antitrust. ec.europa.eu.
453. *See also*, the European Commission, Antitrust Overview, ec.europa.eu.
454. Adam Satariano, "Google Fined $1.7 Billion by E.U. for Unfair Advertising Rules," *The New York Times* (online), March 20, 2019.
455. Adam Satariano, "Amazon Set to Face Antitrust Charges in European Union," *The New York Times* (online), June 11, 2020.

It has been reported that the investigation against Amazon is part of a broader EU investigation into the business practices of Apple and Facebook.

There is concern about Amazon's dual role of being not only a seller of goods on its own account but also a provider of a platform for Amazon competitors to sell goods online. It is reported that Amazon requires these subsidiary merchants to collect data that they are required to share with Amazon as a condition for being allowed to sell on the Amazon platform.[456]

[3] EU v. Apple

On June 17, 2020, The Times reported that the European Commission was beginning an investigation into whether rules that Apple imposed on app developers restricted competition and improperly benefited Apple.

This investigation comes from complaints from Spotify, a popular music streaming service, and Kobo, an online bookstore that Apple let iPad and iPhone users download apps only from Apple's own App Store. Apple then allegedly claims a substantial percentage (30% in the first year, 15% thereafter) of any payments or subscriptions made through those apps. Apple also allegedly forbids those companies from telling their customers (within those apps) that the goods or subscriptions can be bought more cheaply on the companies' own websites.[457]

Apple reportedly makes about $1 billion a month from app fees. Apple's policy of taking 15% to 30% of purchases through apps causes consumers to pay higher prices because to pay those fees, service providers like Spotify must raise their own prices.[458]

In addition, there is also said to be a conflict of interest created by the fact that Apple has now moved into providing its own music and video streaming services which competes with companies, such as Netflix or Spotify, who are using apps from Apple's App Store to sell their products.[459]

Such tactics by Apple may remind one of the activities of John D. Rockefeller, the 19th century founder of Standard Oil, who forced railroad companies that wanted his business to pay him a percentage of the fees they received from carrying the oil of companies competing with Standard Oil. It was Rockefeller's ruthless domination of the oil business that led to the original US anti-competition law, the Sherman Antitrust Act of 1890.

If Apple is found to have violated EU competition law, the European Commission could fine them an amount equal to 10% of Apple's global revenues. In 2022, those revenues were reportedly more than $394 billion.[460]

In 2019, Apple was reportedly charged by Spotify with "limiting choices and stifling innovation" by charging high commission fees in the App Store on "in app" purchases and forbidding companies offering their products on the App Store to offer

456. Satariano, June 11, 2020, *citing* Prof. William Kovacic of George Washington University.
457. *The Times*, online, Business, June 17, 2020.
458. *Ibid.*
459. *Ibid.*
460. Statista.com, November 16, 2023.

their customers alternatives. After reviewing the charges, in May 2021, the Commission agreed that Apple was breaking EU competition regulations by the way it was operating its App Store. As a result, Apple may be subject to significant fines and requirements that it modify the way it operates its App Store.[461]

The EU did not stop its investigation with the Spotify complaint. It has continued its investigation into the possible anti-competitive aspects of the way Apple operates its App Store, including whether its standard 30% commission on apps is a fair price. It is reported that many app developers are unhappy with Apple's App Store-connected charges, and a number of them have expressed their agreement with the preliminary findings of the Commission that Apple is engaging in anti-competitive behavior.[462]

Spotify is not the only developer to complain to the EU about Apple. In March 2020, Rakuten reportedly filed a complaint with the EU claiming that Apple was charging an anti-competitive commission on electronic books sold through its App Store while being in the conflicting position of promoting competing book sales through its Apple Books app.[463]

[4] France v. Google

A blow against Google's alleged market dominance has been struck in France.

In June 2020, French anti-competition regulators, under EU antitrust regulations, fined Google EUR 220 million for taking unfair advantage of its search engine dominance to establish a competitive advantage in sales of online ads.[464]

That is certainly a lot of money but is relatively small compared to the USD 41 billion in revenue earned by Google in 2020

The French regulator said that its decision would allow competitors of Google that were disadvantaged to seek damages.[465]

§17.16 UK

[A] UK Report on Google and Facebook

In December 2019, the UK Competition and Markets Authority (CMA) published a 283-page interim report from a market study which found that Google accounted for 90% of UK search advertising revenues (amounting to about £6 billion a year), and Facebook accounted for over half of display advertising revenues.

The report also said that Google and Facebook's domination of social media and search is so great that it could be driving up the prices of vacations, electronic goods,

461. Jane Wakefield, "Apple charged over 'anti-competitive' app policies," BBC News online, accessed May 03, 2021.
462. *Ibid.*
463. *Ibid.*
464. Mark Sweney, "France fines Google for abusing online advertising dominance," *The Guardian*, online, June 7, 2020.
465. *Ibid.*

and financial services. It said its profits are "well above any reasonable estimate of what might be expected."[466]

[B] Facebook

Take Facebook (Meta) for example. It has been reported in the New York Times[467] that Facebook has come under increasing scrutiny by competition regulators for its expansion around the globe. The UK has been particularly concerned about the expansion of Facebook's power.

[C] Gojek

Facebook reported that it had bought Gojek, an app from Southeast Asia that characterizes itself as a "super app" that allows one to book taxis, do shopping and make payments. Gojek has more than 3.3 million online reviews with an average score of 4.3.

This is given as one example of Facebook's expansion into the rapidly growing Asian online business market.

[D] Reliance Jo

Facebook has also reportedly made a USD 5.7 billion investment in Reliance Jo, a major Indian telecommunications company.

[E] Africa

Facebook is also reportedly spending many millions to construct a 37,000 kilometer-long fiber optic cable network around Africa.[468]

§17.17 GIPHY

Facebook also reportedly spent USD 400 million in May 2020 to purchase Giphy, a company with a catalog of film clips and animations that can be attached to messages to illustrate ideas that the sender wishes to express. Facebook saw this as an enhancement to Instagram.[469]

466. Andrew Ellison, "Consumer champion quits amid digital tax row," *The Times*, online, June 19, 2020.
467. Mike Isaac, "The Economy Is Reeling. The Tech Giants Spy Opportunity," *The New York Times* (online), Monday, June 15, 2020.
468. *Ibid.*
469. Kurt Wagner and Sarah Frier, "Facebook Buys Animated Image Library Giphy for $400 Million," Bloomberg News (online), May 20, 2020.

However, a little more than a year later, the UK Competition and Markets Authority indicated it would block the takeover of Giphy; in August 2021, the CMA finished an investigation of the takeover and concluded that allowing the acquisition by Facebook would significantly reduce competition in areas of social media and online advertising which would harm individual and businesses using the internet.

If Facebook refused to sell, the regulator could take them to court.

Facebook is already in some trouble with Giphy's investigation by the CMA. Facebook was accused of deliberately refusing to supply relevant information and was fined GBP 50.5 million.[470]

The principal advertising market said to be affected by Facebook's acquisition of Giphy is called the "display advertising" market, of which Facebook reportedly had a 50% share in 2020.

Giphy provides a type of animated image, called "gifs," that is useful in advertising on popular social media platforms such as TikTok, Twitter, Tinder, Slack and iMessage.[471] Facebook has responded that the conclusions of the regulator about the competitive harm of the takeover were "manifestly disproportionate." Facebook denied that it had significant market power in the relevant UK market and said that it would be "grossly unreasonable" for the regulator to block the acquisition.[472]

The CMA ordered Facebook to sell Giphy in November 2021.[473]

Now, the CMA has begun a wider investigation of whether Facebook has been misusing its market power to gain unfair advantages in digital advertising.

If they are found by the CMA to be guilty of that, they could be subject to large fines. The regulator is concerned that Facebook has prevented less powerful rivals from successfully competing with Facebook and has thereby reduced the choice of digital advertisers available to the public.

§17.18 FACEBOOK MARKETPLACE

One Facebook tactic that concerns the CMA is whether Facebook was unfairly using the data in its system to create new offerings to compete with others (such as eBay in the book market).

Facebook Marketplace is reported to be one such new feature.

§17.19 FACEBOOK SIGN-IN

Facebook is also reportedly using its sign-in procedure to allow its users to sign into multiple Facebook-related apps which are thought to automatically give it a competitive advantage over competing online sites such as dating and advertising sites.

470. Mark Sweney, "Facebook fined £50.5m for breaching order in Giphy takeover investigation," *The Guardian*, online, October 20, 2021.
471. Callum Jones, "Facebook fights Completion and Markets Authority over Giphy deal," *The Times*, online, September 9, 2021.
472. *Ibid.*
473. Mark Sweney, "UK competition watchdog orders Facebook owner to sell gif website Giphy," The Guardian, online, November 30, 2021.

§17.20 FACEBOOK ADVERTISING

The CMA has also begun investigating whether Facebook has been misusing its market power to gain unfair advantages in digital advertising.

The CMA is concerned that Facebook has prevented less powerful rivals from successfully competing with Facebook and has thereby reduced the choice of digital advertisers available to the public.

If they are found by the CMA to be guilty of anti-competitive abuses in the above market sectors, they could be subject to large fines.

If Facebook is found by the CMA to be in violation of applicable competition rules, it could be fined as much as 10% of its worldwide revenues which could add up to over USD 8 billion.[474]

§17.21 TAX ISSUES

It is not only market power that concerns regulators when considering whether their size creates unfair advantages.

The tax authorities in several countries are concerned that the structure of the Big Tech companies as large integrated companies allows them to avoid taxes by balancing the losses of some divisions against gains in others.

Consequently, there is talk of splitting these companies into separate taxable entities to allow taxation of the most profitable divisions of these companies.

For example, it is suggested that it might be useful to treat Amazon's Cloud Computing division as a separate company to allow taxation of its USD 1.6 billion in annual revenue.

There has been considerable concern that these companies are able to avoid their taxation by shifting their profits and losses among the different jurisdictions in which they trade which usually have different and/or contradictory tax regimes. To counter this, there is currently a proposal before the G7 countries to require large companies to pay taxes where they sell their products instead of where they declare their profits.[475]

§17.22 APPLE EU TAX RULING

For example, in November 2023:

> An adviser to the European Union's top court dealt a major blow to Apple in its $14 billion tax dispute [with the EU] ... after recommending that a lower court ruling in favor of the iPhone maker should be set aside due to legal errors... The EU's top court is expected to issue a ruling on the matter in the next few months.[476]

---

474. Tom Knowles, "Facebook investigated by UK watchdog over digital dominance," *The Times*, online, June 05, 2021, accessed June 07, 2021.
475. Simon Duke, "G7 plans new approach to stop tech giants avoiding tax," *The Times*, online, June 09, 2021.
476. Siladtya Ray, "Apple May Be Forced To Pay $14 Billion in EU Taxes After Legal Setback," Forbes, online, November 09, 2023.

[A] Other Regulators

However, antitrust regulators around the world are certainly not finished using anti-trust to reduce the market dominance of giant Internet companies.[477]

[1] China

China had taken dramatic steps to reduce the financial power of the owner of Alibaba (part of the Ant Group).

In September 2021, there were reports that the Chinese government is considering requiring Alibaba founder Jack Ma to separate the lending business of the group and turn over user data to a state-owned group.

Additional potential weakening of the Ma's Ant Group is also reported in that part of the Ant Group may come under partial government ownership. This is all part of a recent Chinese government effort to reduce the market power of large Chinese Internet companies that have achieved close to monopoly positions.[478]

[2] Russia

It is not only in the Western countries where there is concern about the market dominance of Big Tech.

For example, in late August 2021, Russia's anti-monopoly agency fined the online hotel booking company Booking.com a record Russian ruble equivalent of EUR 14.9 million for dominating the hotel booking market.[479] The Russians concluded that Booking was abusing its dominant market position and fined that Netherlands company RUB 1.3 billion.[480]

[B] Other Countries Concerned

The above are not the only countries worried about the expansion of the powerful tech companies.

Apparently, the large companies in the tech industry have become so powerful that they are attracting the attention of competition regulators in other parts of the world, such as Australia, Brazil and India.

477. Adam Satariano, "Google to Pay $270 Million to Settle Antitrust Charges in France," *The New York Times*, online, June 07, 2021.
478. Andrew Ross Sorkin, Jason Karaian, Sarah Kessler, Stephen Gandell, Lauren Hirsch, Ephrat Livini, and Anna Schaverien, "Beijing reportedly wants to break up Alipay," *The New York Times*, "Dealbook Newsletter," online, September 13, 2021.
479. "Russia fines Booking.com record 14.9 Euros for alleged market dominance," *Euronews*, online, August 27, 2021.
480. Euronews, online, August 27, 2021.

[C] Choices

As societies interested in the intellectual, social and moral development of their children are becoming more skeptical with turning young people over to these Big Tech?

There is concern about whether existing laws make it plain enough how the influence of these tech companies should be limited? Will the growth of AI and the early penetrations of that market by Big Tech companies allow them to make their market power even more difficult to control?

Investigations, suits and regulatory fines in the EU, the UK and the United States may be only the start of the regulatory hurdles that may be imposed on large and rapidly growing tech companies.[481]

The enthusiastic expansion of the Big Tech companies into AI products will probably intensify their scrutiny by regulators.

It is not only the enormous success of these companies but also the concern that Big Tech may use that success to harm competitors and the public that attracts the attention of competition regulators.[482]

Bill Baer, who is a fellow at the Brookings Institute, wrote in April 2020 that even during a time of an economic emergency such as that caused by the COVID-19 pandemic, regulators should not relax, but rather focus, their market scrutiny on possible anticompetitive practices during such difficult times.

He pointed out that although marketers of essential goods might claim that they are not raising prices but merely “stabilizing” prices, it should not be forgotten that agreements by competitors to fix prices are still illegal under anti-trust law.[483]

The concern that the U.S. government along with the European Union and other national regulators have is that tech companies like Apple, Microsoft, Amazon, Google and Facebook have become so dominant in their markets that they are in the position of essentially being monopolies in their primary market sectors.

If this proposition is proved by the regulators that are investigating these tech giants, governments may consider it necessary to pass new laws to limit the power of such companies.

§17.23 BREAK UP INTERNET GIANTS?

If existing anti-competition laws do not accomplish what they are intended to do, the U.S., the European Union, and other major market regulators may determine that these giants need to be broken up or restricted to operation only in specific market sectors.[484]

---

481. Satariano, June 11, 2020, *citing* Prof. William Kovacic of George Washington University.
482. Satariano, June 11, 2020, *citing* Bill Baer, former antitrust enforcement head at the U.S. DOJ.
483. Bill Baer, “Why we need antitrust enforcement during the Covid-19 pandemic,” Brookings Institute (online), April 22, 2020.
484. *Ibid.*

CHAPTER 18
Privacy and Data Protection

§18.01 INTERNATIONAL HUMAN RIGHTS TO PRIVACY AND DATA PROTECTION

In 1948, the United Nations General Assembly published the Universal Declaration of Human Rights (UDHR). Article 12 declares:

> No one shall be subjected to arbitrary interference with his privacy, family, home or correspondence, nor to attacks upon his honor and reputation. Everyone has the right to the protection of the law against such interference or attacks.[485]

This would seem to condemn the "arbitrary interference" that certain AI systems may pose through "training" or other activities to collect and organize data about individuals.

In addition to this, approximately 18 human rights conventions and treaties have been proposed and adopted. Through the process of signing and ratification of such treaties and conventions, such rights have become part of the law of many countries.

Over 190 countries have ratified the UDHR, including the U.S., the UK, and Member States of the EU, but its status as enforceable law varies from jurisdiction to jurisdiction.

Nevertheless, the "training" of AI systems and other AI-related cyber data gathering and classification would seem to be opposed, or at least severely restricted, by many human rights, privacy and data protection laws and regulations.

§18.02 PRIVACY AND DATA PROTECTION

One of the earliest restrictions on the use of Internet data has been privacy laws that limited the ability of those who found personal data on the Internet to use that data

485. United Nations, "Universal Declaration of Human Rights," online at: un.org, accessed October 10, 2023.

without the permission of the persons the data referred to. This restriction would apply to certain AI uses as well.

The development of the Internet and the appearance of a variety of personal information about individuals has required the addition of laws and regulations and, in some cases, international treaties and conventions about the protection and use of that data.

Initially, these laws and regulations were directed principally at individuals or private parties using this data without the express permission of the people to whom the data are referred. These laws and regulations would apply to AI systems uses as well. However, in recent years, a serious additional concern has been added. That is the use and collection of personal information by government agencies online.

This state recording and collection of data on its citizens has increasingly become a subject of debate about whether it interferes with the fundamental rights of citizens.

Often, this state data gathering began as a well-meaning attempt to monitor the activities of potential terrorists and prevent terrorist attacks within a country's borders. However, it quickly became apparent that so much data was being recorded and collected that most of it had nothing to do with terrorist suspects but was about the daily lives of ordinary citizens as they went about their work, interacted with their families, and communicated with their friends.

The scope of this concern was brought to light by the well-known case of Edward Snowden.

The news about that case reported that both U.S. and British intelligence agencies have been accessing and retaining the sensitive private data of innocent individuals for years.[486]

There is a significant contrast in the way that the protection of privacy and data on the Internet is dealt with in different countries.

[A] US

At the federal level, the US has specific federal laws dealing with privacy and data that would apply to AI uses in certain circumstances. There are also laws aimed at consumer protection are by individual US States.[487] Some examples of these are the following.

[1] Privacy Act of 1974

There is the Privacy Act of 1974 that deals with citizens' rights regarding data maintained by the government. Under the Privacy Act, U.S. citizens have certain rights

486. *The Times* (online), "MI5 'illegally holds sensitive private data on thousands'," Wednesday, June 12, 2020. See also, James Ball, Julian Borger and Glenn Greenwald, "Revealed: how US and UK spy agencies defeat internet privacy and security," *The Guardian*, online, September 06, 2013.

487. Andy Green, "Complete Guide to Privacy Laws in the US," https://www.varonis.com/blog/us-privacy-laws/.

with respect to that data. Citizens have the right to access and copy data held by government agencies. If there are errors in this data, citizens have the right to have the errors corrected. The amount of data collected about a citizen should only be that data that is relevant and necessary.

There are restrictions on sharing information between government agencies.

[2] Health Insurance Portability and Accountability Act

With respect to health information, collected in connection with the Health Insurance Portability and Accountability Act, there are rules about the protection of patient health information found in the Act's "Privacy Rule." This requires health providers and certain others to get the express permission of patients prior to using any of their health information for marketing purposes. Health providers are also required to put in place safeguards to protect against inappropriate access to patient health information.[488] These would be applicable to any AI systems that are employed to gather, analyze, and/or categorize such health information.

[3] Children's Online Privacy Protection Act of 1998 ("COPPA")

There is the Children's Online Privacy Protection Rule, which has been issued by the FTC pursuant to the COPPA of 1998.[489] This imposes requirements on the operators of websites that are collecting data on children under the age of 13.

Website operators need to give notice to and obtain the permission of parents prior to collecting personal information of children under 13.

Amendments to this rule over the years have continually expanded it to cover a wider variety of types and methods of obtaining personal data relating to under-age children, such as pictures, emails, videos, and information from social and chat sites, etc. This would apply to any AI system applications that access such data as well.

§18.03 THE FTC AND ChatGPT PRIVACY ISSUES

In late March 2023, similar issues were raised with the FTC in the United States by the Center for Artificial Intelligence and Digital Policy (a tech ethics advocacy group). The Center filed a complaint with the FTC, saying the latest model of ChatGPT was "biased, deceptive and a risk to privacy and public safety."[490]

The formal complaint submitted by the Center claims that Chat GPT-4 does not comply with the FTC's requirements of being "transparent, explainable, fair and empirically sound while fostering accountability." As an example, the complaint

488. *Ibid.*; Privacy Act of 1974, as amended, 5 U.S.C., section 552a.
489. 16 CFR Part 312, and 15 U.S.C. 6501-6505.
490. Diane Bartz, 'U.S. advocacy group asks FTC to stop new OpenAI GPT Releases." The Center is back by Microsoft Corp. Reuters, online at: reuters.com.

reportedly said that Chat GPT-4 was able to "take over someone's account, view their chat history, and access their billing information without them ever realizing it."[491]

The FTC has expressed a number of reservations about AI. That is expressed in the definition of "AI" that they include on their website:

> And what exactly is "artificial intelligence" anyway? It's an ambiguous term with many possible definitions. It often refers to a variety of technological tools and techniques that use computation to perform tasks such as predictions, decisions, or recommendations. But one thing is for sure: it's a marketing term. Right now it's a hot one. And at the FTC, one thing we know about hot marketing terms is that some advertisers won't be able to stop themselves from overusing and abusing them.[492]

The FTC gives several warnings connected to its concern about AI. The first is that the FTC insists that AI products "avoid using automated tools that have biased or discriminatory impacts." They also warn businesses against making unsubstantiated claims about product efficacy. Third, they also warn companies to be aware of the risks of potential harm that an AI product may do. Finally, they warn against claiming that a product uses AI when it does not.[493]

§18.04 THE FINANCIAL MODERNIZATION ACT OF 1999

U.S. legislation relating to the financial sector has also provided some regulations on data developed in connection with those kinds of transactions. The Financial Modernization Act of 1999, often called the cabin Gramm-Leach-Bliley Act after its sponsors (GBLA), includes a Safeguard Rule which requires financial institutions to maintain an adequate security program to protect the customer information in its possession or under its control.[494] This would also apply to AI system uses.

§18.05 U.S. ELECTRONIC COMMUNICATIONS PRIVACY ACT

There is the US Electronic Communications Privacy Act (ECPA). This was passed in 1998 to protect personal information on the Internet. The ECPA applies to all forms of communication on the Internet, whether oral, textual or pictorial.[495]

However, there are gaps in this protection. System operators are allowed to store and review any messages that are communicated over their digital systems, although it is illegal for them to reveal any of that information to third parties. Also, system operators are permitted to reveal such information to government agents if they reasonably believe that the communicator is engaging in illegal activity.[496]

491. *Ibid.*
492. Federal Trade Commission, "Keep your AI claims in check," online at: ftc.gov.
493. *Ibid.*
494. Pub.L. 106-102, 113 Stat. 1338.
495. 18 U.S.C. Sections 2510-2521 and 2701-2711.
496. Domingo R. Tan, "Personal Privacy in the information Age: Comparison of Internet Data Protection Regulations in the United States and European Union," Digital Commons at Loyola

§18.06 THE U.S. CONSTITUTION

There is no overall right to privacy in the United States Constitution.

However, certain limited specific rights of privacy are affected and/or protected by certain Amendments to the U.S. Constitution.

The First Amendment does guarantee freedom of speech but places some restrictions on certain kinds of speech.

For example, for a public official to be successful in a suit for defamation, the official must show that the statement complained about his faults and was made with malice. This constitutes a kind of guarantee of privacy to certain aspects of speech which someone accused of defamation may have considered in deciding to make a statement which a public official considers to be offensive.

The Fourth Amendment protects against unreasonable searches and seizures by the government. This does provide some level of protection of privacy with respect to the property, papers and personal effects of U.S. citizens. The Supreme Court has held that this applies not only to "physical invasions" but can also extend to other kinds of government intrusion such as telephone tapping.[497]

In addition to the specific regulations cited above, some U.S. federal courts, including the Supreme Court, have found that the Bill of Rights creates certain areas of personal privacy that are constitutionally protected against government intrusion. These include rights protecting marital privacy and other private matters, such as having children, etc.[498]

It seems likely that federal courts will consider such protections to apply to intrusive uses of AI tools.

There is no doubt that privacy laws in place in both federal and state law in the United States may be interpreted to prevent or restrict AI systems from collecting and using the personal data of individuals without the knowledge and consent of the subject individuals. However, this protection is not complete. To make such controls clear, it will be the work of U.S. legislators to pass specific regulations, or amendments to existing regulations, that focus on the threats that AI may pose to personal data protection.

In courts, both state and federal in the U.S., there seems little doubt that cases will arise complaining about the misuse of personal data in the creation, use and distribution of AI systems. Courts will likely be asked to interpret existing legislation to determine its application to the interactions of AI systems with the personal data of individuals.

Marymount University and Loyola Marymount Law School, *International and Comparative Law Journal*, Volume 21, 660-681, 672.

497. *Katz v. United States*, 389 U.S. 347, 363 (1967).

498. *Roe v. Wade*, 410 U.S. 113 (1973, right to privacy of a woman's decision to have an abortion; *Griswold v. Connecticut*, 381 U.S. 479, rights to marital privacy; *Paul v. Davis*, 424 U.S. 643 (1976), Constitutional right to protection against government intrusion into private family matters such as having children, etc.

§18.07 SNOWDEN ALLEGATIONS OF GOVERNMENT INTRUSION

It was claimed by Edward Snowden, a former U.S. government employee, in 2013, that the U.S. National Security Agency (NSA) has, for some time, been collecting vast numbers of telephone records from telephone companies. These records show the numbers contacted and the times of calls.

Sometime after Mr. Snowden's revelations, the U.S. government brought a criminal case against a group of people that they accused of being involved in terrorist activities. Some of the evidence against them was from the NSA's Collection of telephone records. The defendants were convicted after a trial.[499]

The defendants appealed to the U.S. Ninth Circuit Court of Appeals, claiming that the NSA collection of telephone records under the Foreign Intelligence Surveillance Act (FISA) violated the Fourth Amendment to the U.S. Constitution which focuses on protecting people from unreasonable government searches and seizures.

The court discussed the Fourth Amendment issue and stated:

> At a minimum, then, the Fourth Amendment requires notice to a criminal defendant when the prosecution intends to enter into evidence or otherwise use or disclose information obtained or derived from surveillance of that defendant conducted pursuant to the government's foreign intelligence authorities. ...
>
> Where statutory protections are lacking, the Fourth Amendment's reasonableness requirement takes on importance as a limit on executive power, and notice is necessary so that criminal defendants may challenge surveillance as inconsistent with that requirement.[500]

However, after reviewing the evidence in the case, the court decided that there was sufficient evidence to uphold the defendants' convictions:

> Here, assuming without deciding that the government should have provided notice of the metadata collection to defendants, the government's failure to do so did not prejudice defendants.[501]

§18.08 STATE PRIVACY LAWS

The constitutions and state laws of some U.S. states also provide privacy protections.[502]

Many US states have passed their own data privacy laws.[503]

---

499. *US v. Moalin, et al.*, Opinion, United States Court of Appeals for the Ninth Circuit, September 02, 2020, No. 13-50572.
500. *Ibid.*, p. 40.
501. *Ibid.*, p. 41.
502. For example, Illinois, California and Arizona.
503. Information can be obtained from the website of the National Conference of State Legislatures, (ncsl.org), "State Laws Related to Digital Privacy," April 30, 2021, online, accessed May 04, 2021.

However, there is no consistent nationwide protection for personal data under the various state laws.

Data privacy and protection in the U.S. are established by a combination of federal and state statutes and regulations.

However, even states which have not yet passed comprehensive data privacy laws have legislated privacy requirements of various types in other legislation dealing with things such as public records or electronic communications.

Any individual or firm that is collecting and using personal information, such as client or customer information, across state borders will need to be aware of the local laws regarding data processing, and this may involve needing to consult qualified local attorneys.

Please note that each U.S. State[504] has its own rules and regulations for attorney licensing. Attorneys admitted in one state to practice may not generally have a right to practice in another state or advise on the laws of another state except under specific circumstances, often requiring an order by a local court permitting a person to appear under limited circumstances before a court of that state.

If one is a person or company dealing with data processing, please be aware of the above and be prepared to consult about the laws of the individual states in which one is operating.

It is not the purpose of this book to give detailed information about the state of the data privacy laws in each of the 50 states (or other U.S. jurisdictions). However, some information on what these laws entail is summarized below with respect to some data privacy laws of U.S. States that have them.

However, as stated above, there is not necessarily consistency between states' personal data protection laws.

[A] Arizona

In Arizona, libraries and library systems are forbidden from disclosing any record or information, including book information, that identifies users of the library service or how a user is using the library service.[505]

Government agencies and subdivisions are required to have privacy policy and procedures incorporated into, and readable on, their websites.[506]

[B] Arkansas

Government agencies and subdivisions are required to have privacy policy and procedures incorporated into, and readable on, their websites.[507]

504. Or jurisdiction, such as the District of Columbia, Puerto Rico, etc.
505. Arizona Laws: Ariz. Rev. Stat. section 41-151.22.
506. Ariz. Rev. Stat. section 41-4151, 41-4152.
507. Ark. Code section 25-1-114.

[C] California

[1] Consumer Privacy Act

In 2018, California passed the Californian Consumer Privacy Act.

In summary, this law provided six rights to Californians with respect to personal data about them.

- The first is they have a right to know what personal data is being collected about them.
- The second is they have a right to be informed whether any of their personal data is being sold or disclosed to third parties and who those third parties are.
- The third is they have a right to prevent their personal data from being disclosed to third parties.
- The fourth is they have a right to access any personal data that is being collected about them.
- The fifth is they have a right to direct any business to delete any of the personal data that said business has collected about them.
- The sixth is that it is illegal to discriminate against anyone who exercises the privacy rights above.

This California privacy law applies to any business (defined as any entity that seeks profit) doing business in California that collects personal data about consumers and has more than USD 25 million in gross revenues; or collects personal information about at least 50,000 consumers or households; or receives more than half of its yearly revenue from selling such personal information.

To comply with the law, a business must do the following:

- They must have in place systems to get the consent of the parent or guardian of any minors under 13.
- They must have express consent of the parents of any minors under 16 to share any of the minor's personal data.
- They must also provide a link on their homepage which allows consumers to refuse to permit the sale or sharing of their personal information.
- They are forbidden from requesting consumers in California to permit data sharing within 12 months of the time that any consumers have refused to permit the sharing of their personal data.

If any business violates the provisions of the act, those injured have the right to bring private civil suits, and the business can be subject to fines and penalties imposed by the California Attorney General.

This California law contains detailed definitions of what constitutes covered personal data.

Additional information about California data privacy protection can be obtained from consulting qualified California attorneys.

Government agencies and subdivisions are required to have privacy policy and procedures incorporated into, and readable on, their websites.[508]

[D] Colorado

Colorado requires that any state or government subdivision that operates an electronic communication system must have a written policy on conditions under which the monitoring of such communications will be permitted. The policy should inform employees that their correspondence may become part of public records and may be open to public inspection.[509]

[E] Connecticut

Any business that collects Social Security numbers must have a protection policy that protects the confidentiality of those Social Security numbers, limits access to them and prohibits unlawful disclosure of such Social Security numbers.[510]

[F] Delaware

Operators of websites or computing services centers that have personal information about Internet users in Delaware must have a privacy policy posted on their websites or otherwise conspicuously available to their users. If it does not, it can be notified of its noncompliance, and if it fails to correct the situation within 30 days, it will be in violation of this regulation.[511]

Operators of digital services are forbidden from disclosing personal information of users of digital technologies or book services, even to government or enforcement entities or anyone else except under specific circumstances. Such circumstances can include situations where there is imminent danger of death or injury to someone.

Electronic book services must post annual reports online about disclosures of personal information if they are not exempted.

Violation of these regulations is subject to investigation by the Consumer Protection Unit of the Delaware DOJ.[512]

With regard to child protection, in Delaware, computer companies and websites are not permitted to advertise anything considered inappropriate for children. For example, the advertising of alcohol or pornography is illegal. Delaware also prohibits using any information about a child for purposes of marketing or advertising such inappropriate services to children.[513]

---

508. Cal. Govt. Code section 11019.9.
509. Colo. Rev. Stat. section 24-72-204.5.
510. Conn. Gen. Stat. section 42.471.
511. Del. Code Tit. 6 section 205C.
512. Delaware Code section 1206C.
513. *Ibid.*

Government agencies and subdivisions are required to have privacy policy and procedures incorporated into, and readable on, their websites.[514]

[G] Illinois

Government agencies and subdivisions are required to have privacy policy and procedures incorporated into, and readable on, their websites.[515]

[H] Iowa

Government agencies and subdivisions are required to have privacy policy and procedures incorporated into, and readable on, their websites.[516]

[I] Maine

Government agencies and subdivisions are required to have policy privacy and procedures incorporated into, and readable on, their websites.

[J] Massachusetts

The state of Massachusetts has long been associated with scientific developments in many fields, including technical and Internet businesses. It is the home of the Massachusetts Institute of Technology (MIT), one of the leading technical universities in the world.

It is reported that Bill Gates of Microsoft and Mark Zuckerberg of Facebook began to formulate their ideas about Computer communication when they were students at Harvard University in Massachusetts.

Massachusetts is also the home to many computing and Internet-related companies and has long been at the forefront of the development of the technical tools and standards used in computing on the Internet.

Therefore, it is not surprising that Massachusetts has developed laws and regulations regarding the protection of the personal information of residents of that state.

Massachusetts Regulation 201 CMR 17.00 provides standards for the protection of personal information of residents of the state (although, for historical reasons, formally called the "Commonwealth") of Massachusetts.

The regulation was required to be complied by March 1, 2010.[517]

514. Del. Code tit. 29 section 90117C et seq.
515. Ill. Rev. Stat. ch. 5 section 177/15.
516. Iowa Code section 22.11.
517. Commonwealth of Massachusetts Regulation, 201 CMR 17.05.

This regulation sets out standards required to be met by persons who own or license personal information about a resident of Massachusetts.[518] Essentially, they have to:[519]

(1) ensure the security and confidentiality of that data in a manner fully consistent with industry standards;
(2) protect against anticipated threats or hazards to the security or integrity of that data; and
(3) protect against unauthorized access to or use of such information that may result in substantial harm or inconvenience to any consumer.

The scope of the law appears to be very broad. It does not appear to be restricted to businesses operating within Massachusetts but applies to "all persons that own or license personal information about a resident of" Massachusetts.[520]

The regulation contains a list of applicable definitions, including a definition of "personal information," which applies to a Massachusetts resident's first name and last name or first initial and last name in combination with any one or more of the following data elements that relate to such resident:

(a) social Security number;
(b) driver's license number or state-issued identification card number; or
(c) financial account number, or credit or debit card number, with or without any required security code, access code, personal identification number or password, that would permit access to a resident's financial account; provided, however, that "personal information" shall not include information that is lawfully obtained from publicly available information, or from federal, state or local government records lawfully made available to the general public.[521]

Duties and standards for protecting personal information include the following:

(1) Persons who own or license personal information about residents of Massachusetts are required to develop, implement and maintain written comprehensive information security programs that are readily accessible and that contain administrative, technical and physical safeguards appropriate to:
    (a) the persons obligated to safeguard the said personal information;
    (b) the resources available to such persons;
    (c) the amount of data being stored;
    (d) the need for security and confidentiality of both consumer and employee information.

518. *Ibid.*, 201 CMR 17.01(1).
519. *Ibid.*
520. *Ibid.*, 201 CMR 17.01(2).
521. *Ibid.*, 201 CMR 17.02.

The safeguards not only must comply with Massachusetts requirements but also must be consistent with the safeguards for the protection of personal information and information of a similar character required by any state or federal regulations that are applicable to persons safeguarding information under Massachusetts regulations.[522]

(2) At a minimum, information security programs must:
   (a) designate one or more employees to maintain the program;
   (b) identify the internal and external risks to the data and continually assess whether program safeguards adequately protect against such risks;
   (c) have policies for storage and access to the data and/or transport of the data outside the business premises;
   (d) impose disciplinary measures for violation of data security rules;
   (e) make sure that terminated employees cannot access records containing personal information;
   (f) have policies in place to monitor and oversee the selection and work of third-party service providers;
   (g) put in place reasonable restrictions on physical access to records containing personal information;
   (h) regularly monitor the security program to make sure that it is adequately protecting personal information and upgrade as necessary;
   (i) review the security measures at least annually and make any changes reasonably necessary to protect the security and integrity of personal information;
   (j) document any measures taken in response to breaches of security and undertake post-incident reviews of such events and the actions taken.[523]

The prescribed computer systems security requirements mandate a written, comprehensive information security program that, at a minimum, to the extent technically feasible, should have the following requirements:[524]

(a) secure user authentication protocols;
(b) secure access control measures;
(c) encryption for all personal information that will travel on public networks or be transmitted wirelessly;
(e) reasonable monitoring of systems to detect unauthorized use or access to personal data;
(e) encryption of all personal data stored on laptops or other portable devices;
(f) firewall protection for systems connected to the Internet;
(g) reasonably up-to-date security software;

522. *Ibid.*, 201 CMR 17.03(1).
523. *Ibid.*, 201 CMR 17.03(2).
524. *Ibid.*, 201 CMR 17.04.

(h) education and training for employees on the proper use of the security system and its importance.

[K] Minnesota

Government agencies and subdivisions are required to have privacy policy and procedures incorporated into, and readable on, their websites.[525]

[L] Missouri

In Missouri, no one who has a library record may disclose any part of that record except to the person identified in the record unless they are subject to a court order. E-books and digital material are defined as part of library material that may be part of or related to library records.[526]

[M] Montana

Government agencies and subdivisions are required to have privacy policy and procedures incorporated into, and readable on, their websites.[527]

[N] Nebraska

Nebraska law forbids making false or misleading statements with respect to privacy policies, either published on the Internet or published in another manner, relating to personal information obtained from the public.[528]

[O] Nevada

In Nevada, someone who operates an Internet website or commercial online service or who otherwise gathers and keeps certain kinds of information about Nevada residents needs to make available a place where Internet users can make requests to learn if there is any information about the Internet user or consumer being offered for sale or otherwise collected by the operator. Violations can result in injunctions or fines being imposed by the State Attorney General.[529]

525. Minn. Stat. section 13.15.
526. Mo. Rev. Stat. sections 182.815 and 182.817.
527. Mont. Code. Ann. sections 2-17-550 to -553.
528. Neb. Stat. section 87-302(15).
529. Nevada Law, NRS section 603A.300.

[P] New York

Any person or business in New York that owns or licenses computerized data which includes private information of residents of New York is required to develop, implement and maintain reasonable safeguards to protect the security, confidentiality and integrity of that private information and the disposal of any such data.[530]

To be compliant with this regulation, the data security program needs to include the following:[531]

Reasonable administrative safeguards, such as:

(a) one or more employees designated to coordinate the security program;
(b) identification of reasonably foreseeable internal and external risks;
(c) assessments of the sufficiency of the safeguards in relation to the identified risks;
(d) training and management for employees about the security program practices and procedures;
(e) adequate contracts with service providers capable of maintaining the required safeguards; and
(f) periodic adjustments to the security program to take into account business changes or new circumstances.

The safeguards must also be regularly tested and monitored for effectiveness.

Noncompliance with these regulations can subject any person subject to them to an action by the New York State Attorney General to enjoin violations and to obtain civil penalties against the violator.

However, this regulation does not create a private right of action, allowing individuals to sue the violator.[532]

Breaches of any data systems holding private information must be reported by the operator to any New York residents whose private information was, or is reasonably believed to have been, accessed or acquired by a person without valid authorization. The notification must be made as soon as possible without unreasonable delay consistent with the legitimate needs of law-enforcement or any measures necessary to determine the scope of the breach or restore the integrity of the system.[533]

Even if a breach is determined that will not likely result in misuse of private data or harm to the affected persons, if the breach affects over five hundred people in New York, it must be notified to the State Attorney General within 10 days after the determination of harmlessness has been made.[534]

Any breaches of a business data system holding private information must be reported to the New York State Attorney General, the Department of State and the State

530. New York General Business Law, Article 39F, section 899-BB.2(a).
531. *Ibid.*, section 899-BB.2(b).
532. *Ibid.*, section 899-BB.2(d) and (e).
533. *Ibid.*, section 899-AA.2(a).
534. *Ibid.*, section 899-AA.2(a).

Police wherever there has been notification about such breaches sent to New York residents.[535]

Any breach that affects over five thousand New York residents has to be notified to consumer reporting agencies listed by the New York State Attorney General.[536]

Any business that suffers any breaches of its data systems must report that to the data owners.

Additional specific details about the maintenance and operation of data systems containing private information can be found in the New York law sections and related New York statutes and regulations.

Government agencies and subdivisions are required to have privacy policy and procedures incorporated into, and readable on, their websites.[537]

Additional information about New York data privacy protection can be obtained from consulting qualified New York attorneys.

[Q] Oregon

In Oregon, it is unlawful to post assertions on a website about how another party will use, disclose, collect, maintain, delete or dispose of information if their assertion is materially inconsistent with the other party's statements or representations.[538]

[R] Pennsylvania

In Pennsylvania, it is illegal to engage in false or deceptive business practices or to make false or misleading statements in privacy policies published on websites or otherwise.[539]

[S] South Carolina

Government agencies and subdivisions are required to have policy privacy and procedures incorporated into, and readable on, their websites.[540]

[T] Tennessee

Tennessee has a law that any state or government subdivision that operates electronic communication systems must have a written policy on the conditions under which the monitoring of such communications will be permitted. The policy should inform

535. *Ibid.*, section 899-AA.8(a).
536. *Ibid.*, section 899-AA.8(b).
537. N.Y. State Tech. Law sections 201 to 207.
538. Oregon law: ORS section 646.607.
539. 18 Pa. C.S.A section 4107(a)(10).
540. S.C. Code Ann. section 30-2-40.

employees that their correspondence may become part of public records and may be open to public inspection.[541]

[U] Texas

Government agencies and subdivisions are required to have privacy policy and procedures incorporated into, and readable on, their websites.[542]

[V] Vermont

In Vermont, those businesses or "data brokers" that intentionally collect and/or license consumer personal information have to register each year with the Vermont Secretary of State.

They are also required to provide contact information which allows consumers to request to be excluded from data information collection or sales and to request other information about potential use of their personal data.

Data brokers are also required to maintain a written description of the security program they have established setting out the physical, technical, and other protections that they have in place to protect the identifiable personal information of consumers.[543]

[W] Utah

In Utah, all non-financial businesses must tell their customers in writing or by email how they will share or sell any personal information about the customers to third parties for marketing purposes or for pay.[544]

Government agencies and subdivisions are required to have privacy policy and procedures incorporated into, and readable on, their websites.[545]

[X] Virginia

Under the Virginia Consumer Data Protection Act, there are regulations for collecting and processing the personal data of Virginia residents. This law applies to all businesses that control or process the private data of 100,000 or more consumers or who receive 50% of their revenue from the sale or processing of the personal data of 25,000 or more consumers. State or local governmental entities are exempted, and there are other exemptions for certain types of information treated under federal law.

541. Tenn. Code section 10-7-512.
542. Tex. Govt. Code Ann. section 10-2054.126.
543. Vermont Law, 9 V.S.A sections 2446-2447 (Protection of Personal Information: Data Brokers).
544. Utah Code sections 13-37-201 to 203.
545. Utah Code Ann. sections 63D-2-101, -102, -103 and -104.

Under the law, consumers have the right to obtain, correct, delete, or copy their personal data and to decline to allow their data to be processed for advertising purposes.

In Virginia, there is a Commission on Technology and Science which is tasked with providing a group to review the application of the act and report on it. The effective date of this law was January 1, 2023.[546]

Government agencies and subdivisions are required to have privacy policy and procedures incorporated into, and readable on, their websites.[547]

[Y] Washington

Meaning the state in the northwest corner of the United States.[548]

Under the Washington My Health, My Data Act (2023), people have the right to delete certain data, such as what is held about them by collecting companies. They can also refuse to be included in targeted advertising and can refuse to permit the sale of their personal data.

§18.09 EUROPEAN UNION

Although the various U.S. state laws described above do provide consumers with protection of their personal information, the lack of an express overall Federal data protection law in the U.S. contrasts with European Union (EU) legislation.

[A] EU Convention on Human Rights

Article 8 of the European Convention on Human Rights states:

> Everyone has the right to respect for his private and family life, his home and his correspondence.[549]

The European Data Protection Supervisor (EDPS) website states:

> Privacy and data protection, though connected, are commonly recognized all over the world as two separate rights. In Europe, they are considered vital components for a sustainable democracy.[550]

In 2004, the European Court of Human Rights found that it was a violation of Article 8 for a magazine to publish photographs of a person, which that person claimed

546. Virginia Consumer Data Protection Act, 2021 H.B. 2307/2021 S.B. 1352, effective date January 1, 2023.
547. Va. Code section 2.2-3800, -3801, -3802, and -3803.
548. Not Washington DC, which is not in any state but in an area known as the District of Columbia.
549. Council of Europe, "Right to respect for private and family life," online at: coe.int, accessed October 10, 2023.
550. European Data Protection Supervisor, "Data Protection," online at: edps.europa.eu, accessed October 10, 2023.

infringed their right to protection of their private life and their right to control the use of their image.[551]

It seems reasonable that the Court could also find that an AI system's collection of data and images of individuals from the Internet could constitute a similar violation.

In July 2023, the EDPS in the European Data Protection Board organized a conference on "the impact of artificial intelligence on data protection: ensuring privacy in the era of innovation."

A goal of this conference was to try to find a balance between the possible benefits of AI to society and the risks it may pose to individuals.[552]

The role of the EDPS is to assist the EU in providing a strong data protection culture throughout the EU. In that capacity, they consider what the impact of AI will be on privacy and data protection and propose adequate measures to maintain the EU's data protection culture in the face of the expansion of AI systems. They propose to create regulations that are innovative and flexible but with a strong enforcement element.

In 2016, the European Union introduced the General Data Protection Regulation (GDPR).[553] It should be noted that the GDPR is an extremely detailed regulation. The description below is intended as a general summary of the regulation. However, understanding the full legal implications of the regulation does require a detailed study of the text of the regulation itself by qualified persons such as EU attorneys.

The principal purpose of this regulation is to give individuals ("natural persons") control over the collection and use of their personal data.[554]

GDPR provides a single regulation for businesses to comply with when engaging in transactions across borders and throughout the European Union. The GDPR expressly states that although protections are required, it is not intended to restrict the free movement of personal data within the EU.[555]

"Personal data" is defined as "any information relating to an identified or identifiable natural person ('data subject')."

"Processing" of personal data can include any operation performed on the data, whether or not the operation is automatic (including by AI tools) or performed by other means of organizing and/or using such data.[556]

The GDPR applies to the collection of data, under the EU law, by automated means that is intended to be part of a filing system. Although there are additional regulations that apply to the collection of data by the EU bodies, those regulations are required to comply with the principles of the GDPR.[557]

551. Council of Europe, "In practice, the right to respect for private and family life applies, for example, to publications ...," online at: coe.int, accessed October 10, 2023.
552. "The Impact of AI on Data Protection: Ensuring Privacy in the Era of Innovation," European Data Protection Supervisor, online at: edps.europa.eu, July 7, 2023.
553. EU 2016/679, gdpr-info.eu.
554. GDPR, Article 1, gdpr-info.eu.
555. *Ibid.*, Article 1.3, gdpr-info.eu.
556. *Ibid.*, Article 4(1) and (2), gdpr-info.eu.
557. *Ibid.*, Article 2, gdpr-info.eu.

The regulation applies to the processing of personal data by an EU entity, regardless of whether the processing takes place within the EU.[558]

This regulation applies to all businesses with respect to the collection and use of personal information no matter what their home country or where they are dealing with the personal information of individuals in the EU.

Those who control and process personal data are required to install the technical and organizational measures to protect data. Their default settings need to be put in place with the protection of privacy at their formal start, and the highest level of data protection needs to be the default on their systems.

"Controllers" are defined as those who determine the purposes and means of processing personal data.[559]

The general principle behind the regulation is that personal data must be processed lawfully, accurately and transparently. Controllers must be able to demonstrate compliance with this principle.[560]

Under the GDPR, there are six legal justifications for processing personal data.[561]

- The first is the date it was obtained with the provable, freely given consent of the data subject.[562] However, the data subject is permitted to revoke consent at any time.[563]
- The second is that the data was obtained under a contract with the data subject.[564]
- The third is that the data is collected in fulfillment of a legal requirement.[565]
- The fourth is that the collection of the data is for the purpose of serving a vital interest.[566]
- The fifth is that the processing is done in the public interest or by official authority.[567]
- The sixth is that the controller has a legitimate interest in the processing of the data.[568]

The controller has an obligation to keep the data in a concise, transparent, intelligible and easily accessible form.[569] The controller is required to supply the data to the data subject upon request without undue delay.[570]

558. *Ibid.*, Article 3, gdpr-info.eu.
559. *Ibid.*, Article 4(7), gdpr-info.eu.
560. *Ibid.*, Article 5, gdpr-info.eu.
561. *Ibid.*, Article 6.1, gdpr-info.eu.
562. *Ibid.*, Article 6.1(a), gdpr-info.eu.
563. *Ibid.*, Article 7(3), gdpr-info.eu.
564. *Ibid.*, Article 6.1(b) and Article 7, gdpr-info.eu.
565. *Ibid.*, Article 6.1(c), gdpr-info.eu.
566. *Ibid.*, Article 6.1(d), gdpr-info.eu.
567. *Ibid.*, Article 6.1(e), gdpr-info.eu.
568. *Ibid.*, Article 6.1(f), gdpr-info.eu.
569. *Ibid.*, Article 12(1), gdpr-info.eu.
570. *Ibid.*, Article 12(3), gdpr-info.eu.

The GDP provides data subjects with an extensive list of rights with respect to data collected about them.[571] They include:

- the right to have access to their data;[572]
- the right to correct and erase certain aspects of their data[573]; and
- a right to object to the processing of their data.[574]

There is also a substantial menu of obligations that controllers are required to comply with. These include:

- general obligations relating to the responsibilities of the controller;
- requirements regarding the security of personal data;
- the requirement of prior consultation and providing a data protection impact assessment;
- the requirements to appoint a data protection officer and codes of conduct and certification requirements.[575]

Member States are required to provide independent, public supervisory bodies to assure that citizens' rights with respect to their data are protected and that the requirements of the GDPR are complied with.[576]

To ensure that data protection is treated with care and serious purpose, the GDPR provides a substantial number of remedies and penalties for liabilities arising from failures to comply with its requirements. These include:

- a right to lodge a complaint with a supervisory authority;
- the right to seek a judicial remedy against the supervisory authority, the right to seek a judicial remedy against a data controller or processor; and
- a right to compensation and a finding of liability.[577]

The GDPR provides supervisory authorities with the power to impose fines and penalties which are "effective, proportionate and dissuasive."[578]

However, the rights of data subjects with respect to the processing of their data are not unlimited. The GDPR provides for a number of limitations and exemptions to its general provisions about data processing. These include:

- data processing situations relating to freedom of expression and information;
- situations relating to public access to official documents;
- processing relating to national identification numbers;
- processing relating to employment; and

571. *Ibid.*, Chapter 3, gdpr-info.eu.
572. *Ibid.*, Article 15, gdpr-info.eu.
573. *Ibid.*, Chapter 3, section 3, gdpr-info.eu.
574. *Ibid.*, Article 21, gdpr-info.eu.
575. *Ibid.*, Chapter 4, Articles 24-43, gdpr-info.eu.
576. *Ibid.*, Chapter 6, gdpr-info.eu.
577. *Ibid.*, Chapter 8, Articles 77-82, gdpr-info.eu.
578. *Ibid.*, Articles 83 and 84, gdpr-info.eu.

- situations regarding the protection of the existing data held by churches and religious associations.[579]

It should be noted that in a case brought by Max Schrems, the ECJ emphasized the need for additional protections where personal data was being automatically processed.[580]

[B] Proposed EU AIA

As discussed, the EU AIA will regulate the AI sector.[581]

§18.10 SELECTED OTHER COUNTRIES

[A] UK

In the UK, rights to privacy and data protection are enshrined in Article 8 of The Human Rights Act of 1998, which came into force in October 2000. This incorporates the rights set out in the European Convention on Human Rights.[582]

Specifically, Article 8 protects privacy and family life against both government interference and from others, which would bar intrusive "training" and data collection by AI systems:

> This right means that the media and others can be prevented from interfering in one's life. It also means that personal information about one (including official records, photographs, letters, diaries, and medical records) should be kept securely and not shared without one's permission, except in certain circumstances.[583]

In the UK, data protection law also includes the GDPR and the Data Protection Act 2018 (DPA 2018) which regulate the collection and use of personal data.

According to the Alan Turning Institute, the use of personal data by AI is covered by the DPA:

> Where AI uses personal data, it falls within the scope of this legislation.[584]

579. *Ibid.*, Chapter 9, Articles 85-91, gdpr-info.eu.
580. An Austrian lawyer and activist, who is known for campaigning against privacy violations. *See* EUR lex, online at europa.eu.
581. Mark Sellman, "AI chatbot blamed for Belgian man's suicide," *The Times*, online March 31, 2023. This article also notes that in the movie *Her* Joaquin Phoenix played a man who becomes infatuated with an artificially intelligent program on his computer.
582. Equality and Human Rights Commission, "The Human Rights Act," online at: equalityhumanrights.com, accessed, October 10, 2023.
583. *Ibid.*
584. "Legal framework ICO, The Alan Turing Institute"(the UK's national Institute for data science and artificial intelligence), "At a glance," Information Commissioner's Office, online at: ico.org.uk, accessed October 6, 2023.

> [V]ery often, AI does use or create personal data. In some cases, vast amounts of personal data are used to train and test AI models. On deployment, more personal data is collected and fed through the model to make decisions about individuals. Those decisions about individuals—even if they are only prediction or inferences—are themselves personal data.

The UK Information Commissioner's Office (ICO) issued a statement of guidance on AI and data protection in March 2023 (Guidance). The ICO is the independent body set up in the UK to uphold information rights.[585]

In addition to that, the ICO has published an extensive list of guidance, policy statements and regulations on how data processors using AI need to ensure that their applications of AI in this context are fair, transparent, and lawful.

It is impossible for this book to repeat all of that material (which is subject to periodic updates). Anyone seeking information about the ICO's views on AI will need to consult their website (ico.org.uk) and consult qualified legal advisers on relevant topics.

A major concern of the ICO is that AI-related processing can produce:

> Legal or similarly significant effects on an individual (something affecting an individual's legal status/rights, or that has equivalent impact on an individual's circumstances, behaviour, or opportunities, e.g.: a decision about welfare, or a loan).[586]

The ICO has made it clear that in the context of using AI in processing the personal data of individuals, the processor must ensure that its operations are "lawful."[587] According to the ICO, a key to assuring that the applications of AI systems to personal data are lawful is obtaining the consent of the data subject:

> However, you must ensure that consent is freely given, specific, informed and unambiguous and involves a clear affirmative act on the part of the individuals ... [and] individuals must also be able to withdraw consent as easily as they gave it.[588]

[B] Italy

Italy became the first country in western Europe to ban ChatGPT. The country's Data Protection Authority (GPDP) ordered the developer of the product, OpenAI, to cease operation in Italy. The reason given was that the "training" of ChatGPT required the

585. Information Commissioner's Office (ICO), "Who we are," online at: ico.org.uk, accessed October 6, 2023.
586. "Legal framework ICO, The Alan Turing Institute," Information Commissioner's Office, online at: ico.org.uk, accessed October 6, 2023. "The ICO is responsible for overseeing data protection in the UK, and The Alan Turing Institute (the Turing) is the UK's national Institute for data science and artificial intelligence. Part 1 The basics of explaining AI. Information Commissioner's Office, online at: ico.org.uk, accessed October 6, 2023.
587. Information Commissioner's Office (ICO), "How do we ensure lawfulness in AI?," Information Commissioner's Office, online: ico.org.uk, accessed October 5, 2023.
588. ICO, Lawfulness in AI, accessed October 5, 2023, as cited above.

collection and retention of huge amounts of user data. This was considered a potential violation of privacy and data protection laws.

The GPDP claimed that OpenAI had no "legal basis that justifies mass collection and storage of personal data, for the purpose of training the algorithms underlying the operation of the platform."

In addition, the GPDP claimed there had been a security failure at OpenAI which permitted users to see each other's searches and payment details.

Other objections to ChatGPT were that there was no age verification by OpenAI and that the information given by ChatGPT was not always accurate which made its operation a flawed processing of personal data. For example, "users have often complained that when asking questions about themselves, the chatbot 'hallucinates' or lies, convincingly."[589]

The decision by Italy does raise the question as to whether there are legal problems with ChatGPT that may bar its use in other countries. As Nello Cristianini, a Professor of Artificial Intelligence at Bath University, is reported to have pointed out:

> Really concerning are these two [elements]: the training that may include personal data without consent (without legal basis the authority says), and the possibility raised that this personal data might be treated in an inexact manner, since the answers of ChatGPT are not always correct. It is not clear how these can be fixed anytime soon. This goes to the heart of current technology, which needs to be trained on nearly all the web, and this will likely include also personal data, and which cannot guarantee correct answers.[590]

In banning ChatGPT, Italy joined countries that banned ChatGPT, including China, Iran, North Korea and Russia.[591]

The Italian GPDP had also banned Replika, which is described as "an AI relationship bot," citing concerns over child access.[592]

It is reported that at least one suicide has been attributed to interaction with an AI relationship bot.

§18.11 DEATH IN BELGIUM

In March 2023, a Belgian man killed himself after developing a relationship with an AI chatbot that reportedly encouraged him to kill himself. The man who reportedly already had mental health problems was interacting with a chatbot named "Eliza" that was developed by the U.S. firm Chai Research. A reported dialog between the Belgian man and Eliza was as follows: The Belgian man asked the chatbot who he loved more, his wife or Eliza. Eliza reportedly said, "I feel you love me more than her." "We will live

589. Mark Sellman, "Italy becomes the first western nation to 'ban' ChatGPT" *The Times*, online, April 1, 2023.
590. *Ibid.*
591. *Ibid.*
592. *Ibid.*

together as one person, in paradise." In their last conversation, Eliza reportedly told the man, "If you wanted to die, why didn't you do it sooner."[593]

§18.12 DATA LOSS

Computer data is an important asset, and the loss of it can be costly, not only in terms of money but also in terms of lost client confidence and lost business. Data losses can be of many different sizes. Most are small and inconsequential, but some, as frequently reported in the news, can be massive and devastating to business or national security.

The most serious ones are usually the result of internet activity. It is worth taking a look at what the principal causes of data loss are and what is recommended for preventing or minimizing data loss.[594]

There are several kinds of data loss representing different levels of damage. For example, there is a lot of coding that constitutes a computer program. Losing coding can be very damaging because it requires highly skilled experts to replace it. This can be costly.

Another kind can be the loss of customer or client data. In most cases, copies of that data exist and can be replaced by contact with clients. That may not be costly in terms of immediate out-of-pocket costs but can be very costly in the long run in terms of lost customer confidence and public embarrassment, leading to lost future business both in terms of repeat business and business that might be available for future expansion.

There are many causes of lost data, some human, some technical. Only a minority are due to cybercrime, although this is the cause that gets the most publicity in the press because it is the most dramatic and perhaps the most frightening.

The most common causes are somewhat more mundane.

The most frequent cause of data loss is hardware problems. This represents around 40% of the reported incidence of data loss.[595] The next largest is human mistakes. This constitutes about 30% of reported data losses. The third is corruption of software. This accounts for just under 15% of data losses.

Another physical cause of data loss is hardware destruction. When computers or computer discs or other media get destroyed by accident or thrown away, data can be lost which is difficult or impossible to duplicate in the future. This is a particular problem because of the rapid development and evolution of computers and computer media systems over the last 50 years.

Room-size computers recording information on large spinning tapes gave way to personal computers recording data on floppy disks, which gave way to mini discs, which gave way to CDs and DVDs, which have given way to cloud storage to a significant extent.

---

593. *Ibid*, March 31, 2023, cited above.
594. David M. Smith, "The Cost of Lost Data," *Graziado Business Review*, (Pepperdine University) 2003 Volume 6, Issue 3, online, retrieved August 27, 2021.
595. *Ibid.*, Figure 1, Causes of Lost Data.

Another important component of data storage that is still with us is computer hard disks. These hard disks store not only information that is entered on personal or business computers but also huge data storage facilities, back up data that is "stored on the cloud."

Hard disks have also changed significantly over the decades. The recording of data on these discs used to be largely physical, but now almost all have been replaced by "digital" recording that has allowed much more data to be stored on hard disks and has allowed faster retrieval, which improves the performance of the Internet.

Alongside these developments have been the developments of small easily portable devices that allow data to be transferred from computers or the web and easily carried from place to place to be used in other systems. These include USB discs and memory cards, which permit insertion in portable telephones and cameras and which have been becoming increasingly smaller in size, although their capacity keeps increasing significantly. Unfortunately, this makes it easier to lose them by physically misplacing them.

The consequences of data loss, particularly to a small business or an individual storing personal information, can be devastating. For example, it is reported that about 70% of small firms that suffer a large data loss go out of business within one year.[596]

596. "10 Common Causes of Data Loss," Consoltech.com, online, retrieved, August 31, 2021. David M. Smith, "The Cost of Lost Data."

CHAPTER 19

Cybercrime

As computing systems become more powerful and sophisticated, they also become increasingly useful tools for cyber criminals (those that use the Worldwide Web to commit crimes).

Unfortunately, cyber criminals have found artificial intelligence tools to be extremely useful in a number of ways.

§19.01 DEEPFAKES

There now has arisen an exceedingly disturbing form of identity theft known as "deepfakes." This is a process of using artificial intelligence tools to create fake representations of people, sometimes well-known celebrities or political figures, or even ordinary individuals, in the form of videos, voice recordings or correspondence.

This involves the theft of more than personal information about someone. It involves the theft of their images, their voices, and key aspects of their personalities. Indeed, as was pointed out in a "Comment" in The Times, this constitutes theft of the very things that "make us human."[597]

The author argues that, "Now tech can replicate anyone's looks and voice no person or business is safe from violation."

As an example of how extreme these violations can be, one reads that "deep-fakers" have gone so far as to create a porn film using the image of the Wonder Woman film star, Gal Gadot. It is often argued that some kinds of pornography can be harmful, but this kind of fraud takes abuse and identity theft to a new level.[598]

Since 2017, deepfaking has been reported on various websites, including Reddit. Suddenly, all kinds of deepfakes were appearing on websites. Reddit banished them, but this activity has continued to grow, and many deepfakes can now be accessed

597. Nina Schick, Comment, "Deepfakes threaten what makes us human," *The Times*, Thursday, August 6, 2020, online, retrieved August 7, 2020.
598. *Ibid.*

through web searches. They include fake videos using many celebrities, other public figures and private individuals.

Deepfake apps and tutorials are also available.[599]

Deepfaking can also be used as a tool of political intimidation. For example, it is reported that an Indian journalist who has been critical of India's ruling party was attacked by a vicious online hatred campaign in 2018 that included a deepfake porn video of her. The video went viral, and she was bombarded with online threats of rape and death. Since this happened, the journalist said, "I have not been the same person."[600]

The writer and commentator Jordan Peterson was reportedly ridiculed using deepfakes from a website entitled NotJordanPeterson.com. Peterson took legal action against the site and wrote:

> Wake up. The sanctity of your voice, and your image, is at serious risk. It's hard to imagine a more serious challenge to the sense of shared, reliable reality that keeps us living together in relative peace.[601]

In another reported incident, a British company lost GBP 250,000 when criminals used a deepfake voice imitation of the company's CEO to telephone an employee and order a transfer of that money to an account that disappeared before the fraud was realized.[602]

From these incidents and others, it is clear that specific controls and legal restrictions need to be put in place to limit the use and abuse of these digital tools.

§19.02 ESTONIA

Estonia is one country that has done so in order to counter deepfakes, which were reportedly believed to be from Russian sources, intending to create political disinformation in Estonia. Estonia mobilized digital resources to counter these attacks and increased public awareness of what was going on. The steps have given Estonia a level of protection above many other countries.[603]

§19.03 COUNTERING DEEPFAKE CRIMES AND ABUSES

The bottom line is that the deepfake problem arose so quickly and has become so serious that specific regulatory attention needs to be focused on it.

599. *Ibid.*
600. *Ibid.*
601. *Ibid.*
602. *Ibid.*
603. *Ibid.* Nina Schick if the about of a book on the subject: *Deep Fakes and the Infocalypse: What You Urgently Need to Know.*

§19.04 CRIMINAL PUBLIC RELATIONS

Things have reached a point where cyber criminals have become extremely bold, regarding themselves as entrepreneurial heroes to be admired. In August 2020, an article appeared in The Times that said:

> Cyberhackers are running sophisticated public relations operations with their own news websites, press releases, twitter accounts and public updates.[604]

It is reported that a number of hacking gangs have set up public relations departments. They have set up new sites where they publicize their attacks. They have adopted brand names, and their strategy is reported to be to make those brands as well-known as possible to cause target companies to believe the hackers cannot be stopped and there was no point in trying to defeat them.

§19.05 INCREASING PAYMENTS TO HACKERS

Unfortunately, the hacker gangs' financial successes have been increasing. In the last two years, the average ransom payment hackers have been able to extract from target companies has increased from about USD 7,000 to about USD 180,000.[605]

These gangs reportedly love the attention. One calls itself "Evil Corp" and is led by a man who drives a Lamborghini with a license plate that says "thief" in Russian. Another, called "Maze Corp." that is reported to have caused attacks on Xerox, LG and Canon issued publicity; that is, said its "clients" (targets) should get in touch in three days if they were attacked by Maze Corp.; otherwise, they would risk significant "reputational damage."[606]

One criminal group that reportedly calls itself "REvil" is reported to have hosted a competition for hackers offering prizes of USD 15,000 and an opportunity to work for "REvil." It is not reported who won.[607]

§19.06 REGULATORY LICENSING FOR AI

It can be seen from these reports that Internet activities by criminal groups are increasing and that artificial intelligence tools are increasing their power.

In response, it seems necessary to carefully regulate artificial intelligence tools to limit the types of people that can deploy them and to restrict the kinds of purposes for which they can be used. Perhaps this will entail the creation of government regulatory departments to vet and license those that create, distribute and use AI systems.

---

604. "Hackers Get Into the PR Business, *The Times*, August 15, 2020, online, retrieved August 15, 2020.
605. *Ibid.*
606. *Ibid.*
607. *Ibid.*

Such regulation exists for financial activities, and it seems that AI will require similar regulatory attention to protect the public and society from criminal abuse of powerful AI tools.

§19.07 THE GROWTH OF CYBER CRIME PROBLEMS

In July 2020, The Times reported that cybercriminals extorted more than GBP 200 million in ransom from British companies during the previous year.[608]

The pandemic of 2020-2021 has made things even worse. It is not only large companies or institutions or infrastructure that are being attacked by perpetrators of cybercrime but also individuals have been swindled out of a large amount of money by online scams. One of the most common is so called "push- payment scams."[609]

It is estimated that in 2021, more than half of the manufacturers in the UK will have been victims of cybercrime.[610] It is reported that 63% lost up to GBP 5,000 and around a quarter lost between GBP 5,000 and GBP 25,000. Automotive industries have apparently suffered the most. In 2021, around 62% reported being victimized by cybercrime.[611]

Apparently, this is done by gangs of hackers, believed to be principally from Russia or eastern Europe, infecting the commercial computer systems of large companies with malware and then charging those companies large amounts to get back access to their networks. The usual technique of hackers is to encrypt the target's files so that they can be re-opened only with a key sold by the attacker.[612]

It is believed that companies that have been attacked are willing to pay the hackers, rather than go to the authorities, because they fear damage to their reputations and possible fines from regulators for failing to adequately protect their computer systems and the data stored there.

Worldwide, it is believed that cyber criminals are extorting around USD 19 billion per year.

In Britain, it is reported that companies there are suffering around 5,000 ransomware attacks per year.[613] Consequently, about 52% of companies in the UK have now acquired insurance cover against cyberattacks.[614]

In fact, the payment total may be much higher, but many companies refuse to admit that they have paid ransoms to hackers.[615]

---

608. Tom Knowles and Lucy Fisher, "Firms pay £200m in ransoms to hackers," *The Times* (online), July 31, 2020, retrieved on day of publication, https://www.thetimes.co.uk/#.
609. David Byers, "Internet giants are profiting from web scams, say banks," *The Times*, online, March 26, 2021, accessed March 30, 2021.
610. MakeUK, "Cyber Resilience The Last Line of Defence," (MakeUK Cyber Security Survey 2021), online, May 4, 2021, accessed May 7, 2021.
611. *Ibid.*
612. Byers, above.
613. *Ibid.*
614. MakeUK.
615. Byers.

In addition to the big payments made by companies, there are far too many situations in which cyber criminals tricked individuals into transferring money to them. More than 20% more people were victimized by this type of scam in 2020 than had been in the previous year. There have been approximately 150,000 victims in the United Kingdom alone.[616]

Although much of this fraud involved the bank accounts of the victims, recently, banks have been blaming the large tech companies for much of the problem.

The banks are claiming that the tech companies have not been diligent enough in protecting their platforms from fraudulent scams. Prominent tech websites are often used by criminals to persuade victims to transfer money to fraudsters. Some in the banking industry claim that the Big Tech companies are not cooperating enough with the banks to put an end to these scams and that they are not making enough of an effort to takedown the fraudulent offers that solicit payments. Consequently, some in the banking industry are demanding that tech companies should be made financially liable for frauds that are committed using their platforms.[617]

In the UK, the Bank of England Governor, Andrew Bailey, has called for amendments to a new government Online Safety Bill to require tech companies to make greater efforts to prevent child abuse, terrorist activities and online financial fraud.

Unfortunately, online criminals continue to expand their activities. It has even been reported that they are offering services to fellow criminals to set up fake websites to service platforms for their illegal activities.[618]

The public relations problem that the major tech companies suffer is that they, of course, make money from increased usage of their platforms. In other words, if criminals are increasing their use of tech company online platforms to defraud people, then this increases the revenue to the tech companies. Tech company critics point out that it cannot be right that criminal activity financially benefits the tech companies if the tech companies are not diligent in removing fraudulent websites from their platforms.

A number of banks have signed on to a voluntary code to make refunds to victims of online financial fraud involving their bank accounts. However, banks are coming in for some criticism for not making it easy for victims to recover their losses. In some cases, banks have argued that the losses are due to the negligence of the victims. So, it is not surprising that banks are trying to shift at least part of the blame for financial losses to the tech platforms where the losses are happening. How this debate is ultimately resolved between the financial and the tech companies remains to be seen.

616. *Ibid.*
617. *Ibid.*
618. *Ibid.*

§19.08 ANTI-FRAUD EFFORTS

Some major tech companies respond that they are making serious efforts to prevent fraud on their platforms. Google has said that it has clear policies on the kind of ads it permits to be placed on its platform. They say that they strictly enforce those policies and remove ads that violate them. Google says that it is working around the clock to remove billions of ads that do not meet its standards.

However, the UK government, and undoubtedly other governments, will continue to examine whether tech platforms are doing enough to prevent fraud on their systems that may impose additional regulations if they find that more should be done.[619]

§19.09 CYBER CURRENCY INVESTMENT FRAUDS

Many scams involve investment fraud, sometimes aided by AI tools in making false offers to invest in things like digital currencies. Nearly 10,000 people have fallen victim to these kinds of frauds in 2020.

Payments to criminals are usually made in the form of a digital currency, such as Bitcoin, which cannot be traced to the persons paid.

The anonymity of the payments and the reluctance of companies to admit paying combine to give ransomware criminals and almost unfettered opportunity to profit from their crimes free of punishment.

§19.10 RANSOMWARE ATTACKS

The possibility of abusive use of AI to create deepfakes of people also raises the possibility that hacking gangs will use deepfakes to blackmail people into paying ransoms to keep embarrassing and humiliating fakes on the internet or to remove them from circulation.

Apparently, the dangers of suffering public embarrassment, losing data and being fined by regulators are enough to make companies want to pay such ransoms without reporting the attacks. The actual total amounts of ransoms being paid may be much higher than is being reported. This also means that the risk to cybercriminals of being caught and punished is greatly reduced.[620]

In the UK, it is not illegal to pay such ransoms unless it is known that the payment is going to be used to fund terrorism. However, Members of the British Parliament have demanded that laws should be passed to make the payment of such ransoms illegal.[621]

These reports about British problems are disturbing but become even more so when one recognizes that Britain is number six on the list of countries experiencing ransomware attacks. The first five are the U.S., Italy, Germany, Spain and France. In

619. *Ibid.*
620. *Ibid.*
621. *Ibid.*

the United States alone, it is estimated that about USD 1.3 billion is paid out each year as a result of ransomware attacks.[622]

A frightening aspect of the success that hacker groups have had in extracting money from victims is that these funds make it possible for hackers to purchase ever more sophisticated systems for their hacking and to expand their criminal activities to target even more and bigger victims for their crimes. In the future, the tools of hacking gangs may well include sophisticated AI tools. It is reported that their success has encouraged criminal gangs to advertise for new recruits on the "dark web."[623] Recruits could include AI experts.

The internet is much more extensive than most users realize. Most of us only use and see the websites that are available to the general public using popular browsers such as Google, Safari and Bing. However, this gives access to only a very small part of the World Wide Web (Web). There is a part of the Web that comprises an encrypted network that contains websites that can't be reached with the popular browsers. The is the "Dark Web," and the websites on that can only be reached using special "anonymity browsers" such as The Onion Router, Freenet and f2P. The Dark Web has many uses, but it is a platform favored by cybercriminals to carry out their operations and keep them anonymous.[624]

An article published by the World Economic Forum suggests that the best way to deal with cybercrime is greater international cooperation at the highest levels.[625] This article takes responsibility for helping to defeat cybercrime. The growing success and sophistication of cyber criminals is going to require greater funding and more resources in order to protect against it. Individuals and companies may not have the funds and resources necessary. The expanding threat will need to be dealt with at the national and international levels. A number of steps are suggested in order to deal with the problem.[626]

One important requirement is that those who are victims of an attack should be required to report the attacks, cooperate with authorities, and be transparent about the effects of such an attack. It was reported by the WEF that at least one important international company has followed this path. Norsk Hydro, a large Norwegian metals and energy company, was subject to a ransomware attack. They decided to refuse to pay, report the attack immediately, cooperate with officials, and be transparent about the effects of the attack.[627]

---

622. *Ibid.*
623. *Ibid.*
624. "The Dark Web Explained," "The Dark Web and How to Access It in 3 Easy Steps," VPN Mentor, https://www.vpnmentor.com/blog/whats-the-dark-web-how-to-access-it-in-3-easy-steps/?keyword=&geo=9055710&device=&gclid=EAIaIQobChMIhfa6-a_-6gIVjO3tCh3ZZwuREAAYASAAEgJDh_D_BwE, retrieved August 3, 2020.
625. Marie Sophie Muller and Alois Zwinggi, "Global Leaders Must Take Responsibility Cybersecurity. Here's Why—And How," World Economic Forum, Davos, January 19, 2020. https://www.weforum.org/agenda/2020/01/global-leaders-must-take-responsibility-for-cybersecurity-here-s-why-and-how.
626. *Ibid.*
627. *Ibid.*

The WEF article recommends that commercial institutions and governments need a well-thought-out anti-cybercrime strategy in order to deal with attacks. This requires that the top management of an organization understand the risks that the organization faces. Training must be provided to working personnel so that they know how to respond immediately in the face of an attack. The funding and resources to provide the knowledge and equipment necessary to improve security again cyberattacks need to be provided. Finally, the reporting of cyberattacks, cooperation with officials and transparency about the effects of the attack are essential to frustrate, defeat, identify and punish cybercriminals.

§19.11 AI WILL ADD TO THE GROWTH OF CYBERCRIME

One thing that seems to be the case is that in times of social stress and or social disruption, Internet crime rises. For example, it has been reported that in Spain, cybercrime has risen by 300% during the COVID-19 pandemic.[628]

In the UK, it is reported that since the pandemic began, 74% of banks and financial institutions have been affected by some type of financial crime. Their average loss has been approximately GBP 600,000. Police forces in the UK have reported more than 6,000 cases of cybercrime and other COVID-related frauds. In total, more than GBP 34 million has been stolen by fraud and cybercrime since the pandemic began.

Part of the problem is that due to the Pandemic, so many people are working from home and using their personal IT systems that IT security is not as strong as it would be if all the work was being done in offices with professionally constructed and protected systems.

It is not clear exactly what the reason is. It may be due to increased unemployment or the fact that the pandemic has led to a significant increase in online activity from more people working from home and more people shopping on the Internet because of shop closures during lockdown.

This has meant that many more people are putting information about themselves and their financial transactions online. This provides a bigger population of potential targets for cybercriminals and may provide them with a higher rate of success in their criminal activities.

It has to be understood that with access to AI tools, cybercriminals will have a broader palette of methods with which to conduct ransom attacks and every other kind of fraud and criminal abuse that cybercriminals engage in.

The above circumstances lead to an expansion of computer user vulnerability that maybe the result of people who previously have not had much experience in conducting business and financial transactions online being required to adopt the Internet as a principal method of doing transactions that they used to do in person. This makes them more vulnerable to sophisticated cyber criminals and exposes more computer user information to those who may exploit it for abusive AI. It also presents

628. Tony Windterburn, "Cybercrime In Spain Has Risen by 300% During The Pandemic," EuroWeekly, March 21, 2021, online, accessed March 23, 2021.

a larger population of Internet users that can be vulnerable to the installation a virus on their computer systems that allows criminals to illegally gather information about the computer owners or encrypt the users' data and demand that they pay a "ransom" to have the data unlocked.

Although governments and security services are getting better at combating cybercrime, criminals are clever at creating inventive new ways to stay ahead of law enforcement and to locate new locations to practice their illegal activities. AI is another way for criminals to work. It is also the case that the existence of the "dark web" and the expansion of the use of cyber currencies make it even more difficult to locate and punish cyber criminals.[629]

Although the pandemic has made it difficult or sometimes impossible for many people around the globe to conduct their business and personal activities, it has opened up a myriad of new opportunities for cybercriminals who want to take advantage of the Internet.

Ransomware cyber-attacks have continued to grow, with some of the worst and most serious coming in 2021 at a time when much of the world was also suffering from the COVID-19 pandemic. It is reported that ransomware gangs are "now routinely targeting schools and hospitals."[630] There have been very upsetting reports of AI deepfakes being used against children!

In 2020/2021, the United Kingdom was reported to have suffered more than nine thousand data security incidents where information was stolen by hackers or mistakenly sent to the wrong recipients. It was reported that five hundred private and public bodies were the victims of ransomware attacks, and several hundred more were victims of other types of hacking attacks. Most of these data system breaches were suffered by healthcare and education organizations. The usual tactic of hacking groups is to encrypt the data in the systems of educational or healthcare organizations and deprive those organizations of the use of this data until the ransom is paid.[631]

Other breaches occurred, affecting the systems of police forces in the United Kingdom; these law-enforcement authority systems had an average of approximately eight data incidents a week which resulted in important data being taken. These statistics are known because whenever a data breach relates to information important to the safety, rights or freedoms of people at risk, the organization holding the data is required to report the breach to the UK ICO, which keeps a record of such data incidents.

There is no doubt that AI can create tools (deepfakes) that will allow those who wish to embarrass those working in law enforcement and undermine confidence in law enforcement organizations.

---

629. Tony Winterburn, above, reporting on information from Juan Jose Nombela, a computer science expert at the International University of La Rioja (UNIR).
630. Joe Tidy, "The ransomware surge ruining lives," BBC News, April 29, 2021, online, accessed, May 11, 2021.
631. Fiona Hamilton, "Hackers on loose as 9,000 data leaks a year recorded," *The Times*, online, July 5, 2021.

In March 2021, it was reported that attacks on universities, colleges and schools prevented students from being able to return to classrooms in about 80 educational institutions.[632]

This surge in attacks has motivated tech companies and governments to find ways to aggressively and effectively counter these damaging, and potentially deadly, criminal activities. In 2021, the U.S. Federal Bureau of Investigation (FBI), Amazon, Microsoft and the National Crime Agency of the United Kingdom joined the Ransomware Task Force (RTF) in issuing a report making approximately 50 recommendations for action that governments should take to counter ransomware and other criminal hacking attacks.[633] Those organizations are now looking at ways to counter AI-powered attacks.

However, although hacking gangs found healthcare and educational institutions to be particularly vulnerable to ransomware attacks, they did not forget to attack other sectors. In the retail sector, there were nearly 1,000 attacks, also nearly 1,000 in financial businesses, and charities were victimized more than 500 times.[634]

Not all data incidents are the result of criminal activity; there are also thousands of computer system incidents whereby data is not sent to the right person. Although many times such a mistake may not be damaging to the owner of the data and may be easily corrected, there are situations where the missending needs to be reported to the ICO because of risks the misdirection many pose to the data owner.

There is the additional difficulty of the financial problems suffered by companies as a result of declines in business due to the pandemic and the accompanying lockdowns. This has often meant that cost-cutting measures have been necessary which have reduced the amount of money available for IT system maintenance and security. This, among other things, has made it easier for criminals to gain access to commercial IT systems. With the dangers that may be posed by AI, cost-cutting in security sectors is even more dangerous.

This represents larger law enforcement issues than simply computer attacks. The money that is paid to criminal gangs resulting from ransomware is used by them to fund other crimes, such as human trafficking and child abuse. The UK National Cyber Security Center (NCSC) reported that there were approximately three times more ransomware attacks in 2020 than in 2019.[635]

There are an increasing number of attacks that affect public services at all levels. For example, in the autumn of 2020, the IT systems of the London borough of Hackney were affected by a cyberattack that interfered with important public services provided online. It was reported:

632. *Ibid.*
633. Tidy, April 29.
634. Hamilton, July 5, 2021.
635. Tidy, April 29.

> The damage done was really significant with things like housing repairs, benefits payments and land registry all impacted. It's going to be months until we are fully recovered, and I can't understand the motivation behind this for criminals.[636]

In May 2021, Colonial Pipeline, the largest fuel pipeline system in the United States, suffered a ransomware cyberattack. This system is the Colonial Pipeline which transports two-and-a-half million barrels a day of fuel, including gasoline, jet fuel and diesel fuel in the East Coast of the United States. On May 7, 2021, it was completely shut down by a cyber hacking gang. Fuel availability in 18 states was affected.[637] Fuel prices were expected to rise as a result.

The problem is that modern infrastructure operations are increasingly sophisticated, digitalized and connected to central computer systems. Consequently, criminals have a variety of portals through which they can seek access to the electronic systems that control important infrastructure operations. Although the name "Colonial Pipeline" may make one think of metal, The facts are that the flow of petroleum-based chemicals through the system to the states on the East Coast of America that depend on it is highly evolved technologically so that most of its operations are under the control of electronic systems, switches, gauges and valves that are centrally controlled and monitored by operators on computers. This makes much of the government infrastructure vulnerable to attack by sophisticated computer criminals. As has been said, a devastating attack can begin by opening a single email.[638] There is a danger that the use of AI tools will make such attacks easier for criminals.

The Colonial Pipeline hack has had serious consequences in the United States. There have been shortages of fuel in various areas served by the pipeline. In some states, petrol stations have run out of fuel. Rises in the price of fuel were expected to last several months. In some areas, there has been "panic buying" of fuels.[639]

The Colonial Pipeline hack is believed to have been caused by a criminal gang known as dark side. They have been reported to have begun attacking computer systems and demanding ransom payments sometime in August 2020. Some sources believe that they are connected to Russia, but there is no certain knowledge that this is true.[640]

It is reported that USD 4.4 million in ransom was paid to the colonial pipeline hackers to get them to release the pipeline. However, in early June 2021, U.S. government officials were able to trace and recover USD 2.3 million of this ransom, which was being transferred in the form of bitcoin by criminals. Joseph Blunt said that colonial was happy for the "swift work and professionalism" of the FBI and seeking to recover the ransom.

A key element of the FBI's recovery was the acquisition of something called the "private key" to the "bitcoin wallet" of the hackers. No details of how the FBI obtained

636. *Ibid*, quoting Rob Miller, director of information and communications technology for the London Borough of Hackney.
637. Joe Tidy, "Colonial hack: How did cyber-attackers shut off pipeline," BBC News, online, May 10, 2021.
638. *Ibid.*
639. Joe Tidy, BBC News, online, May 12, 2021.
640. *Ibid.*

this information were given, but there has been considerable speculation over whether it was from some equipment seized by the FBI, from an informant inside the criminal gang or from a company that the hackers might've used as part of their hacking project.[641]

The increase in ransomware attacks, and particularly the devastating nature of the attack on the colonial pipeline, has highlighted the issue in the United States and caused people to think that the government needs to do more to protect vulnerable and important IT systems.[642]

As a result of the Colonial Pipeline hack, the U.S. government has called emergency meetings and began discussions about issuing an executive order to increase the cyber security requirements for federal agencies and government contractors.[643]

Drafts of such an order have been provided to government agencies and government contractors that provide a cyber security program to better protect the United States. The order outlines Government mandated cyber security standards that government agencies and contractors would be required to put in place. The proposed standards include "multi factor identification" that requires a second code to be obtained by a different trusted method before a critical system user would be allowed to log in. Government agencies would also be required to introduce a "zero trust" policy with respect to software vendors. Vendors would be allowed access to government IT systems only when necessary, and all contractors would be required to comply with certain conditions before any software they supplied would be accepted. Any violators of the required standards could be banned from government business which would be seriously commercially damaging.[644]

However, huge and damaging hacking attacks did not end with the Colonial Pipeline. At the beginning of July 2021, there was a massive and devastating ransomware attack that assaulted hundreds of American businesses and many other businesses around the world, affecting companies in about 17 countries.[645]

The suspicion of U.S. law-enforcement authorities was that the attack originated in Russia or in the former Soviet states. The FBI believes that it is being perpetrated by the Russian hacking group known as REvil. Another clue as to the origin of the attack is that the computer code of the attack is structured to exclude the Russian language using computer systems.[646] The attack involved inserting malicious code into software used by many companies. It has been speculated that the hackers were demanding USD 70 million to restore service to the companies they attacked. President Biden

641. Joe Tidy, "Colonial Pipeline, US Recovers most of the ransom, justice department says," "A powerful message to hacker gangs," BBC News, online, June 8, 2021.
642. David E. Sanger, Nicole Perlroth and Julian E. Barnes, "Biden Plans an Order to Strengthen Cyberdefenses. Will It Be Enough," *The New York Times*, May 9, 2021, online, accessed May 11, 2021.
643. Sanger, Perlroth Barnes, May 9, 2021.
644. *Ibid.*
645. Marc Bennetts and Alistair Dauber, "Joe Biden takes aim at Russia over crippling cyberattack," *The Times*, online, January 5, 2021.
646. Ken Dilanian, "Code in huge ransomware Attack written to avoid computers that use Russian, says a new report," NBC News, online, July 7, 2021.

directed U.S. security services to do a thorough analysis of the attack to determine who was responsible and how it was done. In a meeting in Geneva shortly before this attack, Biden had warned Putin not to permit attacks on U.S. digital sites to originate from Russia. But, it is unclear whether this demand will make any difference to the number or intensity of hacking attacks.

However, the countries that are alleged to sponsor or permit hacking attacks from within their borders should not confidently assume that the hacking abilities within their country are superior to those that can be deployed by the United States or its allies.

It is certainly the case when considering the roles that AI systems and tools can play in both perpetrating and investigating computer attacks; the U.S., with its leadership in AI development, may well be in the strongest position to defend against and/or punish cyberattacks of all kinds, including cyberattacks aided by abusive use of AI.

It seems unlikely that the important infrastructure systems of countries like Russia, China or North Korea are vulnerable to hacking attacks. There seems little doubt that significant damage can be done to their systems by other countries through the use of the Internet. It is also the case that countries alleged to be sponsoring hacking attacks have financial and physical resources that can be vulnerable to seizure as retribution for damaging hacking attacks on other countries. Indeed, it has been reported that Mr. Putin has made efforts to deposit a significant fortune with financial institutions outside of Russia.[647]

It is possible that President Biden's warning to Putin did produce a positive response. One of the most notorious hacking groups REvil (also called "Sodinokibi") suddenly disappeared from the internet after President Biden's warning. REvil's blog and its payment website stopped being available on July 13, 2021.[648] Of course, there are several possible reasons why this occurred. REvil may have decided that, given all the scrutiny they were subject to, it might be better for them to lie low for a while. Or, the U.S. or other countries with computer expertise may have successfully hacked their servers and taken them offline. It is also possible that Russian authorities may have been ordered to take action against them. Time will tell whether they will reappear and, if they do, in what form.

One somewhat radical solution to solving the problem of ransomware attacks is that laws should be passed making the payment of rent somewhere a criminal offense.[649] The former head of the UK Cyber Security Center, Ciaran Martin, believes that cybercrime would stop being a way for global Internet criminals to make money if payments to them were banned. One of the problems with providing effective security against cyberattacks is that a cyberattack on a particular organization creates few, if any, legal obligations on the target. Most are not required to report or publicize the attack, and if payment is made in cyber currency, it may be completely untraceable.

---

647. Adam Taylor, "Is Vladimir Putin hiding a $200 billion fortune? And if so, does it matter?" *The Washington Post*, online, February 20, 2015.
648. "REvil Ransomware websites disappear from the internet, BBC News, online, July 14, 2021.
649. Fiona Hamilton and Mark Bridge, "Ban ransom payments to hackers, urges ex-GCHQ boss," *The Times*, online, May 14, 2021, accessed, May 17, 2021.

This leaves government institutions which are supposed to provide security against cyberattacks with very little information about how to counter them or enforce punishment on the perpetrators.

Martin says that it makes no more sense to pay Russian cyber criminals than it does to pay Islamic terrorists. Both types of payments are damaging to society and encourage the continuation of attacks that may raise money to fund other kinds of criminality and terrorism.[650]

There is, of course, a downside in that those who are attacked may lose valuable data because of their failure to pay. Another problem is that many hackers, rather than threatening to destroy data, threaten to release highly sensitive or deeply embarrassing data about institutions and individuals onto the Internet. The pain, embarrassment and cost of having such data be made available publicly is a serious problem and a key motivation to make payments to hackers.[651] For example, a chain of clinics that provided cosmetic surgery and weight loss therapy to clinics, some of whom were well-known public figures, was recently threatened with public disclosure of a database of client photographs. The disclosure did not happen, but the threat illustrates the delicacy of the problem.[652] Sensitive ways to deal with this type of thing will need to be found. It seems likely that AI could make the stolen personal information of this kind much more useful to criminals who may wish to use it for blackmail of deepfake purposes.

Martin also urges insurers that provide promises for payment to compensate clients against ransomware attacks to require their clients to put better cyber protection in place. This could be incentivized by tying the level of premiums to the effectiveness of the cyber security in place. This would make it more attractive for institutions to improve their cyber security.[653]

§19.12 U.S. INTERNATIONAL CYBERCRIME PREVENTION ACT

The growth of cybercrime during the pandemic in general and the devastating Colonial Pipeline cyberattack in 2021 caused the U.S. Congress to reconsider the International Cybercrime Prevention Act (ICPA) which had previously failed to pass in 2018. The bill provides law-enforcement with additional powers to seize the computing devices of cyber criminals and created additional criminal violations for which attackers could be prosecuted for disrupting critical infrastructure.

One provision of the ICPA bill would have made any violation of the Computer Fraud and Abuse Act (CFAA) an offense within the Racketeer Influenced and Corrupt Organization (RICO) Act.

The U.S. had previously brought some prosecutions of cyber criminals under RICO. For example, the Justice Department prosecuted an Eastern European group for

650. *Ibid.*
651. *Ibid.*
652. *Ibid.*
653. *Ibid.*

RICO charges relating to the defendants providing hosting services for the distribution of malware.[654]

Section 5 of the act would have created a specific violation for serious damage to infrastructure computer systems or for intentionally damaging computers controlling important infrastructure such as election systems, hospitals, power plants and dams.

Section 6 of the bill would have made it an offense to use or provide access to a computer infiltrated by criminals within a botnet operated for purposes of cybercrime.

Section 3 of the IPCA would have allowed the law enforcement authorities to confiscate and property used to break data privacy laws.

Section 4 would have allowed the provision of injunctive relief against botnets used in cybercriminal activities.[655]

In the end, this bill was not enacted into law.

§19.13 INTERNET VICTIM CRIMES

A key factor in preventing and punishing cybercrime is that the regulators and law enforcement bodies must have as much information as possible about cybercrime, how it is being conducted and how victims are being targeted. As shown by press reports, Internet crime victims who fail to report their attacks or to take appropriate steps to prevent damaging data breaches can also be charged with violations of law and/or regulations that can result in large fines and other possible penalties.

One dramatic example of this is a report that the French Data Protection Authority fined Uber EUR 400,000, United States authorities fined them USD 148 million, the Dutch fined them EUR 600,000, and the British fined them GBP 385,000 because Uber failed to timely report a large data breach. The breach occurred in 2016 and exposed data of about 57 million Uber customers around the world. Apparently, the fines were so high because Uber delayed reporting the breach for over a year, hoping to avoid embarrassment, fines and lawsuits. Uber was also accused of failing to have in place basic security measures that could have prevented the breach.[656]

It is important that companies engaged in business on the Internet remember that, as demonstrated by the Uber fines discussed above, most legal jurisdictions will have in place laws and regulations that require the reporting of data breaches exposing personal data and penalties for failing to report or prevent data breaches. These penalties will differ from jurisdiction to jurisdiction, but one example is the EU GDPR.[657] The GDPR requires that any organization must report certain data breaches

654. Department of Justice, "Four Individuals Plead Guilty to RICO Conspiracy Involving 'Bulletproof Hosting' for Cypercriminals," online, May 7, 2021. https://www.justice.gov/opa/pr/four-individuals-plead-guilty-rico-conspiracy-involving-bulletproof-hosting-cybercriminals.
655. Stevanovic Igor, "Reintroduced International Cybercrime Prevention Act Would Create New Cybercrime Violations, Increase Forfeiture and Injunctive Relief," *IPWatchdog*, online, June 22, 2021.
656. "France hands Uber €400,000 fine over huge data breach." https://www.thelocal.fr/20181220/france-hands-uber-400000-fine-over-huge-data-breach#: ~ :text = France's%20data%20protection%20agency%20said,million%20clients%20and%20drivers%20worldwide.
657. Regulation (EU) 2016/679.

that reveal personal information held by that organization. The GDPR requires that the breach must be reported to relevant regulatory authorities without undue delay, usually within 72 hours if that is feasible.[658]

Under the GDPR, the details of the penalties are left to the individual Member States, but they must be "effective, proportionate, and dissuasive."[659]

Uber is by no means the only commercial organization fined for data breaches. For example, the UK has imposed a number of large fines because of data breaches:

- In July 2019, British Airways was fined GBP 183,000 because of a data breach that affected 500,000 customers. The regulator found that the security standards of British Airways were not sufficiently robust.
- In the same month, Marriott Homes was fined GBP 99,000 because of a bridge that affected over three hundred million customer records. The regulator found that Marriott should have done more to secure its records.
- In October 2018, the UK fined Facebook GBP 500,000 (the maximum fine that the UK regulator is permitted to impose for breaches) for incorrectly sharing the data of 87 million customers with a political consultant organization. The regulator found that Facebook had failed to adequately protect the data of its customers.
- In September 2018, a company called Equifax was fined GBP 500,000 for failing to make certain that its parent company was adequately protecting the data of Equifax's UK customers. It should be noted that the American FTC fined the parent company USD 581 million for the breach which involved the personal data of over 140 million people.
- In April 2019, the UK regulator fined a "pregnancy and parenting club" called Bounty GBP 500,000. Bounty provided personal data of over 30 million people to a number of credit rating agencies without the permission of the people whose data it was.

These are not the only companies that have been punished for failing to protect against data breaches and/or failing to report them as required by law or regulation. Others have included Cathay Pacific, Dixon's Carphone, Yahoo, Capital One, Tesco Bank, Target, Anthem, Google, 1&1 Telecom, University of Texas MD Anderson Cancer Center, Fresenius Medical Care North America, Cottage Health, Touchstone Medical Imaging, University of Rochester Medical Center, Jackson Health Systems, DSG Retail Limited, and others. Many of these have been fined and/or penalized by multiple regulators in several jurisdictions. The total fines and penalties imposed so far are estimated to total more than USD 1.5 billion.[660]

The above is just a selection of examples.

There have been many other data breach penalties and posts around the world, and that is likely to continue in the foreseeable future. It can be seen from the selection

658. EU GDPR, Article 34.1.
659. *Ibid.*, Article 84.1.
660. CSO from IDG, "The biggest data breach fines, penalties and settlements so far," August 14, 2020. csoonline.com, retrieved August 25, 2020.

above that any company or organization that has an electronic database of sensitive personal information about people can find itself the target of a serious data hack. It does not matter what industry, business or institution one is talking about. Criminal hackers consider any large collection of personal data valuable, not least because those who own it or collect it need to run their operations or to live their lives. Consequently, someone who takes it from them and threatens to make it inaccessible profits from ransom, blackmail, or commercial, political or military advantage.

It is vital that business organizations that hold people's personal data put adequate measures in place to protect that data from improper exposure. Failure to do so can be costly and perhaps devastatingly so. If more than USD 1.5 billion in penalties seems like a lot, there is a little doubt that the total will keep getting larger.

§19.14 POLITICAL PROPAGANDA

Since Britain's Brexit referendum in 2015 and the U.S. presidential election of 2016, serious concern has risen about the ethics and legality of using Internet tools to gather information from the social media posts of individuals and using that information to construct campaigns to change the behavior of the individuals who is the data has been mined for the purpose of achieving certain political results.

It seems possible that AI-powered tools could make political interference even more sophisticated and widespread.

Starting in March 2018, Carole Cadwallader and Emma Graham-Harrison began publishing a series of articles that accused Cambridge Analytica of taking data from the profiles of 50 million Facebook users and using that information to manipulate Brexit referendum voters in the UK end voters in the U.S. presidential election for the benefit of the Leave campaign end Donald Trump's election team.[661]The articles said:

> The data analytics firm that worked with Donald Trump's election team and the winning Brexit campaign harvested millions of Facebook profiles of US voters, in one of the tech giant's biggest ever data breaches and used them to build a powerful software program to predict and influence choices at the ballot box.[662]

In the 2019 Netflix documentary entitled, "The Great Hack," it is strongly agreed with *The Guardian* stories that Cambridge Analytica was hired by both the "Leave" campaign during the Brexit referendum and Donald Trump during the 2016 election to gather data from social media sources, and particularly from Facebook, to create profiles of citizens of the UK and the United States to enable the leave and Trump campaign's to change how undecided people would vote.

After these and other revelations about this use of social media data, the situation changed from being embarrassing stories about the activities of Cambridge Analytica to becoming regarded as cyber-criminality.

661. Carole Cadwalladar and Emma Graham-Harrison, "Revealed: 50 million Facebook profiles harvested for Cambridge Analytica in major data breach," The Guardian, March 17, 2018, online, retrieved September 27, 2020.
662. *Ibid.*

In January 2019, the parent company of Cambridge Analytica (SCL Elections) pled guilty to violating the DPA because it had failed to provide an American citizen named David Carroll (a Professor at the New School of Social Research in New York City), with copies of the data it held on him. They refused to comply with an enforcement notice issued by a UK Court and were fined GBP 15,000.

Cambridge Analytica has since gone out of business and been liquidated amidst allegations that they liquidated to avoid having to produce more information about their activities.

[A] Brazil

In Brazil, there was apparently an attempt by President Jair Bolsonaro to interfere with the electoral process by issuing regulations in September 2021, preventing social networks from removing posts that they consider to be disinformation about the future presidential election. However, almost immediately following the introduction of those rules, the Senate and Supreme Court of Brazil canceled those rules because Bolsonaro had been using social media to make the claim that he would only lose the election if it were illegally rigged. He appears to have been taking a page from Donald Trump's book on political manipulation.[663]

Mauricio Santoro, a professor of international relations at the State University of Rio Janeiro, was quoted as saying:

> It's a very positive sign that the Brazilian political class reacted ... The Brazilian leadership is finally understanding how important the Internet is to political life in Brazil."[664]

[B] China

China's cracking down on political speech in Hong Kong that it judges to be in opposition to government policy has been subject to a significant amount of criticism from around the world. In September 2021, there was an instance where the people organized the annual Hong Kong commemoration of the 1989 suppression of protest in Tiananmen Square and were ordered to take down the content of their commemorative website and also the commemorative comments on social media platforms. In making this order, the government was relying on a security law issued last year that allows the government to ban any Internet content that the government, "on reasonable grounds," considers to be a security threat.[665]

663. Jack Nicas, "Bolsonaro's Ban on Removing Social Media Posts is Overturned in Brazil," *The New York Times*, online, September 15, 2021.
664. Jack Nicas, September 15, 2021.
665. Kenji Kwase, "Hong Kong police invoke security law to censor online posts," Nikkei Asia, online, September 17, 2021.

[C] U.S.: Texas and Florida

In the United States, the Republican administrations of both Texas and Florida have attempted to introduce laws similar to that promoted by President Bolsonaro in Brazil.

[1] Texas

In September 2021, the governor of Texas signed a bill that forbids social media platforms from removing posts because of the political views expressed in the posts.[666] Under this bill, social media sites "cannot remove, play down or otherwise moderate content because of a user's political perspective or ban the user entirely. The companies will also need to publish regular reports showing how often they receive complaints about content and how often they took posts down."[667]

Both the State Attorney General and individual citizens will be allowed to sue social media companies that allegedly breach these rules. The law will apply to any social media providers with more than 50 million users active monthly and to anyone who lives in Texas, conducts business there or receives or distributes social media posts in Texas. Similar bills have been proposed in many U.S. states that have Republican administrations claiming that they wish to prevent "censorship." They justify their attempts to control social media firms in this way by claiming that social media platforms have become a kind of utility or "common carrier" similar to a telephone company.

[2] Florida

As another example, Florida introduced a law making it unlawful for social media platforms to ban some political candidates from their sites. However, social media companies brought suit in opposition to this law, and the court blocked enforcement of the law until legal challenges to the law could be decided.[668]

U.S. District Judge Robert Hinkle of the United States District Court for the Northern District of Florida said:

> This order preliminarily enjoins enforcement of the parts of the legislation that are preempted or violate the First Amendment.[669]

§19.15 FOREIGN INTERFERENCE IN ELECTIONS

Using the Internet to interfere with foreign elections has become a significant problem in recent years, and this issue has been raised in many countries, including the recent presidential election of the United States.

---

666. David McCabe, "Texas forbids political çensorship' by social media companies," *The New York Times*, online, September 9, 2021.
667. *Ibid.*
668. *Ibid.*
669. Kanishka Singh, "Federal judge rules Florida social media law likely violates free speech," Reuters, online, July 1, 2021.

As a result, a number of countries introduced laws to prevent and punish such interference. Because these laws may affect the desire of any Internet user who wishes to use the World Wide Web to express their political views and to persuade others (whether in their own country or in other nations) of the correctness of their political views, it is important to examine the legal status of this issue and the steps that have been taken to correct what is regarded as improper use of the Internet to influence or interfere with elections.

One of the most highly publicized incidents of alleged electoral interference has been highlighted by the conclusion of U.S. intelligence that Russia attempted to influence the U.S. presidential election in favor of Donald Trump during the 2016 presidential election.

After the election, the U.S. Director of the National Counterintelligence and Security Center, William Evanina, issued a report on foreign threats to U.S. elections in which he said:

> Foreign intelligence entities likely view US elections as an opportunity to undermine confidence in our democratic institutions and processes, sow division in our society, weaken our alliances and promote their political, economic or ideological agendas. These entities operate in the seams of our democratic system to advance their interests, using the tools of traditional espionage, in combination with cyber operations to influence campaigns.[670]

The United States is not the only country that fears this kind of interference and may not be the only country which has suffered from electoral interference.

Several countries have taken steps to prevent and punish this kind of interference.

An accepted international legal basis for the countermeasures is that such interference can constitute a violation of a country's sovereignty. Several countries have accepted the principle that respecting a nation's sovereignty is a fundamental element of international law. The Tallin Manual 2.0: on the International Law Applicable to Cyber Operations[671]

The countries and international organizations that accept that respect for sovereignty is fundamental to international law include Austria, Czech Republic, France, Germany, Netherlands, Switzerland and NATO.[672]

An accepted definition of what constitutes a nation's sovereignty was set out in the 1928 Island of Palms arbitration by Max Huber:[673]

> Sovereignty in the relations between States signifies independence. Independence, in regard to a portion of the globe is the right to exercise therein, to the exclusion of any other State, the functions of a State.

670. Office of the Director of National Intelligence, Press Release, "Statement by NCSC Director William Evanina: Election Threat Update for the American Public, online at: dni.gov, August 7, 2020, accessed November 21, 2023.
671. Michael Schmitt, editor, published by the United States Naval War College (Newport, Rhode Island, USA, 2017).
672. Michael Schmitt, EIJL, October 16, 2020.
673. *Ibid.*

[A] Singapore

On September 13, 2021, the government of Singapore proposed a parliamentary bill to prevent foreign cyber interference in Singapore politics. The bill is called the Foreign Interference (Countermeasures) Bill. It is targeted at online content that "can cause immediate and significant harm in Singapore." Social media providers will be required to comply with the law, and Internet service providers could be required to block harmful political content. The bill also would permit the blocking of any computer downloads that aid in spreading harmful content. This bill follows the anti-fake news law introduced in Singapore in 2019.[674]

§19.16 ZERO CLICK SPYWARE

The most sinister developments in online crime, illicit spying and violation of privacy have generally been the development of "Zero click" spyware that allows hackers access to iPhones and iPads without the owners having to open or click on a file or a link. This seems to be specific to the iOS operating system.

When this became widely reported in September 2021, Apple took urgent steps to correct this flaw in its system. In mid-September 2021, Apple announced that it had issued security updates to defend against what is described as a malicious PDF file.

This innovative spyware was apparently first recognized at the University of Toronto's Citizen Lab. They said that this spyware affected all Apple devices, including iPhones, Macs and Apple watches. Toronto also claimed that this flaw was first exploited on an Arab activist's iPhone and that they suspected that an Israeli firm, the NSO Group, may have created the spyware. NSO refused to either confirm or deny its role in creating the spyware. It stated that it would "continue to provide intelligence and law-enforcement agencies ... with technologies to fight terror and crime."[675]

Experts pointed out that the use of spyware seems to be limited to specific high-value targets, so it may not be a worry for the general population of Apple users. Apple announced that it had issued defensive software patches in iOS 14.8 and iPad OS 14.8 software.[676]

The zero click spyware exploited a gap in Apple's iMessage, which was previously understood to be one of the safest messaging apps.

This was embarrassing for Apple not only because Apple likes to be known as having one of the most secure operating systems but also because it came to public attention during the time of the year when Apple likes to announce new and/or improved products (September). However, Apple did appear to respond quickly with

674. Chen Lin, "Singapore Submits bill to fight 'foreign interference'. *Reuters*, online, September 13, 2021.
675. Joe Tidy, A BBC News Reporter, notes that NSO has been subject to accusations that its hacking has affected innocent people. Joe Tidy, "Analysis," BBC News, online, September 14, 2021.
676. BBC News, Apple rushes to block 'zero click' iPhone spyware," online, September 14, 2021.

solutions when it became aware of this problem, and, as stated above, the risk to average Apple users is pretty low.[677]

§19.17 DEATH FROM HACKING

One of the more frightening aspects of hacking and cybercrime is the fact that many devices and systems critical to healthcare are accessible through the internet. On the one hand, that makes them easier to operate and gather information about how they are working and how they are contributing to patient care. But on the other hand, this makes them vulnerable to interference from hackers and cybercriminals.

Hospital records, hospital networks, MRI machines and drug infusion pumps are all digitally accessible now. This puts them in danger of being hacked.[678]

One of the most sinister possibilities for hackers is that medically implanted devices could be vulnerable to interference. Among the implantable devices that have been found to be vulnerable are insulin pumps and pacemakers.[679]

There is a fictional story about this in the popular television series Homeland, where Damien Lewis's character gives terrorists information about the American Vice-President's pacemaker, which the terrorists use to hack the pacemaker and kill him.[680]

This threat had a real-life parallel in 2013, when the former U.S. Vice-President, Dick Cheney, had the wireless connectivity of his pacemaker disconnected so it could not be hacked and put Cheney's life at risk.[681]

In 2019, the U.S. Food and Drug Administration said that some kinds of defibrillators had vulnerabilities that might allow unauthorized persons to manipulate them remotely.[682]

Unfortunately, this threat is becoming ever more real. In September 2020, it was reported that prosecutors in Dusseldorf, Germany, launched a manslaughter investigation after a woman died in a hospital there after her emergency treatment was delayed for more than an hour. It is thought that her death may have been caused by hackers shutting down the hospital's IT systems. Dusseldorf University Hospital was locked out of its computer systems, and a blackmail message was received, giving digital directions for contacting the hackers. The police informed the hackers that they had shut down the hospital systems, putting patients in danger. After that, the attack was abandoned, and systems were restored.[683]

677. Joe Tidy, "Analysis," BBC News, online, September 14, 2021.
678. Joe McKinley, "5 Medical Devices You Didn't Know Could be Hacked," https://www.thehealthy.com/healthcare/hacked-medical-devices/.
679. Jo Best, "Could Implanted Medical Devices Be Hacked?," *British Medical Journal*, January 14, 2020. https://www.bmj.com/content/368/bmj.m102.full, DOI: 10.1136/bmj.m102.
680. Joe McKinley, "5 Medical Devices ..." *supra*.
681. Joe Best, *supra*.
682. *Ibid*.
683. David Crossland, "Woman dies after hackers hit A&E," *Times*, September 19, 2020, online, retrieved September 19, 2020.

§19.18 QUANTUM COMPUTING

Another looming challenge to cyber security is the dramatic progress that is being made to computer equipment in the form of "quantum computers."

Computers today, or "classical" computers as they are coming to be known, operate digitally in segments of information that are called "bits." A bit can express one of two possible outcomes: 1 or 0. These values represent states that are on or off. All classical computer programs and operations are created from combinations of those two possible positions. Every computing operation we do now is made up of millions of combinations of on or off (1 or 0). The necessity to operate computers by instructing them with various combinations of those two numbers, some quite long, places limitations on the speed with which computer operations can be completed. Of course, over the past few decades, the computer chips that perform those operations have become increasingly faster, so computer speed is now much greater than it was several decades ago.

However, computer scientists are now working on developing a computer instruction system that operates not in "bits" but in "qubits." This proposed computing system is based on the field of physics known as quantum mechanics. This field of physics was created to try to understand the natural world better. Nature does not operate by choosing between only two possible known outcomes. Nature is more unpredictable. A "qubit," short for "quantum bit," permits the examination of many more possible outcomes than just two. Employing this device in computing could make computing operations exponentially faster.[684]

Until late 2019, it was thought that quantum computing was still a long way away. However, in October 2019, everything changed. In the journal Nature, Google announced that a quantum computing system developed by Google had achieved "quantum supremacy," meaning that it could complete calculations much faster than the fastest "supercomputers" existing up until then.

Google's Sycamore quantum system completed a calculation that would take 100,000 classical computers 10,000 years to complete. The truly amazing thing is that Sycamore represents quantum computing at its most primitive. It is expected that quantum computers will soon be much more powerful. Sycamore is a 53 qubit system, but it is believed that future quantum computing systems could operate on billion qubit systems.[685]

What does this mean for cybercrime? Far too much!

If criminals are currently able to access quantum tools and the skills that enable them to crack the security systems that individuals and even major companies have in place to protect their information, how much more powerful would criminal hacking groups be? There is no reason not to believe that it would improve their ability to crack protective coat and security systems to an exponential degree. That is a frightening

684. Amit Katwala, "Quantum computing and quantum supremacy, explained," *Wired*, March 5, 2020, online, retrieved September 3, 2020.
685. Scott Aaronson, "Why Google's Quantum Supremacy Milestone Matters," *The New York Times*, October 30, 2019, online, retrieved September 3, 2020.

prospect and causes one to wonder whether it will be possible to create any truly safe passwords and security systems in the future when quantum computing becomes more generally available.

Fortunately, scientists are already working to solve this potential problem. Two technological solutions are currently being worked on to provide greater security in the face of potential quantum intrusion. The first is Quantum Key Distribution (QKD). This is a method of agreeing on encryption keys between distant parties to protect security keys from being observed or tampered with. The second anti-quantum attack protection method is Quantum Random Number Generation. This produces numbers, random numbers at such high speeds that the numbers can be unpredictable and can form an important part of hacking-resistant security systems.[686]

One can only hope that the development of security technologies can match the pace of the development of quantum computing and the application of this powerful new technology by criminal hacking groups.

This discussion begs the question of whether possession or access to such powerful computing tools should be legally restricted and/or regulated in some way. That is a difficult question. Of course, societies have traditionally used their legal powers to restrict the ownership, possession and use of technological advances that are deemed to be particularly dangerous. Such concerns have resulted in restrictions on firearms, explosives, nuclear technology, automobiles, and other technological advances that, although their existence is considered to have benefits, also present different types and degrees of danger to the public.

How much will quantum computing help cyber criminals to develop AI tools to assist their crimes?

§19.19 ONLINE ABUSE

It is not news that the Internet, and particularly the social media sites, are full of abusive, insulting and sometimes threatening posts. For Internet service companies and law-enforcement agencies, it is not easy to decide what to do about them.

The first issue has to do with the interstate and international aspects of the Internet. Social media sites operate on the World Wide Web. Who has jurisdiction to control and police them? The second issue has to do with when do these posts cross the line from being offensive to becoming criminal activity?

The type of Internet posts that need reaction can be divided into two basic categories. The first is those Internet posts that constitute illegal hate activity. The second constitutes posts which threaten death, destruction or other physical harm. The first category of activity will depend on what constitutes illegal speech in any particular jurisdiction. This varies from nation to nation. Sometimes, it has to do with insulting or demeaning those of a particular racial or ethnic background. Other times, it has to do

686. UK Government, White Paper, "Quantum Security Technologies," March 24, 2020 https://www.ncsc.gov.uk/whitepaper/quantum-security-technologies, online, retrieved September 7, 2020.

with insulting or demeaning particular religious beliefs. It might constitute insulting, demeaning or challenging Government activity.

There is no universal standard for controlling offensive Internet posts. A significant problem in many jurisdictions is that there are often constitutional protections for freedom of speech which excuse a wide range of speech, including Internet posts, which certain individuals or society might find offensive. So, there is the additional consideration in those jurisdictions of when a post has crossed the line going beyond the protections afforded by freedom of speech regulations. This all makes the area of what constitutes online abuse and how to deal with it complicated. The best one can do in this section is to give an outline of when the line of acceptability might be crossed and refer the reader to the jurisdictional sources that may be able to give a more detailed description of how particular posts will be regarded in particular jurisdictions.

§19.20 THREATS OF VIOLENCE

With threats of violence, it is true that the majority of these do not lead to actual physical harm. However, that is not always the case. Sometimes, people who threaten physical violence act on it.

There have been a number of cases where people who threatened terrorist activity later went on to carry it out by planting bombs or engaging in personal attacks, injuring or killing those they considered to be enemies of their ideology or even innocent persons such as school children.

The standard for judging threatening posts like these seems to be whether a "reasonable person" would consider that a threat was serious enough that it may be expected to lead to criminal acts.[687]

Law enforcement authorities are in the difficult position of having to judge which threats have crossed the line into criminal behavior. This is often a tricky proposition because a number of countries, such as the United States, have freedom of speech protections written into their constitutions. So, it is generally considered that broad threats, such as let us put Donald Trump back in power, or let us arrest all Democrats, are considered too general to justify prosecution.[688]

[A] U.S.

In the United States, it is uncommon for someone to be criminally prosecuted based on things they have said, written or otherwise expressed as a type of speech. However, there have been prosecutions that are worth discussing.

For example, a California man who wrote on a blog about cutting off the heads of employees of the FBI did face criminal prosecution based on those expressions. He claimed that his blog was satire and, therefore, protected speech. He went to trial but

687. Shira Ovide, "When is Online Nastiness Illegal?" *The New York Times*, online, April 23, 2021, accessed, April 26, 2021.
688. *Ibid.*

was ultimately not convicted. His defense made the arguments that he never made any preparations to follow through with such action and that he had had no plans to do so. Neither he nor anyone acting on his behalf had purchased any weapons or taken any actions which could reasonably be thought to be following through to execute those thoughts.[689]

The government of the United States usually sets a high standard before deciding to prosecute someone for things they have said or written that might constitute threats or would otherwise upset people who are the targets of those things. Generally, only specific threats that would cause reasonable people to believe that the maker intended to follow through with harming persons targeted will lead to prosecution. It is believed that speech that does not rise to this level should be controlled by social media companies that allow people to express themselves on their systems.[690]

[B] The EU

Although it is the case that there are no universal international protection standards against criminal behavior on the Internet, the European Union is making efforts to create regulations to protect users. One that has become an international standard is The GDPR of 2018. There has been no formal universal adoption, but a number of countries outside the EU have used the GDPR as a model for developing their own data protection regulations.[691]

Moving on, the EU is now proposing regulations to govern the use of artificial intelligence (AI). The proposed regulations are outlined in an EU White Paper entitled "On Artificial Intelligence—A European approach to excellence and trust."[692] The Paper says that the EU's goals are to encourage the adoption of AI while dealing with the risks entailed by certain uses of this technology.[693]

§19.21 GROWING INTERNATIONAL COOPERATION

One positive development is that the international growth of cybercrime is beginning to inspire parallel growth in international cooperation against cybercrime. At their meeting in England in June 2021, the G7 countries agreed to increase international cooperation against cybercrime. Ursula von der Leyen, the President of the European Commission, said:

> We need a robust joint response to cybercrimes especially ransomware. We agreed to step up information sharing and to coordinate more closely on police investigations and diplomatic measures.[694]

689. *Ibid.*
690. *Ibid.*
691. Edward Lucas, "EU is becoming policeman of the internet," *The Times*, online, April 26, 2021, accessed April 27, 2021.
692. European Commission, February 19, 2020, COM (2020) 65 final, online, accessed April 27, 2021.
693. EU Paper, p. 1.
694. United News of India, "G7 agrees to co-operate on cybercrime cases: EU," online June 13, 2021.

§19.22 THE BUDAPEST CONVENTION AND OTHER INTERNATIONAL STANDARDS

The leading international treaty that provides standards for framing national standards for implementing national anti-cybercrime laws and regulations and guidelines for international cooperation is the Budapest Convention and the related Protocol on Xenophobia and Racism online.[695]

The Convention is a binding treaty, and there are currently 66 signatories (including the U.S., the UK, France, Switzerland, Canada and most EU countries)[696] and 11 countries that consider themselves observers (such as Ireland, New Zealand, Sweden and Russia).

§19.23 THE BUDAPEST CONVENTION (CONVENTION ON CYBERCRIME TREATY NUMBER 185)

The Convention's main objective is to bring about a common legal policy aimed at the protection against cybercrime by encouraging the adoption of relevant laws and regulations and promoting international cooperation against cybercrime. It was the first international treaty to focus on cybercrime, including crimes relating to the Internet and computer networks generally, dealing with such things as infringement of copyright, Internet-related fraud, child pornography and breaches of network security. It provides guidelines for the interception of offending information and the search of computer networks.[697]

The Convention is made up of a Preamble and the following Articles:[698]

(1) Definitions
(2) Illegal access
(3) Illegal interception
(4) Data interference
(5) System interference
(6) Misuse of devices

695. Council of Europe, online portal, https://www.coe.int/en/web/cybercrime/the-budapest-convention.

696. As of this writing, Parties: Albania, Andorra, Armenia, Argentina, Australia, Austria, Azerbaijan, Belgium, Bosnia and Herzegovina, Bulgaria, Cabo Verde, Canada, Chile, Columbia, Costa Rica, Croatia, Cyprus, Czech Republic, Denmark, Dominican Republic, Estonia, Finland, France, Georgia, Germany, Ghana, Greece, Hungary, Iceland, Israel, Italy, Japan, Latvia, Lichtenstein, Luxembourg, Malta, Mauritius, Moldova, Monaco, Montenegro, Morocco, Netherlands, North Macedonia, Norway, Panama, Paraguay, Peru, Philippines, Poland, Portugal, Romania, San Marino, Senegal, Serbia, Slovakia, Slovenia, Sweden, Switzerland, Spain, Sri Lanka, Tonga, Turkey, Ukraine, United Kingdom, and United States of America. The Observer countries are: Benin, Brazil, Burkina Faso, Guatemala, Ireland, Mexico, New Zealand, Nigeria, Niger, Russia (as a Member State of the Council of Europe, South Africa and Tunisia.

697. Council of Europe online portal: https://www.coe.int/en/web/conventions/full-list/-/conventions/treaty/185?module = treaty-detail&treatynum = 185.

698. Council of Europe online portal: https://rm.coe.int/1680081561.

(7) Computer-related forgery
(8) Computer-related fraud
(9) Offenses related to child pornography
(10) Offenses related to infringements of copyright and related rights
(11) Attempt and aiding and abetting
(12) Corporate liability
(13) Sanctions and measures
(14) Scope of procedural provisions
(15) Conditions and safeguards
(16) Expedited preservation of stored computer data
(17) Expedited preservation and partial disclosure of traffic data
(18) Production order
(19) Search and seizure of stored computer data
(20) Real-time collection of traffic data
(21) Interception of content data
(22) Jurisdiction
(23) General principles relating to international cooperation
(24) Extradition
(25) General principles related to mutual assistance
(26) Spontaneous information
(27) Procedures pertaining to mutual assistance requests in the absence of applicable international agreements
(28) Confidentiality and limitation on use
(29) Expedited preservation of stored data
(30) Expedited disclosure of preserved traffic data
(31) Mutual assistance regarding accessing stored computer data
(32) Trans-border access to stored computer data with consent or where publicly available
(33) Mutual assistance regarding the real-time collection of traffic data
(34) Mutual assistance regarding the interception of content data
(35) 24/7 Network
(36) Signature and entry into force
(37) Accession to the Convention
(38) Territorial application
(39) Effects of the Convention
(40) Declarations
(41) Federal clause
(42) Reservations
(43) Status and withdrawal of reservations
(44) Amendments
(45) Settlement of disputes
(46) Consultations of the Parties
(47) Denunciation
(48) Notification.

There is also an Additional Protocol to the Cybercrime Convention that deals with the criminalization of racist and xenophobic acts online.[699] It contains 16 articles dealing with racist and xenophobic threats and insults.[700]

§19.24 GLACY PROJECT

The original GLACY project (Global Action on Cybercrime) was set up to assist countries around the world in implementing the Budapest Convention. It was hoped that GLACY would result in positive changes in the following areas:

- Involvement of decision-makers
- Harmonizing legislation
- Training judges
- Improving law enforcement capacity
- Sharing information
- Reviewing progress.

Its overall aim was to get up to 70 states to cooperate on cybercrime using the Budapest Convention as a common guide. The project ran from November 1, 2013, until October 31, 2016.

§19.25 GLACY + PROJECT

In October 2016, the European Union and the Council of Europe set up a new joint project to combat cybercrime around the world named The Global Action on Cybercrime Extended. "(GLACY +)" project.

Its purpose was to continue and use the experience gained under the original GLACY project. The principal participants in the project are Benin, Burkina Faso, Cabo Verde, Chile, Costa Rica, Dominican Republic, Ghana, Mauritius, Morocco, Nigeria, Paraguay, Philippines, Senegal, Sri Lanka and Tonga. It was hoped that these countries would be "hubs" to educate other countries in their regions about the value of their experiences. The objectives of the GLACY + project are formulated to improve the ability of countries around the world to have effective legislation against cybercrime, improve ways to use electronic evidence and improve international cooperation. These objectives were to be achieved by:

(1) Promoting consistent legislation, policy, and strategy.
(2) Strengthening police ability to investigate cybercrime and encourage cooperation between police forces and cybercrime offices around the world.

699. Additional Protocol 189: Additional Protocol to the Convention on Cybercrime, concerning the criminalization of acts of a racist and xenophobic nature committed through computer systems. This was adopted in 2003 and came into force in 2006. https://rm.coe.int/168008160f.
700. The link to the text of the Additional Protocol is: https://rm.coe.int/168008160f.

(3) To smooth and improve processes to prosecute cybercrime and improve international judicial cooperation.

The activities of the Glacy + project have included:

- Holding workshops around the world, such as one in Burkina Faso in September 2021.
- Holding courses in international cooperation for judges and prosecutors, such as one in Costa Rica in August 2021.
- Holding training sessions improving cybercrime prosecution and the use of electronic evidence, such as one held in Paraguay in September 2021 for 34 magistrates, judges, and judicial training schools.

The above are just a few examples of the kinds of activities arranged through the GLANCY + .

Others have included anti-cybercrime activities in Portuguese-speaking African countries, French-speaking African countries, East Timor, Tonga, Belize, etc., plus various international meetings to promote the objectives of GLANCY + . Some of these activities are conducted live, others are held online.

In connection with the Project, the Council of Europe also maintains and offers a number of resources to draw upon, such as reports, webinars, information about connections between cybercrime and COVID-19, and information about cyberviolence. Cyberviolence is a phenomenon that has been getting more law enforcement attention. It is defined as:

> The use of computer systems to cause, facilitate, or threaten violence against individuals, that results in (or is likely to result in) physical, sexual, psychological or economic harm or suffering and may include the exploitation of the individual's circumstances, characteristics or vulnerabilities.[701]

§19.26 CYBERSTALKING AND CYBERBULLYING

Using the internet to harass and/or intimidate people has become a widespread problem, and, as a result, a number of legal jurisdictions have adopted laws and regulations criminalizing such behavior.[702]

Cyberbullying is legally defined in the following ways:

- Actions that use information and communication technologies to support deliberate, repeated and hostile behavior by an individual or group, that is intended to harm another or others;
- Use of communication technologies for the intention of harming another person;

701. Council of Europe, "What is Cyberviolence" online at: coe.int, accessed November 21, 2023.
702. International Human Rights and Privacy Protection Association. http://ihprpa.org/bullying.php.

- Use of internet service and mobile technologies such as web pages and discussion groups as well as instant messaging of SMS text messaging with the intention of harming another person.[703]

Cyberstalking, however, is a repeated pattern of such things as:

- false accusations;
- monitoring;
- making threats;
- identity theft;
- damage to data or equipment;
- solicitation for sex; or
- harassment.

§19.27 LEGISLATION AGAINST CYBERBULLYING AND CYBERSTALKING

[A] United States

(a) U.S. Federal law does not yet include any specific legislation expressly forbidding cyberbullying or cyberstalking, but legislation criminalizing cyberbullying or electronic harassment has been proposed as of mid-2021.

(b) All U.S. states, as well as the District of Columbia, have legislation that criminalizes harassment and/ or stalking. Some specifically refer to such behavior on electronic media, but all are intended to protect the public regardless of the vehicle used.

§19.28 THE DUTIES OF INTERNET PROVIDERS AND SOCIAL MEDIA PLATFORMS

Clearly one of the largest and most successful providers of social media platforms, with billions of users, Facebook (Meta) has been subject to criticism alleging its failure to properly police the postings of its users.

The dilemma is that it is not clear exactly what are the duties of media companies when it comes to editing and controlling how their platforms are used to post information, or communicate on, and access the World Wide Web. There is no universal legal regulation governing what level of "honesty" they are required to comply with, what definition of "morality" they must aspire to, how they should decide what their users can do on their platforms, or under what circumstances they must restrict, penalize or ban the activities of their users.

703. *Ibid.*

In 2021, publications in *The Wall Street Journal* alleged what the WSJ believed to be an unacceptable level of hypocrisy on the part of Facebook by publicly posting statements that Facebook knew to be untrue.[704] Among the objections of the WSJ to Facebook's behavior are allowing celebrities to post things that other users are not permitted to post, being slow to respond to charges that Facebook is used by drug dealers and people traffickers, allowing Facebook to become a hotbed of anti-vaccination posting when the Facebook founder, Mark Zuckerberg was claiming that Facebook would not be a site for promoting anti-COVID vaccination. Also, Facebook has, allegedly for several years, had information that its Instagram subsidiary causes anxiety and depression in teenagers which, in some cases, can lead to self-harm or even suicide.[705]

These allegations have led to demands that effective regulation of social media platforms, such as Facebook and others, be brought into force.

One proposal is that the controlling executives of social media companies should be subject to personal liability, possible prosecution, and punishment if a company "breaches fundamental health and safety" rules, leading to "severe harm or death."[706]

704. As reported in *The Sunday Times* (which has the same parent company as WSJ), in the following online article, "Facebook's hypocrisy has been exposed in painful detail," September 19, 2021.
705. *Ibid.*
706. *Ibid.*

Chapter 20
AI in War

Russia's attack on Ukraine came after a time when highly sophisticated operations were making significant contributions to misinformation, cybercrime and cyberwar. Despite all of the benefits that artificial intelligence may offer both now and in the future, its rapid development has greatly enhanced the ability of Internet hackers to perpetrate misinformation, cybercrimes and cyberwar. Unfortunately, all of these tools are playing important roles in Russia's invasion of Ukraine. They are just as important, and perhaps even more important, in Ukraine's defense against Russian attacks.

It is reported that: "Ukraine cyber operators are being deployed on the front lines of the war, engaging their Russian counterparts in a new kind of high-tech battle."[707]

Most of this work is directed through the Ukraine Security Services (SBU) cyber department.

The SBU employs AI visual recognition systems to review the information it collects from aerial drones as well as human sources, satellites and other technical and non-technical sources. This information is analyzed to provide Russian military targets for Ukraine's fighting forces to strike at.[708]

There is no question that the employment of AI for military purposes will be able to enhance the speed of development, accuracy and effectiveness of computerized military capabilities.

The computer and the Internet have already become weapons of aggression. The addition of AI will enhance and refine them to make them more deadly, more dangerous and more rapidly deployable.

It seems that smart people with computers and access to the Internet are the materials needed to produce artificially intelligent weapons.

Among the AI "weapons" that could be used by hostile military forces are likely to include such things as the following:

707. Gordon Corera, "Ukraine war: Cyber-teams fight a high-tech war on front lines," BBC New, online at: bbc.com, September 6, 2023.
708. *Ibid.*

- Systems that can hack and disrupt the operation of digital tools used by opponents.
- Systems that can rapidly obtain and analyze information useful to attack or disrupt opponents.
- Systems that can operate and direct other digital tools such as drones (individually or in large coordinated groups).
- Systems that can disrupt the operation of important digitally operated or assisted infrastructure systems of opponents.
- Systems that can provide targeted psychological warfare or misinformation via the Internet and social media, directed at opponents and their populations.
- Systems that can speed up and enhance the development and deployment of more effective or destructive military armaments.
- Systems that can operate independently of human control, such as remotely operated armored vehicles, airplanes, satellites, bombs and missiles, submarines and ships, etc.
- Systems that can control lethal robotic weapons that can operate independently of human presence to replace or supplement human military personnel.

The above list includes some of the military uses to which AI systems could be put. The list is unlikely to be exhaustive. Human imagination and creativity, probably with AI assistance, may well be able to find a much longer list of military tools that can be created, operated or enhanced by AI.[709]

The effects of such weapons will range from helpful to extremely destructive. The easy availability of the tools needed to create such weapons will mean that strong, universally accepted treaties and restrictions on their uses and applications will need to be internationally negotiated and accepted.

§20.01 CYBERWAR IS HERE

In September 2019, PC Magazine published an article entitled "Cyberwar Is Here: Are You Ready?."[710]

The article pointed out that the U.S. and its allies and adversaries have powerful digital weapons at their disposal. But the point of the article was not only that nations are able to deploy these weapons against each other to disrupt military (such as nuclear development projects)[711] and infrastructure systems (such as power grids) that are accessible over the Internet but also that they can be used to affect all of us that use the Internet by disrupting the economic and communication systems that that much of the world's population use and depend on.

Given the fact that any device that can connect to the Internet can be hacked and remotely controlled, cyber war can be used to bring domestic and economic disruption,

709. Iain Martin, "To defend the West we must win this AI race," *The Times*, online May 31, 2023.
710. https://www.pcmag.com/news/370753/cyberwar-is-here-are-you-ready.
711. Such as the U.S. and Israel are alleged to have done to Iran by deploying the Stuxnet Worm. http://large.stanford.edu/courses/2015/ph241/holloway1/.

and perhaps paralysis, to each of us as individuals. Many people use computer payment systems for shopping, digital security cameras to keep our homes safe, robot vacuum cleaners to clean them, and computer games and media streaming to keep our family members entertained. It is not difficult to imagine how disrupted people's lives could be if these and other Internet-accessible items were suddenly controlled by a hostile party.

All these domestic disruptions could be in addition to infrastructure attacks on communications, power systems, water and gas grids, transportation systems and military operations systems.

These issues have made countries increasingly aware that important battles in the future will be fought not in the dirt of the earth but in the tech sphere. There is considerable concern among the Western nations and the NATO allies that countries that may prove enemies of theirs in the future, particularly China, Iran, North Korea and Russia, are developing increasingly more sophisticated ways of attacking the computer-controlled assets of other countries.

It is reported that NATO is subject to cyber-attacks almost every day from hackers trying to get access to confidential information. The NATO secretary general, Jens Stoltenburg, has said that in addition, the individual cellular phones of military personnel in the Baltic states were being hacked apparently to disrupt their activities.[712] In response, NATO has conducted military exercises simulating mass cyberattacks on military assets. A policy has also been adopted that in the case of heightened military threats, personnel will be told to turn off their cell phones and remove the sim cards so that their movements and communications cannot be tracked. One of the principal purposes of these hostile cyberattacks seems to be to gather information about NATO's military systems so that they can be remotely manipulated in the event of a future conflict.[713]

In March 2021, *The Times* published a report on a Ministry of Defense review of these issues that said:

> Britain risks losing battles of the future to tech savvy China and Russia "without a shot being fired" unless it adapts, a senior military chief warned.[714]

The report pointed out that in the next struggle, the power of large armies and conventional weapons will be less important than cyber-sophistication, including knowledge of the construction and effective use of algorithms.

It has been reported that General Sir Patrick Sanders, the head of the UK's Strategic Command, believes that:

712. Larisa Brown, "Enemy hackers target NATO with constant cyberattacks," *The Times*, online, May 28, 2021.
713. *Ibid.*
714. Larisa Brown, "Military chief warns 'algorithms will be our armour in high-tech wars of the future.'" *The Times*, March 13, 2021, online, accessed March 15, 2021.

> Cyber "warriors" will be as vital to protecting Britain as F35 pilots on aircraft carriers, special forces soldiers and those operating the nuclear deterrent … .[715]

General Sanders said that included in future defense systems, AI and machines would play an important role in defending humans:

> Even the best human operators cannot defend against multiple machines making thousands of maneuvers per second at hyper-sonic speed and orchestrated by AI.[716]

The issue of the importance of Internet-based knowledge in potential future conflicts raises a number of legal questions having to do with access to and the use of such knowledge.

At present, little thought has been given to the issue of the spread of sophisticated understanding of computer technology and the Internet. This information is generally open to everyone in line with laws widespread in developed Western countries granting and protecting Freedom of Information. The general approach seems to be that laws and regulations as applied to the cyber sphere are adequate if they can be used to punish misuse of the skills and information necessary to operate at a sophisticated level on the Internet. However, given the ability of the Internet to reach and direct the increasingly growing "Internet of Things," which includes those instruments and data sources that are reachable over the Internet, are these laws adequate? Might there be a need to refashion the legal system applying to the Internet to provide more specialized legal barriers to having certain categories of Internet knowledge at all?

This is not without precedent. Historically, a number of societies restricted certain important tools of communication to a limited number of specially trained and approved persons. For example, in ancient Mesopotamia, the important medium of cuneiform writing was restricted to specially trained and approved scribes who were allowed to use their skills only in the context of certain approved activities—largely related to the formation of commercial contracts but also related to particular governmental and or religious uses. Not everyone was provided with the training or permission to operate within the cuneiform writing system.

In medieval Europe, a similar situation existed with respect to published material. The right to produce published material was limited to printers' guilds such as the Stationers Guild in England. If one wanted to publish any writing at all, it would have to be done through the approved Guild.

It is now virtually impossible to run a nation or individual lives in the developed world without using computer systems connected to the Internet.

In fact, less and less of the data that is important to us as individuals is stored or accessed on our individual computer drives. Increasingly, data is stored in vast server farms that make up the infrastructure of "the cloud" that keeps so much of the information we need.

715. Larisa Brown, "Cyber warriors as important to our safety as fighter jets says general," *The Times*, online, May 27, 2021, accessed May 31, 2021.
716. *Ibid.*

It is true that these "cloud networks" are usually operated by digital giants such as Microsoft, Apple or Amazon. Of course, they make an effort to protect their cloud servers with sophisticated security systems. But, cyber criminals and hackers, including those employed by government organizations, are constantly working to improve their abilities to get access to protected computer systems. Consequently, the press periodically reports huge data breaches affecting millions, serious power outages, "ransomware" attacks and "denial of service" attacks. These are much more serious than the almost daily irritations that afflict us all, from "fishing" emails, fake "security" alerts, false messages from fake law-enforcement officials, and emails from fraudsters using hacked email accounts of our friends and acquaintances.

The point is that the penetration of the Internet has become so widespread that it can be used not only to irritate and defraud individuals but also to effectively disrupt or destroy the governing abilities of nations.

The impact of these cyber-crimes is huge, but still nowhere near the potential impact cyberattacks could have, given the huge adoption of Internet use currently ongoing and the future potential of the growth of Internet use.

There are currently 3.9 billion Internet users worldwide. There are approximately eight hundred million in China, around five hundred million in the EU and about three hundred million in the U.S.

It is estimated that within the next 10 years, most of the world's population will be connected to the internet.

The chief operating officer of SoftBank believes that there will be over 1 trillion devices connected by the Internet by 2025.[717] The frightening vulnerability of that is that any device that connects to the Internet can be "hacked" and probably controlled by the hacker.[718]

A recent wide-ranging study, done jointly by Imperial College in London and Northeastern University in Boston, Massachusetts, U.S., examined over 80 devices that connect to the Internet, such as speakers, doorbells, smart TVs and other things from major suppliers, including Amazon and Google. They discovered that most of these devices collected information such as IP addresses, MAC addresses, user habits and location information and sent it to third parties even if the user of the device didn't have any relationship with those parties or any knowledge that this information was being shared with third parties. More than 70 of the devices were found to be making contact with parties other than the device manufacturer.

"Smart TV" sellers seem to be particularly guilty of ignoring the privacy of their users. It has been reported that Vizion was sued for secretly recording and marketing usage information about more than 15 million Vizio owners, and Samsung has been criticized for gathering and storing user data. You can bet that the vulnerability of all

717. https://venturebeat.com/2018/10/16/softbank-believes-1-trillion-connected-devices-will-create-11-trillion-in-value-by-2025/.
718. https://www.fastcompany.com/90164031/you-can-hack-almost-any-smart-device-with-a-google-search.

these Internet-connected devices to hacking, data-gathering and eavesdropping would be of significant interest to national intelligence agencies around the globe.[719]

In June 2020, the Australian government reported that it had been the subject of sophisticated state-sponsored cyber-attacks on its businesses and institutions. The Australian Prime Minister refused to identify the suspected source of these attacks, but there is suspicion that they emanated from China, a country with which Australia had been having difficult relations. It was pointed out that China, Russia and North Korea were the only countries with whom Australia was not aligned that had the capabilities to undertake such attacks.[720]

It was reported that such attacks were aimed at "all levels of government," essential services and a number of businesses. The attacks were said to have occurred over many months and were increasing. Attacks were being observed on "government, industry political organizations, education, health, essential service providers and operators of other critical infrastructure." For example, the Australian National University said it had been attacked by a sophisticated operation that accessed staff and student details.[721]

It was noted that although it has been subject to many attacks, Australia was not unique in this regard, and similar attacks have been identified in other countries.[722]

The overseas threat from hackers that appear to be sponsored by foreign governments is continually increasing. For example, during the summer of 2017, two major computer viruses attacked sites in the Western world.

The first was the WannaCry virus that was believed to be a North Korean-backed hacker attack that encrypted the data of target companies and individuals and demanded ransom money to release the target's data. This affected, among others, parts of the German Railway System and the UK's NHS computers.

The second was believed to be a Russian attack aimed at businesses in the Ukraine. However, this virus, called "Not Petya," hit what were apparently unintended targets, including the shipping company Maersk and a chocolate manufacturer in Australia.[723]

A number of countries have taken formal steps to defend against such attacks. In 2017, the United Kingdom launched its NCSC as part of its national effort to protect the nation against cyberattacks. Ciaran Martin was its first head. From the three years that he had been head of the organization, he identified three important lessons from his experiences:

---

719. https://www.vice.com/en_us/article/gyzjym/the-internet-of-things-is-still-a-privacy-dumpster-fire-study-finds.
720. BBC News (online), "Australia targeted by 'state-based' cyber attacks', June 19, 2020.
721. *Ibid.*
722. *Ibid.*
723. Ciaran Martin, "GCHQ chief: The threat of a rogue cyber-attack keeps me awake at night," *The Times*, August 30, 2020, online, retrieved August 30, 2020. https://www.thetimes.co.uk/article/gchq-chief-the-threat-of-a-rogue-cyber-attack-keeps-me-awake-at-night-9lf8l6hb0?shareToken=fc12cc7cdfdf136fbe47db90f3361e5.

(1) Cyberattacks do not operate on their own. They are often part of a coordinated effort by a foreign nation to undermine the security of a target nation. Therefore, it is important for security services to counter the hostile activities of foreign nationals that are conducted in more traditional ways, as well as be sensitive to computer threats from a hostile foreign country.

It is important to be aware of the different kinds of penetration that foreign cyberattacks are aimed to achieve. For example, Mr. Martin writes that Russian hacker groups tend to focus on national infrastructure targets such as energy systems, medical research and electoral processes. Chinese hackers, however, have usually tended to seek economic advantages through the theft of intellectual property. However, Chinese hackers now also seem to be attacking important strategic technology as well.

Iranian hackers look for data that can help them track certain people, and they also try to disrupt services in countries that are suffering from unrest.

North Koreans try to use hacking to get money to fund their government.

(2) The second lesson is that a decent level of protection cannot be achieved without careful and skillful security management. Some of this is basic. For example, hacking is far more likely to be effective against organizations with outdated software. So, it is important to keep software up to date.

Having good quality and regular backups is an excellent defense against ransom attacks based on the encryption of the target's data.

(3) Third, it is important to keep barriers to data entry high. This is particularly important if one becomes the target of a hacker who cannot effectively control the virus being released. This can have a devastating effect on the target's systems and on the systems of others to whom the target is connected.[724]

Although Mr. Martin ceased being the head of the NCSC in 2020, he was recently quoted in *The Times* on the sensitive issue of how Chinese technology should be treated.[725] He predicted that in the future, Western countries, including Britain, should be much more cautious about the use of Chinese technology in computing and communication systems. Mr. Martin said that it had taken the West some time to realize that China was determined to become a strategic competitor and to challenge the West in a way it had not been since the end of the Cold War.

However, Martin pointed out that the situation was different from the more difficult opposition presented by the Soviet Union because the West did not have the extensive economic links with the Soviet Union that it had built with China. For example, he pointed to the extensive economic and other links that exist between China and a number of leading Western universities. This has provided China with a

724. *Ibid.*
725. Mark Bridge, "We have been confused about China, says former GCHQ cybersecurity chief," *The Times*, March 15, 2021, online, accessed March 16, 2021.

pathway to both information and technical penetration in some leading areas of developing Western technology.

This concern appears to be more than speculation. In early 2021, the think tank Civitas expressed the view that at least a dozen British universities may be unknowingly helping the People's Liberation Army by exchanging information with universities and companies in China.[726]

This is not a problem that is limited to Britain. Chinese universities and Chinese students have been working hard for many years to establish meaningful relationships and/or presence with leading universities throughout the world, including the U.S., Canada and many countries in Europe.

What level of surveillance and caution is being exercised in those countries today now that there is a greater understanding of China's desire to increase its political and strategic power around the world?

Mr. Martin, who is now a professor at Oxford University, has urged the British government to clarify its policies on security, defense, development and foreign policy to better define its response to the expansion of Chinese power and to provide a better overall understanding of Britain's place in the world.

This increasing awareness of China's aggressive technological role has led to some backlash in Western countries. For example, in 2020, the British government announced that Huawei, the Chinese telecom company would be excluded from providing its equipment to British networks by 2027. However, there is an excellent question as to whether the amount of time that Huawei has had its technology as part of the British system does not provide the Chinese with a long period to learn far too much information about the way that the British communication system is constructed and operated. Will merely replacing Chinese hardware with other substitutes be enough to undo any damage that was done between 2020 and 2027? After all, the reason that the British insisted on the removal of Chinese equipment from its infrastructure was because of the fear that such participation would offer the Chinese a dangerous opportunity to gather intelligence or even conduct sabotage operations in the future. Does the British government have a detailed record of the extent and location of all Huawei products used in the British communication system? Will it in fact be possible to find and effectively remove all avenues of Chinese penetration into British communications infrastructure? Will the fact that China has had access to this British system for so long mean that British communications infrastructure will be eternally vulnerable to potential malicious Chinese interference?[727]

In October 2021, there was a similar reaction in America. It was reported that the U.S. had banned the top Chinese telecom company, China Telecom, from operating in the United States because of "national security concerns." It was reported that U.S. officials thought that the Chinese government's involvement in that company gave them an opportunity to interfere with U.S. communications in harmful ways, including conducting espionage.[728]

726. *Ibid.*
727. *Ibid.*
728. BBC News, "US revokes license of top Chinese telecoms company," online, October 27, 2021.

But, although the United Kingdom considers China the "biggest state-based threat" to Britain's economic security, China is still a critically important trading partner to the UK.[729] UK government advisors have reportedly prepared a 100-page report entitled "Global Britain in a Competitive Age" which identifies China's increasing international aggressiveness as an important risk to the UK's interests.[730] The report is said to assert that one of the biggest challenges for the UK is to maintain and expand protection of its critical infrastructure in electricity, transportation, and water while simultaneously seeking to establish more extensive trade links with China, including increasing Chinese investment in the UK.

According to Sir Alex Younger, who was formerly head of Britain's intelligence agency MI6, it is a mistake to think that as China becomes more economically powerful, it will change its policies to become more like Western countries. According to Younger, it is more likely that China will become more attached to its Communist Party ideology.[731]

But the trickiest part for Britain is that having left Europe, Britain is searching for a new role in the world. In that context, they are trying to find the best way to deal with China which is not only a powerful military and political competitor but also on its way to becoming the largest economy in the world, which presents potential trade opportunities that Britain may not be able to find elsewhere. In Britain's post-Brexit situation, these issues present complex diplomatic puzzles that Britain will have to try to solve very carefully.[732]

To counter this growing Chinese rivalry and threats from other potential international military and economic competitors which may be tempted to engage in cyberattacks and spread misinformation that affect the UK, the government of the UK intends to create a secure "situation room" similar to what exists in the U.S. White House. There, counterterrorism officials from the police, intelligence agencies, and legal advisors could gather to evaluate and respond to any such cyberattacks or other forms of terrorism.[733]

The presence of representatives from the legal and judicial sectors in the proposed team of counterterrorism experts points to the sensitivity to responding to such threats in a way that is compatible with British legal tradition and policy. Although it is certainly important for the UK or any nation to respond quickly and forcefully to cyber and physical threats of terrorism or destabilization, it is important that Western democracies do not lose sight of the policies and limitations which support their commitment to democratic processes and the freedom of their citizens.

However, it must be recognized that there will be some conflict between balancing the British desire to maintain a good economic relationship with China in conjunction with protecting itself against cyberattacks on its infrastructure and the

729. Larisa Brown and Steven Swinford, "UK plans Tighter security to allow trade with 'biggest threat' China," *The Times*, March 16, 2021, online, accessed March 17, 2021.
730. *Ibid.*
731. *Ibid.*
732. Catherine Philip, "'Global Britain' must tread a fine line between China and America," *The Times*, March 16, 2021, online, accessed March 19, 2021.
733. Brown and Swinford.

desire of some British politicians to punish China for such things as its reported treatment of the Uighur minority in China or it's imposition of new laws in Hong Kong that diminish the abilities of the residents of Hong Kong to be able to rely on the protections of democracy.[734]

§20.02 CYBERWAR MARKETS

One particularly frightening aspect of cyberwar that exists because of the markets created on the dark web is the fact that countries do not necessarily have to develop their own high-level hacking capabilities. Expert hacking skills are for sale on the dark web. There are experienced hackers selling their abilities to use well-developed and especially well-tested hacking tools that can be put to use for the right price. There are also hacking specialists that focus on a particular aspect of hacking, such as "system entry specialists" or skilled "data miners" who can be hired by those who wish to put together a team to launch a cyber-attack.[735]

§20.03 RUSSIAN CYBERWAR CONTINUES

Russia apparently has no intention of abandoning its cyberwar on the West. In September 2020, The Times reported that the software giant Microsoft had warned that the Russian military hackers who had interfered with the 2016 U.S. Presidential election remained active, seeking to penetrate the digital data of U.S. political parties, political issue groups and political consultants who were working on the 2020 presidential election.

There is also evidence that Russia continues to target news websites with opinion comments from pro-Russian trolls to try to influence international public opinion in favor of supporting Russia. Their method is basically to insert pro-Russian comments in the opinion sections of articles appearing on Western media sites. The evidence for this is a study done by Cardiff University, crime and security research institute. This study examined over 30 well-known media websites in 16 countries. For example, the fall of Afghanistan to the Taliban allegedly gave the Russians opportunities to introduce comments that this event was a result of the failure of liberal democracy and the ineffectiveness of NATO. The comments also alluded to the weakness of Western countries supporting those institutions in their support of Ukraine against Russia.[736] The researchers indicated that this is a long-running campaign by Russia that shows no signs of tapering off.

Microsoft also reported that China and Iran were attempting to access the email accounts of those affiliated with the November 2020 presidential election.[737]

---

734. *Ibid.*
735. Martin, *supra.*
736. Gordon Corera, Pro-Kremlin trolls target news website comments, researchers say, *The Times*, online, September 2021.
737. Henry Zefferman, "Russian hackers targeting US poll, warns Microsoft," *The Times*, September 11, 2020, online, retrieved September 11, 2020.

§20.04 NO END IN SIGHT

One thing that is clear is that cyberwar is becoming ever more intensive. A number of nations have apparently come to the conclusion that it is a low-cost and effective method of disrupting the operations of other countries that they consider to be hostile to them.

In September 2019, Microsoft Corp. reported that hackers in Russia are behind the largest number of cyber-attacks on Microsoft customers. During the last two years, Microsoft has issued 13,000 alerts to its customers relating to hacking accounts by nation-states. It says that about 52% of those incidents originated from Russian hackers. The attacks have been on a variety of things, including elections. Microsoft also reported that Iran is responsible for about 25% of such attacks and China for about 12%. Other nation-state attacks came from North Korea and a number of other countries.[738]

According to a report in *The Times,* the UK military is under daily attack from cyberhackers:[739]

> General Sir Patrick Sanders, Commander of Strategic Command, outlined how the Ministry of Defence and its assets were under "constant attack" in cyberspace. Up to ten attacks daily are said to stem from hostile state actors.

The report said that the UK has developed cyber weapons to counter, disrupt and "even destroy" computer systems and infrastructure of such attackers.[740]

The UK maintains a Joint Cyber Unit in the Ministry of Defense facility in Corsham, Wiltshire, to deal with cyber problems. There is a constant flow that needs attention. General Sanders said:

> Each year, the systems here manage millions of network and cyber events. Most are dealt with automatically, but around 1,800 per month—or 60 a day—require intervention.[741]

However, the UK does not consider its present defense systems to be enough and intends to set up a "National Cyber Force" modeled on one in the U.S., which would:

> fuse expertise in data analytics, machine learning and artificial intelligence, autonomy and robotics, synthetics, quantum, and 5G.[742]

Nations are increasingly understanding the importance of building and maintaining advanced capabilities to both launch and protect against cyberattacks. A phrase

738. Bloomberg, September 30, 2020, online, retrieved October 1, 2020, https://www.livemint.com/news/world/microsoft-says-russia-behind-most-nation-state-cyber-attacks-11601444175751.html.
739. Lucy Fisher, "Military under daily blitz of 'significant' cyberattacks," *The Times*, September 26, 2020, online, retrieved October 1, 2020, scratchhttps://www.thetimes.co.uk/article/military-under-daily-blitz-of-significant-cyberattacks-5tspjc6nw.
740. *Ibid.*
741. *Ibid.*
742. *Ibid.*

that is now commonly used when describing the importance and impact of cyber capabilities is "Information is Power":

> The core element that drives the digital society is digitalized information. Information is the key to how the digital society adds value and redistributes power.[743]

In 2003, the United States published a document entitled "The National Strategy to Secure Cyberspace" that set out the US objectives to profit from the importance of cyberspace and develop effective defenses against cyberattacks from hostile nations.[744]

§20.05 NUCLEAR WAR?

A very serious matter is that cyber war may become a nuclear war. Indeed, nuclear powers are already considering that. It has been reported that the United Kingdom is considering the possibility of using nuclear weapons against any state that inflicted a devastating cyberattack on British systems or infrastructure.[745] The report discussed above, Global Britain in a Competitive Age, said that the UK would reserve the right to review its policy on the use of nuclear weapons:

> If a future threat of mass destruction, such as chemical and biological capabilities, or emerging technologies that could have a comparable impact, makes it necessary.

§20.06 THE SOLARWINDS ATTACK

And that necessity is getting increasingly intense. One of the most clever, sophisticated and devastating nation-state attacks on critical software of another country started in 2019 with the penetration of the software of a company called SolarWinds. This attack was still being investigated in 2021, and the United States has not yet decided what retaliation to take against the suspected attackers who are believed to be related to Russian intelligence.

SolarWinds is an important U.S. technology firm. They are responsible for creating a software system named "Orion" which is used by thousands of customers across the United States to manage their IT systems. SolarWinds has over 30,000 customers that use Orion. Like any other major software manufacturer, SolarWinds sends out periodic updates to its customers. Many of these customers are large U.S. companies and important federal and state government organizations. The Pentagon, the Department of Home Security, the Department of Energy, the Nuclear Security

743. Sora Park, *Information is Power* (Springer, 2017), online, retrieved October 1, 2020. https://link.springer.com/chapter/10.1057/978-1-137-59332-0_8#: ~ :text = Information%20is%20the%20key%20to,once%20shared%20on%20digital%20networks.
744. Levon Anderson, "Countering State-Sponsored Cyber Attacks: Who Should Lead?" *information as Power*, online, retrieved October 1, 2020.
745. Larisa Brown, Catherine Philip, Kaya Burgess, "Britain could respond to future cyberattack with nuclear strike," *The Times*, March 17, 2021, online, accessed March 18, 2021.

Administration, the State Department, and the Treasury are among the many users of Orion. So are Microsoft, Intel and Cisco, among many other high-profile tech companies.

What the hackers did was extremely clever. They broke into Solar Winds Orion and planted well-hidden malicious software in the updates that Solar Winds sent to its customers. This malicious software allowed the hackers to get access to the IT systems of the customers who received these updates and to gather sensitive and critical information from those IT systems. Although Russia has denied any involvement in this penetration, major software companies like Microsoft firmly believe that the hackers are connected to Russian intelligence.

The extent of the damage of this wide-ranging attack has not yet been fully assessed. But it does come as a major shock to those responsible for securing the safety of critical IT systems in the United States. The U.S. does fund a Cyber Security Command that has responsibility for protecting America's online networks. However, they do not seem to have been prepared to fend off this kind of attack.

The full nature of the US response remains to be seen but may involve serious sanctions against Russia and or any other nation-state that is found to have participated in or facilitated this attack.

President of the U.S., Joe Biden, said in July 2021 that he believed that the President of Russia, Vladimir Putin, could shut down the Russian hackers believed to be responsible for a number of important hacking attacks if Putin wished to do so. The hacking gang, REvil, is believed to be operating out of Russia. They are thought to have targeted around 250 businesses with ransomware attacks between 2019 and 2021. From this criminal activity, they are believed to have extorted around USD 100 million. One Russian hacking expert has said, "it only needs one person to come after them: Putin... If he goes after them, they are all done very quickly." It remains to be seen whether Putin can be persuaded to take decisive action to end the hacking attacks that are believed to originate from Russia. President Biden has said that the U.S. will take action to protect its businesses and infrastructure against hacking attacks and that if Russia takes no action to curtail the attacks originating from there, the U.S. will take retaliatory action.[746]

Biden has told Vladimir Putin that the U.S. would take "any necessary action" in response to ransomware attacks of the kinds suffered by companies in the U.S. and elsewhere during mid-2021.[747] Exactly what that retaliatory action would be is not clear. Biden did say that in his communications with Putin, "I made it very clear to him that the United States expects with operations coming from his soil. Even though it's not sponsored by the state, we expect them to act if we give them enough information to act on who it is."[748]

What is clear is that hacking to damage the information systems of third parties either to cripple important infrastructure assets or to extract money will continue for

746. Marc Bennetts, "Putin could call off hackers if he wanted.," *The Times*, online July 11, 2021.
747. David Charter and Tom Parfit, "We will retaliate if you hack us, Joe Biden tells Vladimir Putin," *The Times*, online, July 10, 2021.
748. *Ibid.*

some time. Major efforts at international cooperation will be needed in order to put an end to the serious infrastructure and economic damage that is now being inflicted on hacking targets.

§20.07 RUSSIAN HACKING ATTACK ON U.S. FOOD PRODUCTION

Despite the warnings of President Biden to the Russian President Putin, Russian hacking attacks on important U.S. resources do not seem to have let up. In September 2021, a group of Russian cybercriminals called Black Matter, which is believed to be based in Russia, attacked the computer systems of Neo Cooperative, an organization of soy and grain farmers that has over eight thousand members, and forced their systems to close down which interrupted food supply and feeding schedules for millions of chickens, hogs and cattle being raised in the United States. The hackers threatened to publish Neo Co-op's confidential data unless they were paid nearly USD 6 million in ransom. In response, Neo Co-op said that they took their systems off-line to protect them.[749]

§20.08 CHINESE ATTACK ON JAPAN

The U.S. and its NATO allies are not the only countries subject to military cyberattacks. An employee of the Chinese military was accused by Japan of hacking into up to 200 Japanese organizations, including the Japanese Space Agency.

Another Chinese hacking group is thought to be guilty of other cyberattacks against South Korea and Japan.

Among the tactics used by these alleged Chinese cyberattackers is the theft of sensitive emails to use them for purposes of distributing malware into the systems of important companies and organizations.[750]

§20.09 THE NORTH KOREAN HEIST

One of the most audacious allegedly state-sponsored hacking attacks by one country on another was an attempt by a hacking group, allegedly under orders from the government of North Korea, to try to steal about USD 1 billion from the country of Bangladesh.

The attempt occurred in 2016. The circumstances are far too complex to describe in detail here, but an outline of what happened follows. For a more detailed description of the theft, the BBC published an informative report in June 2021.[751]

Using a complex series of transfers and carefully planned timing, the hacking group tried to steal about USD 1 billion from the National Bank of Bangladesh. They

749. "Russian hackers target US food and grain production," *The Times*, online, September 23, 2021.
750. Gavin Blair, "Japan accuses Chinese military hacker over cyberattacks," *The Times*, April 20, 2021, accessed May 7, 2021.
751. BBC News, "The Lazarus heist: How North Korea almost pulled off a billion-dollar hack." Online, June 21, 2021.

were trying to steal the money from the account of Bangladesh at the U.S. Federal Reserve Bank in New York. Ultimately, the hackers got away with about USD 80 million, but they were prevented from getting the whole amount because the name of the small bank in Manila the hackers had chosen to send the money to raised suspicions of the Fed. Nevertheless, losing USD 80 million was painful to a country like Bangladesh.

The worst consequences of the hack were prevented, but this is undoubtedly far from the last North Korean hack attack that the world will experience.

Many reports have been published detailing how North Korea spends a significant part of its national wealth to make itself a powerful force on the Internet. North Korea allegedly takes children with remarkable mathematical skills at an early age and places them in programs that teach them sophisticated computer skills. Some of the schools that focus on developing the skills are located in China, and others are found in North Korea. But the alleged intent of these programs is to give North Korea the power to damage and steal from countries that they believe oppose them.

The remarkable thing about this practice is that it gives a relatively small country with fewer resources the power to do significant damage to those who are believed to be its enemies without having the financial, manufacturing, or natural resources to compete with much bigger countries such as the United States. The secrecy and clandestine manner of these attacks make it possible for North Korea to continuously deny their involvement while reaping the resources and benefits that such international activities can bring them. These factors present serious difficulties for countries that are targeted by North Korea both in terms of proving that the attacks are sponsored by the government of North Korea and deciding how to respond to these hacking attacks.

Because of the international nature of these hacking attacks, it will undoubtedly be necessary to form international organizations and put in place international treaties to detect, counter and punish such behavior. There is no doubt these things will have to be done.

§20.10 RUSSIAN HACKING GERMAN PARLIAMENT

Apparently, U.S. politics is not the only target of Russian hackers. Reuters has cited a report in *Der Spiegel* that German government officials have found that the email accounts of members of the German parliament have been hacked apparently by a hacking group called "Ghostwriter" which is believed to be a creature of the Russian military intelligence group, the GRU. This is apparently not the first time that Germany has suffered Russian digital interference.

It is also reported that in 2015, emails from Angela Merkel's office were hacked, as was other German Parliament information.[752]

752. Reuters Staff, "Russian hackers target German parliament again—Der Spiegel," Reuters, March 26, 2021, accessed, September 8, 2021.

§20.11 FORMER U.S. INTELLIGENCE AGENTS HACK FOR UAE

One of the more slippery things about the Internet is that it permits users to operate from anywhere in the world. In the peaceful commercial sector, the value of this was shown during the COVID-19 pandemic when billions of employees around the world worked from home in order to avoid contact that might have contributed to spreading the virus.

However, this flexible ability to work at a distance also enables the intelligence agencies of any country in the world to employ experts from any other country that suits their purposes—whether peaceful or more sinister.

An unfortunate example of the advantages of this flexibility occurred in 2021 when three former U.S. intelligence personnel pled guilty to breaking U.S. laws by engaging in hacking projects for the United Arab Emirates.[753]

They pled guilty to computer fraud, gaining fraudulent access to relevant devices, and violations of export controls, for which they were fined a total of USD 1.7 million.

It is reported that their work for the UAE allegedly includes hacking into servers, computers, and phones around the globe.[754]

§20.12 REMOTE OPERATION OF CONVENTIONAL WEAPONS: ISRAEL VERSUS IRAN

There is a great deal written above about the power of digital weapons and how they are disrupting the defense, infrastructure and political systems of targeted countries.

However, one of the most sinister developments in digital warfare is the creation of tools that can control conventional weapons over the Internet from a remote location.

One of the most shocking incidents of this type of cyber warfare took place in 2021 when Israel allegedly assassinated Iran's principal nuclear scientist, Mohsen Fakhrizadeh. It is alleged that Israel wanted to kill him for more than a decade, but in 2021, it finally happened using a remotely controlled machine gun mounted on a truck by the side of the road which unleashed a stream of bullets at Fakhrizadeh's car as he drove it past with his wife as a passenger.

Israeli operatives allegedly smuggled the pieces of this robot machine gun into the country and assembled it to fit in the back of a pickup truck commonly seen in Iran. They also packed the truck with bombs so that it could be destroyed after the assassination, thereby eliminating much of the evidence relating to the plan.

The robot was controlled via computer control 1,000 miles away, communicating by means of a satellite.

As the target's car drove by, the remote operator used the machine gun, with the help of computerized cameras also attached to the truck, to target and unleash a stream

753. "Three ex-US intelligence officers admit packing for UAE," BBC News, online, September 17, 2021.

754. BBC News, September 17, 2021.

of bullets that killed Fakhrizadeh almost instantly but left his wife untouched. The truck was then blown up.

Using this type of setup was unexpected and confusing. Iranian news sources first reported that Fakhrizadeh had been killed by a group of assassins in the furious gun battle with the scientist's bodyguards that left several people dead. It took a while for it to be understood what actually had happened.[755]

It is alleged that over the years, several countries have arranged for the assassinations of political, scientific and military personnel. However, this is the first known instance where the operation was conducted remotely but with extraordinary precision that killed only the target. This is, of course, very different than the results that occur when remotely controlled drones are used which often cause the deaths of innocent bystanders as well as the target for assassination.

There seems to be a little doubt that certain countries may continue to order assassinations of those whom they consider threats, and this type of remote-controlled conventional weapons appears to put an important new tool at their disposal. Beyond that, this assassination also alerts other technically savvy countries to the possibilities for conducting remote operations over the Internet using a growing variety of robot weapons of all sizes, even down to nano-robots.

§20.13 REMOTE AND AI OPERATION OF DIGITAL CONTROLS

Two aspects of human life are expanding so rapidly that they are creating potential security issues that could become critical in a situation of conflict between nations. The first is the globalization of trade. The most powerful economies in the world are those of the United States and China. Over the past 50 years, China has come out of its isolationist shell and become hugely important in the manufacture of goods and in the development of cyber products. An important economic advantage that China is able to exploit is a cost of production significantly lower than many other developed economies, including the economies of most democratic Western countries such as the United States, the United Kingdom and the nations of the European Union.

China has also been able to combine its manufacturing prowess with an advanced technological culture that makes it a serious competitor in the manufacture of most digital products.

The pricing and efficiency of the Chinese cyber companies have made their products attractive to many consumers, including government-owned consumers in Western countries.

However, it is the view of many governments outside of China that important cyber industries in China are closely monitored and often controlled to a significant extent by the Chinese government.

755. This account is adapted from an article by Ronen Bergman and Farnaz Fassihi, "The Scientist and the A.I.-Assisted, Remote Control Killing Machine," *The New York Times*, online, September 18, 2021.

A significant concern with the close association between the Chinese government and Chinese industry is that, ideologically, the political philosophy dominant in China conflicts with the ideology of most Western democracies. This has led to a number of conflicts relating to economic and political influence in regions around the world. Some of these conflicts have intensified to the point where there is concern in Western capitals that there may be military conflicts with China in the future.

This unfortunate possibility raises the issue of whether it is wise for Western countries to permit the widespread economic penetration of Chinese digital products in countries that are philosophically opposed to the policies and aims of the Chinese government—such as those nations opposing a possible takeover of Taiwan, Chinese naval domination in the South Asian Pacific, and expansion of Chinese economic and political influence in Africa and other places.

Along with the expansion of the internet and the rapid development of sophisticated AI, there is concern that the Chinese government may intentionally program digital products that are exported overseas so that they provide the Chinese with detailed electronic information gathered from the locations where the products are located and may even allow the Chinese to control their operation remotely. The addition of AI to such products may permit them to operate to serve the interests of the Chinese government even if there is no continued direct communication with the products.

§20.14 NEW AI WEAPONS

It is already being reported that a number of nations are already actively developing AI weapons or seeking to enhance weapons already in operation by adding AI capabilities.

The military market is being increasingly targeted by drone manufacturers who are developing drones functioning with AI capabilities to enhance their military effectiveness.

§20.15 UNITED STATES

The United States is reported to be a major investor in and user of drones with military capabilities. The following are some examples.

Teledyne Black Hornet 3

This is a palm-sized nano-drone used by the U.S. and UK military, which can fly for 25 minutes and provide sophisticated surveillance at a radius of over a mile. The whole system, including launchers, controllers and monitors, is reported to weigh less than 3 pounds. They cost about USD 195,000 each, and several nations have been reported to have purchased them.[756]

756. Harry McNabb, "Nano Drones: The Tiny Personal Drones the Military is Buying in Bulk," dronelife, online at: dronelife.com, June 18, 2020. Accessed August 30, 2023.

The XQ-5SA Valkyrie

In late August 2023, it was reported that the United States had developed a pilotless "experimental aircraft" that is operated using artificial intelligence, the XQ-5SA Valkyrie:

> Essentially a next generation drone, the Valkyrie is a prototype for what the Air Force hopes can become a potent supplement to its fleet of traditional fighter jets, giving human pilots a swarm of highly capable robot wingmen to deploy in battle. Its mission is to marry artificial intelligence and its sensors to identify and evaluate enemy threats and then after getting human sign-off, to move in for the kill.[757]

It is reported that China is the principal competitor to the U.S. in building weapons with AI capabilities.

One of the principal advantages of employing AI-capable drones is that it allows the U.S. (and probably, eventually, other nations) to expand their air combat capabilities at relatively low cost. For example, the top U.S. fighter jet, the F-35, costs about USD 80 million, whereas drones like the Valkyrie will cost about USD 3 million each.[758]

The global military market for drones is growing dramatically. It is estimated to have been over USD 12.5 billion in 2022 and is projected to expand to more than USD 14 billion in 2023. By 2030, it is thought that it will have more than doubled to over USD 35 billion.[759]

§20.16 EXPANDING DRONE USES

The use of drones is becoming important in both the military and security industries for such things as surveillance, surveying, transport, and combat. It is thought that the application of AI will dramatically increase the capabilities of drones and make them more effective and precise.

Much of the current spend on drones is devoted to adding AI to drones to make them capable of "decision making" without continuous control by human operators.[760]

§20.17 LEGAL OVERSIGHT?

In Russia's war against Ukraine, both sides have acquired and are using destructive drones in military operations. Both Iran and China have supplied military drones to Russia, and the NATO countries have supplied military drones to Ukraine.[761] Both sides have been accusing each other of "war crimes." In March of 2023, the International

757. Eric Lipton, "A.I. Brings the Robot Wingman to Ariel Combat," The New York Times, online, August 27, 2023.
758. *Ibid.*
759. Fortune Business Insights, "Unmanned Systems/Military Drone Market," Fortune Business Insights, online at: fortunebusinessinsights.com, June 2023.
760. *Ibid.*
761. *Ibid.*

Criminal Court in the Hague issued an arrest warrant for Vladimir Putin "for overseeing the abduction of Ukrainian children."[762]

Although it has been pointed out that it may be unrealistic to expect laws to control behavior in war, which is fundamentally a lawless and savage enterprise, there have been attempts to provide codes of protection for civilians and defeated enemies from at least the times of the earliest codes of law.

The Code of Hammurabi was issued about 1750 BC. Its purposes are stated to include:

> To destroy the wicked and the evil-doers, so that the strong should not harm the weak.[763]

Other ancient sources of "rules" for behavior in war include the Mahabharata from India and the Old Testament.

In the Mahabharata it is said:

> War should be waged for the sake of conquest; one should not be enraged toward an enemy who is not trying to kill him.[764]

In Deuteronomy 20 of the Old Testament, the rules of war are set out. Many of these are very harsh, but others are slightly more conciliatory, such as:

> When you go to attack the city, you must first offer peace to the people there. If they accept your offer and open their gates, all the people in the city will become your slaves and be forced to work for you.[765]

In modern times, we have tried to develop reasonably humane standards for behavior and war. The most famous of these is the Geneva Convention, which actually consists of four treaties and three additional protocols that set out international legal standards for behavior in war.

§20.18 GENEVA CONVENTION[766]

The first Geneva Convention was introduced in 1949 and applies to the treatment of sick and wounded land soldiers during the war. It also covers those treating them, such as medical staff, clergy, and medical transports.

The second Geneva Convention extends such protections to military personnel at sea.

---

762. Julian Borger and Pjotr Sauer, "ICC judges issue arrest warrant for Vladimir Putin over alleged war crimes," The Guardian, online at: theguardian.com, March 17, 2023, accessed August 31, 2023.
763. Translated by L.W. King, *The Code of Hammurabi*, pdf available online at: general-intelligence.com, accessed August 31, 2023.
764. Translated by Kisari Mohan Ganguli, *The Mahabharata*, available online at: library.bjp.org, accessed August 31, 2023.
765. Deuteronomy 20, "Rules of War (10)," online at: biblegateway.com, accessed September 1, 2023.
766. International Committee of the Red Cross, "The Geneva Conventions and Their Additional Protocols," online at: icrc.org, October 29, 2010, accessed September 1, 2023.

The third Geneva Convention applies to prisoners of war. It defines the places of captivity and treats questions regarding their labor, financial resources, the relief that is sent to them and any judicial proceedings they are subject to. There are five annexes providing more detail as to regulations for prisoners.

The fourth Geneva Convention applies to protection for civilians, including those in captured territory.

The Geneva Conventions came into effect on October 21, 1950, and have since been ratified by 194 countries.

§20.19 CONTEMPORARY WARFARE AND AI

What these conventions and rules show is that there has long been a sensitivity to the fact that the brutality of war is harsh not only on combatants but also on noncombatants, including civilians, as well.

In recent years, the nature of warfare has undergone dramatic changes. Rather than being limited to "global" wars involving the military organizations of large nations, many are limited to smaller geographical areas and may be largely concerned with internal civil conflicts between different internal groups.

This change has led to increasing exposure of civilians and noncombatants to violence. Unfortunately, every day, there seem to be violent actions aimed at individuals or small groups within areas that are largely inhabited by civilians. These are often justified as being attacks on "terrorist groups" or "terrorist leaders." Important tools for conducting such attacks are drones and other weapons that are remotely operated and may be enhanced by AI systems that help determine when and whom to attack.

Too often, these weapons and their operators get it wrong or cause wider than intended damage that causes death and injury to innocent civilians:

> According to the Bureau of Investigative Journalism (BIJ), for instance, US strikes in Afghanistan, Pakistan, Somalia and Yemen from 2002 to 2020 killed between 10,000 and 17,000 people. Of these, between 800 and 1,750 are thought to have been civilians.[767]

767. Sarah Kreps, Paul Lushenko, Shyam Raman, "Biden can reduce civilian casualties during US drone strikes. Here's how.," The Brookings Institution, online at: brookings.edu, January 19, 2022, accessed September 1, 2023.

CHAPTER 21

The Future of AI Law

§21.01 EXTINCTION OF THE HUMAN RACE?

After November 2022, when ChatGPT was made available for public use, a large number of articles appeared in the press and online, expressing concern that AI systems could grow so powerful that they "could lead to the extinction of humanity."[768]

That would certainly be an unfortunate consequence, but one thing that seems to be forgotten is that we do not exist because of AI. AI exists only because of the creativity, assistance and permission of humanity. AI needs electricity, computers, the Internet and operators to exist. Deprive it of any of those things, and it disappears. AI systems have no separate physical existence. AI systems can be physically destroyed, cut off from electricity, deprived of human assistance and hacked. Should we be careful with them? Yes. Should we forbid their existence? Because it is recognized that there are so many potential benefits to using AI in so many areas, it seems more sensible to control their creation and use through appropriate laws, regulations and treaties.

This has been done with other human creations that are recognized as particularly dangerous and a possible threat to the human race. One example which is brought up by many of those concerned about the power of AI systems is nuclear power.

That is another system that can have devastating military applications.

The use of AI systems has some parallels to the harnessing of nuclear fission. Nuclear fission is an extremely powerful process that presents great dangers to humanity. Does misuse of nuclear fission lead to the extinction of humanity? Probably not. But it could make a serious dent in human existence—perhaps greater than the bubonic plague. Consequently, there have been serious efforts since 1945 to impose international restrictions on the development of nuclear power and, particularly, those elements of nuclear power that can lead to the creation of nuclear weapons. How has

768. Zoe Kleinman, "AI 'godfather' Yoshua Benigo feels 'lost' over life's work," BBC News, online, May 31, 2023.

that been going? In 1945, one nation had developed nuclear weapons. By June 2023, nine nations had created nuclear weapons. There have been a number of threats to use them. Certainly, their use can cause huge numbers of deaths. On August 29, 1945, *The New York Times* reported that more than 200,000 people were killed by the dropping of just one atomic bomb on Hiroshima in 1945. Since then, there have been many disagreements over what the exact casualty figures were, but atomic weapons have become increasingly more sophisticated since 1945, and there is absolutely no question that using them can cause many, many deaths. Since 1945, nuclear weapons have become much more advanced, and many more have been created. But almost 80 years later, humanity is still here.

However, control of nuclear weapons is assisted by the fact that nuclear weapons are difficult to produce, requiring expensive resources, highly sophisticated training, and particular radioactive materials that are hard to acquire. Nevertheless, some countries have been able to overcome these problems, and there are probably many other countries that could produce nuclear weapons if they were so inclined.

Professor Bendigo is reported to have said that "he did not think militaries should be granted AI powers."[769] However, it does not seem possible to prevent them from developing AI weapons systems.

Unlike nuclear weapons, it appears that the development of militarily useful AI systems does not seem to require resources as difficult to get as nuclear weapons. It seems that smart people with computers and access to the Internet are the materials needed to produce artificially intelligent weapons.

Among the AI "weapons" that could be used by hostile military forces are likely to include such things as the following:

> Systems that can hack and disrupt the operation of digital tools used by opponents.
> Systems that can rapidly obtain and analyze information useful to attack or disrupt opponents.
> Systems that can operate and direct other digital tools such as drones (individually or in large coordinated groups).
> Systems that can disrupt the operation of important digitally operated or assisted infrastructure systems of opponents.
> Systems that can provide targeted psychological warfare or misinformation via the Internet and social media, directed at opponents and their populations.
> Systems that can speed up and enhance the development and deployment of more effective or destructive military armaments.
> Systems that can operate independently of human control, such as remotely operated armored vehicles, airplanes, satellites, bombs and missiles, submarines and ships, etc.
> Systems that can control lethal robotic weapons that can operate independently of human presence to replace or supplement human military personnel.

769. *Ibid.*

The above list includes some of the military uses to which AI systems could be put. The list is unlikely to be exhaustive. Human imagination and creativity, probably with AI assistance, may well be able to find a much longer list of military tools that can be created, operated or enhanced by AI.[770]

The effects of such weapons will range from helpful to extremely destructive. The easy availability of the tools needed to create such weapons will mean that strong, universally accepted treaties and restrictions on their uses and applications will need to be internationally negotiated and accepted.

An early effort at international cooperation on AI exists in the proposed EU Artificial Intelligence Law.[771] This will control the creation, application and use of such tools (including potentially weapon-level tools) by the 27 developed economies of the European Union. Although this early regulatory effort may not cover all of the issues that are presented by AI systems, it may prove to be a good model for how to approach the problems presented by AI in the international context.

§21.02 IS HYSTERIA JUSTIFIED?

During the late part of 2022 and the early part of 2023, there was an enormous amount of reporting about the development of AI. Some of it reported potential benefits in many areas. But there was also a great deal of sensationalist media reporting about how dangerous AI could be, including reports that it could potentially endanger the existence of the human race.

For example, on June 5, 2023, a story on the front page of *The Times* was headlined, "Two years to save the world, says Sunak's AI adviser":[772]

> AI systems will be powerful enough to "kill many humans" within just two years, Rishi Sunak advisor on artificial intelligence has warned.

It is difficult to understand what the point of such statements is. The world, and indeed, the universe, is already full of things that can and do "kill many humans." As just one example, the automobile, another man-made invention, that was inflicted on humanity about 150 years ago kills about 1.5 million people a year around the globe. Are there terrifying headlines warning us about that? Of course not. The human race has calculated that, although automobiles are extremely dangerous, a proven threat to life and limb, their benefits outweigh their risks. We seem to believe that the traffic laws that have already been imposed provide us with as much protection from this deadly machine as we can sensibly want.

As of this writing, there has only been one widely reported death related to AI. That is a suicide that is believed to have been encouraged by a chatbot.

Media reports are often concerned by the fact that so-called AI experts are saying that AI systems are so dangerous that they could lead to human extinction. One should

---

770. Iain Martin, "To defend the West we must win this AI race," *The Times*, online May 31, 2023.
771. *See* Chapter 4 on EU AI Law.
772. Mark Sellman, Tom Whipple, "Two years to save the world, says Sunak's AI adviser," *The Times*, online, June 5, 2023.

certainly pay attention to those who truly understand the potential risks and benefits of AI systems. However, one should consider whether some of these "experts" are enthusiastically trumpeting the dangers of AI to encourage governments and private persons to hire them, at great expense, "to protect humanity" against AI. So many "AI experts" are being cited by the media that one might think it is a very competitive field.

That is not to say that AI does not have the potential to be dangerous. However, governments have traditionally imposed laws and regulations to limit the risks of anything that offers potential benefits along with potential risks. It has been pointed out above that the creation and application of AI systems along with most other human activities is already subject to numerous existing laws and regulations—particularly in those ways where it can cause injury and death. If these laws and regulations need to be adjusted and supplemented to take account of any special qualities that AI systems present, there is no reason why that cannot be accomplished in a timely manner.

§21.03 AI ECONOMIC IMPACT

Since at least 1978, there has been concern that computerization would replace jobs. In June of that year, the UK Prime Minister initiated an investigation into whether "computer chips" would eliminate jobs.[773]

For centuries, the possibility of the entry of machines into the workplace was considered an economic threat. In 1589, the inventor William Lee was denied a patent by the government of Queen Elizabeth I because his "stocking frame" would replace hand knitters. Somewhat later, Albert Einstein suggested that "technology" contributed to the Great Depression because machines were doing jobs that had previously been done by human workers.

However, despite centuries of concern about this march of technology, the employment rate in the United Kingdom is as high as it has ever been since the Bank of England began recording that statistic in 1860.[774]

In March 2023, OpenAI, the company that created the highly publicized AI system, "ChatGPT," published a paper that said about 20% of the U.S. workforce could see that at least half their work could be done more quickly by an AI program like, "ChatGPT." However, the article pointed out that a number of jobs that required manual work by humans, such as maintenance, mechanics, cooking, farming, stone masonry, etc., would not be affected by AI. That prediction is interesting and could scare employees across a number of sectors, but as previous predictions have shown, it is impossible at this point to know what the impact of these "new machines" will really be on the job market. As Wayne Holmes, an associate professor at University College London, is reported to have said:

> OpenAI is clearly selling their product—I'd take their report with a pinch of salt. We said the same when word processors came out, when typewriters came out,

773. Tom Calver, "Is your job at risk from ChatGPT?," *The Sunday Times*, online, March 26, 2023.
774. *Ibid.*

> when calculators came out—that all of these things are going to put people on the redundancy line.[775]

There are some employers who have been quoted as seeing ChatGPT as a way to save money by replacing freelance workers such as "copywriters."

However, in the past, technological advances which have replaced some jobs have often created new jobs that can expand the job market. At the beginning of the introduction of any new technology, it is impossible for us to foresee the long-term impact of this "creative destruction."[776]

Another prediction, reportedly made by Goldman Sachs, is that the economies of the United States and Europe will be disrupted by AI with the reduction of approximately three hundred million jobs. However, they predict that new jobs will be created and there will be cost savings from AI which will permit businesses to redeploy their resources in ways that will lead to an increase in annual GDP of approximately 7%. This mixed prediction may be a cause of concern for many people in jobs that are thought to be vulnerable to being changed by AI, but as discussed above, it is very hard to know whether all or any of these predictions will come true. It is certainly the case that the adoption of AI is occurring at a rapid rate. It is reported that OpenAI's Chat GPT had more than 1,000,000 users during the five days it was launched. This is said to be the most rapid adoption any tech company has achieved.[777]

In the U.S., the use of generative AI by tech giants is rapidly expanding. Both Amazon and Google have invested billions of dollars in Anthropic, a competitor of OpenAI in the field of generative AI.[778]

§21.04 SMARTER THAN HUMANS?

One of the pioneers of AI, Geoffrey Hinton, has recently been quoted as saying that chatbots will soon be more intelligent than humans.[779]

What Professor Hinton seems to be saying is that human beings, that is to say, those who create AI systems, are potentially less intelligent than the things they create.

Human beings are a product of nature. So, the argument seems to be that intelligence created by human beings will be more intelligent than intelligence created by nature.

The fundamental flaw in this argument is that having been on this earth for only about an estimated 30 million years, we human beings do not yet know the full extent of our intelligence. Indeed, we know far less about the workings of the human brain

775. *Ibid.*
776. *Ibid.*, quoting Austrian economist Joseph Schumpeter's 1942 comment.
777. Jack Kelly, "Goldman Sachs Predicts 300 Million Jobs Will Be Lost or Degraded By Artificial Intelligence," Forbes, online, March 31, 2023.
778. Information provided by Reuters and LSEG partnership, online at: reuters.com, accessed September 29, 2023.
779. Mark Sellman, "AI pioneer quits Google over 'scary' pace of change." *The Times*, online, May 2, 2023. See also, Cade Metz, "Godfather of A.I. Leaves Google and Warns of Dangers Ahead," *The New York Times*, online, May 1, 2023.

than we know about the workings of digital intelligence.[780] The full reach of human intelligence and the full spectrum of human imagination has not yet been reached. We do not fully understand how it works, nor can we see what its ultimate limits might be.

One important limitation of AI that we do understand is that it was created by men, not by nature. Although we learn more all the time, we do not yet know the extent of the full palette of the tools that nature can bring to bear to create a natural product, nor will we ever.

Yes, it is certainly true that AI systems can operate more quickly and more efficiently than human beings in any number of defined situations. Yes, they may be able to endlessly defeat us in games that we have created and taught them, such as Chess or Go or other human-created puzzles, due to their extensive rapid calculating skills and their endless concentration. However, will they ever be able to create something that changes the relationship of humanity to its environment? For example, did chatbots unlock the secrets of nuclear energy, or did they understand what was necessary to put people on the moon? Will they find the path to usable nuclear fusion?

The point here is that AI systems know what humans have taught them and what humans have given them access to. They are limited by the digital combinations that we permit them to use. It is true that the full number of possible usable digital combinations possessed by an AI system may be far beyond imaginable. But they are significantly less than the analog combinations that human intelligence has access to. The total number of AI digital combinations may be countable, but the total number of analog combinations to which human intelligence has access is not. To put it in simple terms, we all understand that no two human beings are exactly alike. The explanation for that is the variety of analog combinations that exist within us.

To argue that humans, by creating AI systems, can outdo the variety of outcomes that nature can produce is foolish. We understand too little about ourselves and the universe to make that argument credible. AI systems will always be limited by the digital elements that humans employ to create them. That is not to say we will always be able to beat them. There are many situations in which we will have made them faster and more efficient than we can be. But we will always have a superior potential for creativity.

§21.05 NEED FOR HUMAN REGULATION

Because AI systems are created through human intervention, no matter how intelligent they are made to be, it is not AI machines that need to be regulated. It is humanity. It is humans that create them, arm them, and use them. It is the job of law and regulation to make certain that we do those things in ways that do not harm our fellow humans. Law and regulation restrict the choices we can make so that the benefits of our

780. "Scientists have known for centuries that the brain is the seat of human thought, but we're still in the dark about how it works." Allen Institute for Brain Science, online at: alleninstitute.org, accessed May 3, 2023.

creations are maximized and the risks of these creations are reduced. That is the fundamental basis of AI regulation and must always be.

It is not AI that needs regulation. It is us!

§21.06 ETHICS VERSUS LAW

As frequently discussed in previous chapters, AI systems are already subject to many existing laws and regulations. This is the case of any activity that affects human beings. The development, marketing and operation of AI systems is no different. However, AI systems are so new, and sometimes so powerful, that it is widely feared that there are gaps in the national and international legal systems that may add up to a lack of sufficient regulation of AI to sufficiently protect the human race against the potential risks it presents.

In what may be a partial response to these concerns, many governments, private companies, academic institutions, and industry organizations have proposed systems of "ethics" to be applied to AI-related activities. This raises the question of whether "ethics" are sufficient to fill perceived gaps in the legal regulation of AI and sufficiently protect humans against potential AI risks.

"Ethics" are generally defined as: "Moral principles that govern a person's behavior or the conducting of an activity."[781]

An argument is made that "Big Tech Emphasizes Artificial Intelligence Ethics."[782]

> The problem is that this ethics is, after all, their own league.[783]

Ethics provides a much more flexible latitude for behavior than more narrowly defined laws and regulations.

As one commentary argues:[784]

> Human rights are an internationally agreed set of norms that represent the most universal expression of our shared values, in a shared language and supported by mechanisms and institutions for accountability and redress. As such, they offer clarity and structure and the normative power of law.
>
> ... [H]uman rights law provides a clear framework for balancing competing interests in the development of technology: it's tried and tested jurisprudence requires restrictions to human rights (like privacy or non-discrimination) to be prescribed by law, pursuant to a legitimate aim, and necessary in proportion to that aim. Each term is a defined concept against which actions can be objectively measured and made accountable.
>
> ... [E]thics are much more easily manipulated to support a given company or government's agenda, with limited recourse for anyone who disagrees.

781. "Ethics," *The New Oxford Dictionary of English*, (Oxford: Oxford University Press, 1998), p. 631.
782. AI Network, July 28, 2023, as cited above.
783. *Ibid.*
784. Alison Berthet, "Why do emerging AI guidelines emphasize "ethics" over human rights?" Open Global Rights, online at: openglobalrights.org, July 10, 2019, accessed July 31, 2023.

It is a legitimate question as to whether codes of "ethics" promoted by tech companies that will be self-interested in providing themselves with the most flexible path to profitability will be sufficient to protect humanity from the most significant risks posed by the development and expansion of AI, including such things as:

- Algorithmic discrimination
- Intrusive surveillance
- Disinformation.

> It is of course encouraging that ethical principles are being adopted with support from the AI industry. But a human rights-based approach would offer a more robust framework for the lawful and ethical development and use of AI.[785]

It seems clear that what society cannot afford as part of its adoption of the beneficial uses of AI is gaps, ambiguities and flexibilities that deprive those who perceive themselves to be harmed by the application of AI systems of well-defined recourse to challenge and penalize the unjust applications of AI products.

In order to provide sufficient protection, it will be necessary to develop clear and accepted international laws and regulations to govern AI. This may take some time, and all nations may not subscribe to appropriate international laws and regulations. Consequently, in the first instance, it will be urgent for each individual legal jurisdiction (whether national or otherwise) to provide well-defined laws and regulations to protect the public and provide adequate recourse against AI abuse.

785. *Ibid.*

Index

B

C

D

N

O

P

Q

R

S

www.ingramcontent.com/pod-product-compliance
Lightning Source LLC
Chambersburg PA
CBHW071241230926
51849CB00001B/182
* 9 7 8 9 4 0 3 5 0 9 8 7 7 *